Inside Organizations

Inside Organizations

Anthropologists at Work

Edited by
David N. Gellner and Eric Hirsch

Oxford • New York

First published in 2001 by
Berg
Editorial offices:
150 Cowley Road, Oxford, OX4 1JJ, UK
838 Broadway, Third Floor, New York, NY 10003-4812, USA

Berg is an imprint of Oxford International Publishers Ltd.

Library of Congress Cataloging-in-Publication Data
A catalogue record for this book is available from the Library of Congress.

British Library Cataloguing-in-Publication Data
A catalogue record for this book is available from the British Library.

ISBN 1 85973 482 0 (Cloth)
1 85973 487 1 (Paper)

Typeset by JS Typesetting, Wellingborough, Northants.
Printed in the United Kingdom by Biddles Ltd, Guildford and King's Lynn.

Contents

Contents

Notes on Contributors

Simone Abram is Lecturer at the Dept of Town and Regional Planning of the University of Sheffield. In 2000, she was Visiting Fellow at the Institute for Social Anthropology at the University of Oslo, where she also conducted fieldwork in a local district council. She is editor of *Anthropological Perspectives on Local Development* (Routledge/EASA 1998) and *Tourists and Tourism* (Berg 1997).

Malcolm Chapman is Senior Lecturer in Leeds University Business School. His anthropological studies have concentrated upon the Celtic fringe of Europe, particularly Scotland and Brittany, and some of his work in this area was summarized in *The Celts – The Construction of a Myth* (Macmillan, 1992). In 1989 he read for an MBA at Bradford University Management Centre, and has since been making a living bringing anthropology to business studies, and business studies to anthropology. He has been research consultant to a major 'Know-How Fund' project in Poland, helping to build strong regional business schools in diverse locations outside the capital.

David N. Gellner is Reader in Social Anthropology in the Department of Human Sciences, Brunel University. His main research has been on religion, social organization, politics, and ethnicity in the Kathmandu Valley, Nepal. He has also carried out fieldwork in Japan. His most recent book is *The Anthropology of Buddhism and Hinduism: Weberian Themes* (Delhi: OUP, 2001).

Christine Hine is Director of the Centre for Research into Innovation, Culture and Technology (CRICT) at Brunel University (http://www.brunel.ac.uk/depts/crict), and also lectures in Communications and Media Studies within the Department of Human Sciences at Brunel. Her research interests focus on the use of information and communication technology in scientific research, the sociology of computer-mediated communication, and the development of ethnographic methodology for the study of computer-mediated communication. She has recently published an ethnographic study of a media event on the Internet (*Virtual Ethnography*, Sage, 2000), and is currently exploring the use of computer-mediated communications by scientists.

Eric Hirsch is Senior Lecturer in the Department of Human Sciences, Brunel University. He has conducted field research in Papua New Guinea and in Greater London. His current research is concerned with the historical ethnography of landscape, power, and property relations among the Fuyuge people of highland Papua; and with historical and ethnographic issues in the connections between new technologies and new forms of social relations. A second edition of his co-authored *Technologies of Procreation: Kinship in an Age of Assisted Conception* (Routledge) appeared in 1999.

Sharon Macdonald is Senior Lecturer in the Department of Sociological Studies, University of Sheffield. Her recent publications include *Reimagining Culture: The Politics of Display* (ed.) and *Approaches to European Historical Consciousness* (ed.). She has carried out ethnographic fieldwork in the Scottish Hebrides, at the Science Museum, London, and in Franconia, Germany.

Stella Mascarenhas-Keyes is currently working at the University of Surrey as a researcher in the School of Educational Studies. She holds a PhD in Social Anthropology and an MA in Higher and Professional Education. She was previously Visiting Lecturer at the School of Oriental and African Studies, London University, and Consultant Educational Researcher and Developer to the National Network for Teaching and Learning Anthropology. She is principal author of the *Report on Teaching and Learning Social Anthropology in the UK*. She has undertaken a number of research and training consultancy appointments for various organizations and co-ordinated an applied research project in the voluntary sector.

David Mosse teaches anthropology at the School of Oriental and African Studies, University of London. He has worked as a reseacher and consultant on participatory rural development in India where he previously worked for Oxfam. His ethnographic work has focused on popular religion, social organization, dalit movements, and indigenous irrigation. He is currently involved in watershed development work in south India and research in the anthropology of development.

Martin O'Neill was born in south Wales and has worked in the ambulance service both in Sheffield and in Wales. He read anthropology and sociology at the University of Wales Swansea, and was awarded a PhD scholarship by the School of Health Science, Swansea, for an ethnographic study of the Ambulance Service. Since 1999 he has been attached to the School of Social Sciences in Cardiff, carrying out ethnographic work both in former coalmining communities and on health inequalities in the south Wales valleys.

Alexandra Ouroussoff is Research Fellow in the Department of Accounting and Finance, London School of Economics, and has taught in Brunel University and the University of Kent. She has done extensive fieldwork in a number of multi-national corporations in Britain and, more recently, in France. Her publications include 'The Problem of Consciousness in Political Rhetoric' (in C. Shore and S. Nugent (eds) *Anthropology and Cultural Studies*, Pluto, 1996).

Melissa Parker is Lecturer in Social Anthropology and Director of the International Medical Anthropology Programme at Brunel University. She has undertaken research on a broad range of topics in medical anthropology, including tropical health and well-being, female circumcision, war and the mind, sexual networks and HIV-transmission in the UK, and gender and sexuality.

Simon Pulman-Jones is Director of Ethnography for the Sapient Corporation, Chicago. He completed his PhD in anthropology from the London School of Economics in 1996. He has worked as an anthropological consultant for the London Business School and various other institutions. Before going to university he worked as a film-maker and script-writer. His PhD was entitled 'Confronting Difficulty: A Day-Care Unit In London For Children With Complex Behavioural Problems'.

Bob Simpson is a Senior Lecturer in anthropology at the University of Durham. He has a long-standing research interest in Sri Lanka where he carried out doctoral research into healing rituals and the transmission of ritual knowledge. He subsequently carried out research into many aspects of divorce and separation in the UK and published numerous articles and a book (*Changing Families: An Ethnographic Approach to Divorce and Separation*, Berg, 1998) on contemporary family life. More recently he has undertaken research into kinship and the new reproductive and genetic technologies in the UK and Sri Lanka.

John Van Maanen is the Erwin Schell Professor of Organization Studies in the Sloan School of Management at the Massachusetts Institute of Technology. He has been a visiting professor at Yale University, the University of Surrey, and INSEAD (Fontainebleau). He has published in the general area of occupational and organizational sociology. Cultural descriptions figure prominently in his studies of the work worlds of patrol officers in the United States, police detectives in London, and park operatives in Disneyland. His books include *Tales of the Field* (1988) and, most recently, *Qualitative Studies of Organizations* (1998).

Acknowledgements

This book grew from a project sponsored by the National Network for Teaching and Learning Anthropology, directed by Sue Wright. Project FDTL 124/96, originally conceived by Professor Adam Kuper, rejoiced in the sober title 'Short-term ethnographic research in industrial and organizational settings in connection with undergraduate work placements and Master's dissertations'. (The keen ethnographer of anthropologists' organizations might begin by deconstructing it.) The aim of the project was to improve the teaching of ethnographic methods (a) to Brunel Human Sciences undergraduates, all of whom have to do two 5–6-month work placements as part of their degrees (and many attempt to do some ethnography), and (b) to MSc students in medical anthropology and the anthropology of childhood, all of whom have to write an ethnographically based dissertation. We began by drawing up a wish list of all the anthropologists we knew who had done research in organizations, and then invited them to come and speak to our students during the academic year 1997–8. We were delighted by the number who responded positively and by the quality of the presentations. Although in many cases substantially reworked, this volume contains chapters by nearly all our speakers; Martin O'Neill's ethical case study (Chapter Eleven) and John Van Maanen's Afterword were added subsequently.

We are grateful to Adam Kuper and Sue Wright for their support and guidance, to the National Network for Teaching and Learning Anthropology for funding the project, to the contributors for their cooperation and patience, and to Eric Macfarlane, Mitchell Sedgwick and Lola Martinez for advice. Perhaps our greatest debt is to the generations of Brunel students whose work-placement experiences have fed our interest in the ethnography of organizations, and in particular to those students who participated when the chapters of this book were originally presented.

David N. Gellner and Eric Hirsch
Brunel

Introduction: Ethnography of Organizations and Organizations of Ethnography

Eric Hirsch and David N. Gellner

Ethnography

Social anthropology has some claim to have discovered ethnography as a method (Stocking 1992), and to be the only discipline so far to have put it unequivocally at the centre of its research activity. But can methods devised and refined in the early days of anthropology for the study of non-industrial societies be as successful and revealing in the study of organizations in the industrial world? What are the problems and what are the implications of using ethnography in such settings? And what are some of the solutions? It is with these questions that the present collection is concerned.

Ethnography is now a popular term. There is ethnography of the classroom (Hammersley 1983), ethnography of television audiences (Morley 1988), ethnography of medical students (Sinclair 1997), and ethnography of the police (Young 1991). But what exactly is it? Undeterred by the almost religious mystique with which some anthropologists used to surround the term, we may say that 'ethnography' refers (1) to a set of activities, a way of doing research work 'in the field', and (2) to the *product* of those activities. It is the activity which comes first. Thus the practice of *ethnographic fieldwork* – fieldwork in which the researcher engages with the people being studied, shares their life as far as possible, and converses with them in their own terms (ideally in their own language, i.e. without an interpreter getting in the way) – gives rise to *an ethnography*. This was conventionally a book, sometimes called an *(ethnographic) monograph*, that describes in detail the social life of a particular place or institution. It is our impression that usage number (2) – talk of '*an* ethnography' – is confined to anthropological circles, whereas the other usage – ethnography as participant observation, i.e. as qualitative field-research method – is much more widely known, being current in sociology, psychology, geography, and organizational studies.[1]

---

1. For an excellent survey of the increasing impact of ethnographic method within organizational studies, see Bate (1997). He distinguishes ethnography (1) as an activity from (2) ethnography as a kind of intellectual effort or paradigm, and (3) ethnography as narrative style; or, more pithily: ethnography as respectively doing, thinking, and writing. We tend to think that there is no one ethnographic style of thinking or writing, but rather different styles of thinking and writing based on ethnography.

The emergence of ethnography as a method in so many different disciplines in recent years can hardly be put down simply to the influence of anthropology. More important is the general intellectual history of the human sciences, which may broadly be characterized as a long march away from positivism: that is, away from attempting to model them upon, and justify them in terms derived from, the natural sciences.[2] Thus, apart from any specific demand for doing ethnography, there has been, quite independently in different disciplines, the discovery of 'the client's point of view', which may be seen as an aspect of growing democratization or critique of established relations of power.[3] This development in the human sciences doubtless reflects a still broader cultural democratization. Bate (1997: 1162) quotes the BBC journalist, Michael Buerk, reflecting on his reports of the first Ethiopian famine fifteen years earlier: today the victims would have to be given the chance to speak for themselves, to put their own point of view.

Yet, despite this evidence that many disciplines are beginning both to be dissatisfied with the jejune results of positivist paradigms and to be aware that careful ethnographic work is likely to bring far greater insight, there are reasons to believe that ethnography will always have an air of subversiveness about it. Alongside the postulated general cultural movement towards democratization, there is a countervailing trend towards control, measurement, and quantification of outputs. Any 'method' that insists it lacks a cut-and-dried technique, any discipline that grants a central position to the voices of the 'client' and refuses to prejudge what they might say, will always be suspect to powerful organizations.

One of the aims of this introduction is to consider the various 'moments' involved in conducting ethnography – the ethnographic process – particularly as these are relevant to the study of organizations. As we intend to show, the practical issues involved in such studies (e.g. access) cannot be divorced from important questions of theory (e.g. how boundaries are constituted).

Organizations

Organizations are many and various, but they all have explicit rules, a division of labour, and aims that involve acting on or changing everyday life. Weber famously posited his ideal type of bureaucracy as the most rational – that is, the most efficient and dispassionate – form of organization, because of its high degree of special-

---

2. Anthropology, of course, also participated in this long march. Malinowski had justified his ethnography in positivist terms, as did Radcliffe-Brown even more unequivocally. But the practice of ethnography has survived and flourished, long after Malinowski's positivist defence of it has withered away (Stocking 1992: 240–1).

3. See Mayer and Timms (1970) for social work, Chambers (1983) for international development, and Mitchell (1993) for psychotherapy.

ization and its rule-governed behaviour. Sociologists ever since have delighted in showing, with ethnographic attention to the everyday and the small-scale, how participants in bureaucracies act to undermine efficiency, either by sticking blindly to the rules, or by secretly undermining them and the chain of command. Weber's ideal type may well have been flawed when taken as an account of how bureaucracies actually work, and he may well have been mistaken to imply that the more bureaucratic an organization is, the more efficient it is. But Weber's ideal type captured an important insight, namely the organizational aspiration to be separate from the values and norms of non-bureaucratic, everyday life. Organizations are based on rules that are consciously set up and sometimes changed. Unlike other social institutions,

> Even the smallest organizations necessarily involve conscious monitoring and control of the relationship between means and ends on a fairly regular basis. Such monitoring and control implies a conscious disciplinary process whereby organizational leaders adapt internal structures to their perception of external conditions (Morgan 1990: 5).

Whereas organizations are ubiquitous in the modern world, in the societies where anthropologists began to do ethnography there was plenty of social organization but few or no organizations. Indeed British social anthropology came to be identified with the demonstration of how predictable social life could be carried on without the specialized order-enforcement agencies (police, courts) familiar in 'developed' countries. In the 'tribal' world, social organization focused on the household and on kinship. There was little that went beyond it, little that aspired to separate people from the realm of kinship: age sets, unions of shamans, occasional messianic movements perhaps, but not much else; and even these did not usually involve anything akin to a salaried personnel. In the modern world, by contrast, organizations are everywhere, including those three that, even as the early ethnographers worked, were already being introduced into the societies they studied: the church, the school, and the hospital.

Given that anthropology began as the study of the non-modern in societies without organizations of the sort described, can it contribute anything to their study? In fact social anthropologists in Britain have long carried out, or been connected to, studies of industrial and other organizations, even though these studies have rarely been acknowledged as part of the history of the discipline (Wright 1994). The same has been true on the other side of the Atlantic: American anthropologists were centrally involved, for instance, in the controversial Hawthorne Studies in Chicago during the 1930s (Gillespie 1991). This volume aims to show how anthropologists in Britain today are bringing a distinctive ethnographic expertise to the study of modern organizations (in many cases having first served an apprenticeship doing a classic 'village study').

As implied above, organizations, of whatever kind, usually have some sort of governing ethos. Recent managerialism has tried to codify this ethos, to impose a 'mission statement' which would encapsulate this ethos and 'martial the troops' by means of a single 'culture'. This crude Durkheimianism has recently been usefully contextualized and critiqued by Wright (1998). In contrast to business managers, anthropologists are inclined to look for evidence of different views and divergent interests, even if these are based on shared assumptions about how things should work out (Edwards 1994). Despite a shared governing ethos, many organizations experience, at the same time, entrenched factional 'warfare' between constituent parts (see Chapters Six, Seven, Ten below). Such factions often come together and act as one when the institution as a whole faces opposition or scrutiny from outside.

Organizations do not exist in a vacuum. They operate in a wider context which both provides them with the aims they pursue and sets limits to the way they may operate. This context may be recurrent government funding shortages in the National Health Service or elsewhere (Chapters Four, Six, Seven), it may be the capitalist market (Chapters One and Two), competition between laboratories and individuals for results (Chapter Three), political competition for resources (Chapter Ten), the need to be able to demonstrate 'doing good' through measurable indices (Chapter Eight), or the spread of managerialism to government-funded agencies. Rather than working inside an organization, the anthropologist sometimes researches at the 'interface' between organizations and 'the people' (Chapters Five, Eight, Nine), a situation for which anthropological skills and awareness can be argued to be particularly suited.

In his afterword John Van Maanen discusses some long-standing and recent lines of inquiry in the ethnography of organizations. He not only suggests a way of thinking about different ways of studying organizations, but also, in reviewing much recent work by anthropologists or social scientists influenced by anthropology, provides a valuable bibliographic survey of the field. Rather than attempt to duplicate what Van Maanen has done so effectively, here we concentrate instead on some of the key issues involved in the ethnographic study of organizations. These practical issues and their theoretical implications have concerned the contributors to this volume, as well as many of the authors discussed by Van Maanen.

Inside or Outside? Issues of Access

Conventional fieldwork in places such as Melanesia, Asia, Africa, or Latin America often involves lengthy negotiations with state and local bureaucracies regarding access to field sites, length of stay, and so on (Clifford 1997: 22–3; Law 1994). These negotiations and the documents and persons involved are usually left out of ethnographies. But some anthropologists are now beginning to include descriptions of this process of gaining access because it has come to be realized that the behaviour of such organizations provides important insights into the way particular places are locally conceptualized, bounded, and resourced. The organizations studied here have many formal similarities to these 'gatekeeper' organizations in non-Western contexts. And indeed similar issues of access arise: boundaries and identities have to be negotiated, and the duration of stay and focus of research have to be cleared, as several of the following chapters illustrate. For the ethnographer, adaptability to the circumstances is essential, since, as Buchanan *et al.* (1988: 56) remark, 'negotiating access for the purposes of research is a game of chance, not of skill'.

Shared assumptions within organizations often mean that there are precise expectations of the researcher who stays at length within it. Ouroussoff's experience of general indifference to her research providing she fulfilled the duties of her job (Chapter Two) may be untypical. Large organizations often have experience of management consultants. This may mean that the anthropologist is regarded as a potential enemy by staff, who assume that he or she is a management consultant whose report will recommend redundancies (Chapter Four); everyone expects a report with an executive summary listing bullet points for action. That there should be such a report is in some versions of 'applied' anthropology the whole point (Chapters Eight and Ten).

Particular individuals may refuse access; but the planners, whom Abram (Chapter Nine) expected to be hostile, surprised her with their openness. Certain categories of individual, as has often been described in the sociology of marginal groups and as Parker (Chapter Seven) vividly illustrates, simply do not wish to be studied. Some organizations, such as research laboratories (Chapter Three), have an established procedure for integrating interested outsiders, but once the outsider appears to take on 'insider' status, problems of appropriate categorization become apparent. The longer the researcher hangs around, the more he or she participates, the harder it is to assimilate him or her to the conventional model of a researcher armed with clipboard and questionnaire. People who were comfortable at first may start to worry about the researcher as the research goes on.

Access is therefore not something to be negotiated once and then forgotten about (as the apparatus of ethics committees confronting medical researchers might suggest). It is, on the contrary, something that has to be both scrutinized for the way it transforms the research and continuously negotiated throughout the time of fieldwork. It is inconceivable, for example, that in-depth open-ended interviews could be conducted without the researcher explaining what he or she is about and gaining the interviewee's consent and cooperation. It is the impossibility of inter-viewing without consent which is – quite apart from ethical considerations – the main objection to covert ethnography (Sanjek 1985). It may be, however, that despite the ethnographer's attempts to explain him- or herself, he or she continues to be slotted into the easily understood category of student, a role sufficiently close to the researcher's that it can conveniently be accepted (Chapter Nine); in many cases, of course, researchers actually *are* students.

It is widely agreed that successfully conveying a sense of 'being there' to the reader is a mark of good ethnography.[4] But what does 'being there' mean or entail? In discussion, Malcolm Chapman made the point that no one (no authority) can stop you renting a flat in a French village, whereas there are numerous barriers to gaining access to a business, for example. And yet, the mere fact of residing in the village does not mean that people will let you into their homes or their lives. Particular thresholds or boundaries need to be transcended. What are these? They are certainly spatial (e.g. being 'let in') and temporal (e.g. people allowing one to be a part of their activities). The most significant, perhaps, is that one has gained some insight or understanding into 'the native's point of view', i.e. into how the world looks or is perceived from the perspective of the people themselves. What is this context, what are its boundaries, how are these determined and how are these connected to the local understanding thereby attained? They are certainly spatial and temporal, but this lived experience of space and time is structured as such through particular concepts, ideas, statements, and the way these are realized in particular social relations. These are the connections at the basis of ethnography and upon which ethnographies (whether the brief case studies found here or the expanded examples developed in monographs) are constructed: they 'speak to the truth of how things relate to one another' (Strathern n.d.: 9).

Specifying Ethnography

What are the differences between doing ethnography and doing interviews? Both can result in the creation of 'an ethnography', so students are understandably perplexed and want to know how they can tell that they are really 'doing ethnography'. Is only sustained participant observation in an organization for at least one year necessary before research can be called ethnography? This is a question which goes right to the heart of current debates between anthropology and fields such as cultural studies that also advocate ethnographic research.

Chapters One and Two, both conducted in business organizations, take up different positions on this issue; and the issue recurs elsewhere in the volume. Chapman (Chapter One), while recognizing participant observation as the ideal, believes that repeated interviewing can achieve ethnographic depth. Ouroussoff (Chapter Two) argues that research based on interviews can only result in ethnography if it is unusually sensitive (e.g. Le Witta 1994). Others suggest that

4. Geertz (1988), Miller (1997: 16; cf. Chapter Four below), Bate (1997: 1163).

interviews

the relationship between ethnography and interviews is more of a continuum (Chapter Three).

Where anthropologists cooperate with economists to conduct research in manufacturing businesses, even such minimally qualitative procedures as semi-structured interviews are perceived as radical (Chapter One). Is it then a question of what one is trying to achieve in the research which dictates whether 'immersion' or more scheduled encounters are appropriate? Furthermore, should the ethnographer pursue his or her enquiries into what happens 'after hours', outside of work, and how this is connected with life inside the organization? There are certainly advantages to so doing, but only a few of the contributors to this volume were able to achieve this. The ethical questions that arise from doing ethnography are not the main focus of this book, but they cannot be avoided. We include an evocative personal account of practical and ethical problems which the ethnographer trying to combine observation and participation may face – dilemmas that became especially acute in this case because the ethnographer routinely found himself in life and death situations (Chapter Eleven).

Perhaps the key to doing ethnography, whether based on a long-term stay or interviews, is the achievement of an empathetic of understanding similar to the therapeutic situation (cf. Chapter Six). This still leaves unanswered the question of the distinctive nature of an ethnography (cf. Thornton 1988, Strathern 1991). It lies, we argue, in its commitment to *methodological* holism – that is, to accepting that in principle anything in the research context can be relevant and could potentially be taken into account – while simultaneously recognizing that *descriptive* holism – the assumption that all social contexts are tightly interconnected social wholes (cf. Clifford 1988: 104) – is in most cases misleading. Indeed some have argued that descriptive holism is ideologically loaded and especially inappropriate in the light of today's increasingly 'multi-sited' contexts of ethnography (Marcus 1995). The consequence for the researcher is clear: he or she needs to adopt a curious kind of cross-eyed vision, one eye roving ceaselessly around the general context, any part of which may suddenly reveal itself to be relevant, the other eye focusing tightly, even obsessively, on the research topic. This is what Miller (1997: 17) calls the commitment to holistic analysis and Hine (Chapter Three) calls 'learning from looking elsewhere' in order to achieve a 'rich', contextualized understanding of whatever it is that one is supposed to be researching.

Finding a Focus

Ethnographic research conventionally takes shape around an initial plan or proposal of research, sometimes based on preliminary knowledge of the fieldwork site(s). However, there is often a disjunction between such intended research and what happens in practice. Regardless of the extent to which a plan is adhered to, how does one set about establishing an appropriate focus? The potential data are infinite; one cannot befriend, or even interview, everyone (unless the organization studied is extremely small); so where should one direct one's attention? This can be an extreme problem (Chapter Ten) but in most cases the people themselves within the organization – those with whom one is having day-to-day contacts and/or interviewing – will suggest the most appropriate focus. To be in a position to appreciate this, one needs to be open-minded and attentive, prepared to engage with 'native' categories and representations. Each organization will have its own preoccupations whether they be objects and visitors (Chapter Four), managing disturbed children (Chapter Six), or sexuality and suffering (Chapter Seven). This is why the ethnographer has to spend time being open to the concerns of the people studied, to spend time *not* being directive. It often then turns out that a small set of key concepts provide the crucial insights needed to gain an 'ethnographic' understanding of the organization (e.g. Simpson's discussion of the metaphors used by divorcing couples in Chapter Five). Such key concepts appear to 'hold things together' or to define the terrain that is being contested.

Focus is achieved with effort and empathy. Recorded information/data and one's recollected perceptions provide the critical, interactive setting where 'themes' are enabled to emerge out of a particular focus. In short, one is searching for a 'pattern' both in the data/perceptions and by implication in how the people studied present order and systematize their lives. Although ethnographers try to be systematic in some respect or other (surveying all households in a locality, or interviewing all the nurses on a ward, for example), this has less importance than the methodological holism mentioned above. To know every nook and cranny of a place is neither conceivable (even Malinowski was not able to produce a synthetic portrait of the Trobriands) nor, fortunately, necessary. To suggest this is to highlight an important tenet of anthropological description and understanding: that the focus derived from those with whom you have entered into relations is a focus they in turn use to order their lives and relations within (say) the particular organizational context.

It is clear, as many have argued, that a degree of reflexivity is essential for the ethnographer. The researcher has to be clear about his or her objectives and the limitations he or she is working under. Otherwise it will appear, as every practising anthropologist has surely felt, that one has failed to gather 'enough data'; at the same time one is faced by 'too much data' and the problem of how to 'write it up'. These paradoxes and frustrations are doubtless avoided by followers of more formal methodologies.

Doing Ethnography

It is part of the point of ethnography that there will never be, and cannot be, total agreement over what is the best way to go about it. But this does not mean that nothing can be said. For the sake of argument we can start from the position of Bate (1997) and expand. Bate suggests that good ethnography

1. conveys the sense of 'being there' (discussed above);
2. produces details and conclusions that are unexpected (we would add that this is the payoff for the – to some people – frightening prospect of research with open-ended questions);
3. reflects the polyphony – the multiple voices – of the real world;
4. offers a model or theory: it is not just for entertainment.

This last feature, or something like it, is necessary to distinguish anthropology from travel writing or journalism. Certainly much travel writing conveys better than many anthropologists do the sense of being there: but whose sense of being there? The very best travel writing – one thinks of V.S. Naipaul's *India: A Million Mutinies Now* – conveys a vivid sense of place and of the very many people whom the author met and spoke to. It might be accepted as a kind of ethnography since it is so evidently (at least overtly) about Indians and not about the author himself. However, it is less than wholly candid about how the material was collected, and it does not really offer a 'model' or theory.

To Bate's list one might add that good ethnography displays at least some of the following virtues. It

5. contextualizes its findings (the methodological holism discussed above);
6. pays attention to questions of power and inequality, by examining the ways in which some participants' voices and models prevail over others' (Chapters Eight and Nine);
7. emphasizes both what people say and what they do, and looks for connections and disconnections between the two (Miller's commitment to treating people as material agents: see Chapter Four);
8. does not restrict itself to 'front-stage performances', but pays equal attention to what people do and say when they are 'off duty' and not being watched (Chapters Eight, Eleven);
9. looks closely at how language is used (see especially Chapters Three, Four, Five, Nine);
10. is reflexively aware of the ethnographer's ambiguous position: empathetically trying to get at the points of view of numerous people – specialist and lay, old and young, male and female, powerful and relatively powerless – and at the same time attempting to put these together into some kind of overall pattern;
11. does not simply seek confirmation of what is already known (i.e. does not selectively pick ethnographic illustrations for a position already worked out), but always presents the material in sufficient richness that it can be worked

over by someone else with different interests and different theoretical dispositions; in other words, the writer attempts to make a contribution to 'the ethnographic record' as 'the central shared heritage of anthropology' (Kuper 1994: 117).

Putting it Down and Writing it Up

There are several problems confronting ethnographer of organizations which the more traditional anthropologist may not have had to face. In the first place, in order to carry out the research he or she may be employed in the organization and therefore have to write reports and carry out tasks like any member of the organization. Mascarenhas-Keyes (Chapter Ten) argues that the researcher should adapt the way in which conclusions are presented to the style and ethos of the organization in question, to ensure that they have maximum chance of being taken up. Mosse, on the other hand (Chapter Eight), suggests that there is an irresolvable tension between studying *inside an organization*, and therefore accepting its aims and agenda, and critically *studying the organization itself.* Anthropologists working for organizations may find that their notes on the organization become a kind of covert research which it is hard to publish. Inevitably, different ways of writing, perhaps even different ways of interpreting material, are appropriate for different audiences: these are likely to include the organization itself and academics, as well as various kinds of more popular readership.

But what should be done when these audiences merge into each other? As Chapman remarked in his oral presentation, Godfrey Lienhardt did not have to worry when writing *Divinity and Experience* that the Dinka themselves would read and assess it (though by the time he died many Dinka had indeed come to Britain and of these many must have read it). The researcher on organizations today knows that any ethnography that is recognizable will immediately be read by the people it is about, and every word must be weighed in consequence. As Macdonald describes (Chapter Four), the kind of publication thought appropriate by those studied may be of a very limited and esoteric kind, so that if the researcher publishes a more accessible description of the field site, it may be met by anger or outrage. These are tangled ethical and pragmatic issues, which have to be faced by the anthropologist studying organizations. Those studying more remote peoples may once have been saved from having to confront them, but this is rarely so today. Even the Ik have begun to protest at the way Colin Turnbull depicted them in *The Mountain People* (Turnbull 1972; Heine 1985).

In this book, the various chapters are 'finished products' and little space is devoted to the question of why the text was written up in one way rather than another (Van Maanen 1988, 1995). They are the outcomes of a series of strategic decisions about how best to describe and interpret the categories and lived experience of those with whom the authors had the privilege of being engaged, in either short-term or long-term relations. These strategies are in part dictated by the established literature and in part by the particular theme or set of themes found significant for presentation; literary techniques for presenting an interesting narrative and argument cannot, of course, be ignored. Intrinsic to this is the issue of closure: all understandings are partial but once this is recognized it is then appropriate to write as if one has achieved a relatively complete understanding of the themes and materials to hand. These may be superseded by subsequent research, but for the particular moment of description and interpretation, it is useful to imagine one has captured the (partial) truths. In short, although a textual entity has been created, one has, more importantly, produced an approximate representation of the way people present and live their lives.

Conclusion: Issues of Symmetry and Complexity

Latour (1993) advocates a 'symmetrical anthropology': this refers to the idea that all institutions and organizations should be studied in exactly the same way, on the basis of the same assumptions. A high-tech scientific laboratory can and should be studied exactly as is a tiny island community: each, he argues, is a particular configuration or network of actors, where the actors can be humans as much as artefacts, lines on paper, or any other created object. Latour claims that what distinguishes such networks is not their difference in kind (science vs non-science) but their relative size or scale and stability. In short, particular actor-networks have the capacity to achieve greater length and durability, but the difference is merely quantitative. For Latour scientific institutions are qualitatively no different from other institutions.

Latour's argument is both sophisticated and seductive. In many respects its spread among social science disciplines parallels the spread of ethnography as a form of research technique and written text. His book *Laboratory Life*, co-authored with Steve Woolgar, was a key text that marked the beginning of ethnography in the post-Kuhnian revision of the study of science. However, as Strathern (1996) has pointed out in her discussion of Latour and actor-network theory more generally, there are important qualitative differences between networks in the way they are 'cut' or bounded. This, in turn, has to do with the socio-historical emergence and continuity of particular conceptual regimes which are simultaneously regimes for ordering the world. Strathern's particular example is 'ownership' and 'property' and the way it places limits or 'cuts' the networks, for example, in scientific discoveries and their patents. This she compares to forms of 'cutting networks' in Melanesian mortuary rituals which are not predicated on Western ownership/property notions. At one level, these networks may appear to be 'symmetrical': Melanesian 'stopping of flow' and patent claims on discoveries or inventions in the West. But once the details of concepts and action on the ground, so to speak, are brought carefully under scrutiny we see important differences that cannot be glossed over. This is as true for the institutions and organizations themselves as it is for the way they come to be represented in ethnography.

complry Id

There is more than symmetry at stake here: there is also the fact, attested above, that organizations have a view of themselves, both for internal and for external consumption. This means that organizations are not just the sum of their participants' interactions: organizations acquire a life and a momentum independent of the people who make them up. Much organizational time and effort goes into controlling and disciplining those on the inside. These controls can be both subtle and complex (as Macdonald's Chapter Four illustrates). Whether this complexity should be taken to encompass different and incommensurable aims and attainments, or whether, on the other hand, there should be some uniform method for assessing different organizations, some single way – suitably adjusted for different types of organization – of judging their output and assessing whether they produce 'value for money' is one of the crucial issues in the field (Strathern n.d.).

With the exception of Mosse's Chapter Eight, all the chapters deal with organizations within the Euro-American context (and even the 'aid' organizations are Western-based). In a rough and ready fashion it is possible to separate the various case studies of this book into three broad categories or types: (1) those concerned with 'science', where the aim is to produce replicable results (Chapter Three; cf Rabinow 1996); (2) those concerned with business, which is oriented to the market and making a profit (see Chapters One and Two); (3) those concerned with agencies of the state, including the provision of welfare, where the aim is to embody and fulfil the wider values of the society (most of the other chapters).

However, the moment such a division is made, qualifications have to be noted. In the case of science, the laboratory is driven to produce results, but the funding and/or output is often market-driven and so we immediately see the influences of business/capitalism. In the case of the firm a not dissimilar problem emerges. For businesses, the explicit objective is profit or market penetration, but if the firm rides roughshod over the welfare of its staff and/or its consumers then it may soon see profits fall. Finally, state and welfare organizations are increasingly being judged as much by their market efficiency as by their 'care', and 'care' itself is increasingly measured in terms derived from the market. In short, within one organization we can perceive the contours of other, separate but also partially connected, kinds of organization.

When does the partially connected nature of organizations described here become relevant to the non-Western contexts conventionally studied by anthropologists? Perhaps this has always been the case but the Malinowskian tradition 'blocked out' the organizational features of colonialism and missions.[5] The ethnography of organizations may have been ignored by anthropologists in the past because it appeared to capture only a part of people's lives, instead of the 'full' view supposedly attained in a village setting. Furthermore, studying organizations has always seemed the preserve of other specialists: sociologists, economists, historians. Chapman (Chapter One) records his worry that, when doing fieldwork in Brittany, he should perhaps have been studying the local factory and hospital, rather than the more anthropologically conventional, but locally marginal, topics of ethnic identity and fishing.

It is our belief that the same methods can be used for village-level, organizational, and multi-sited ethnography. The chapters below show in a variety of different contexts how this is done, what specific problems arise, how they are addressed, and what the implications are of particular responses to these problems. Whether *the results* of that ethnography are to be seen as demonstrating similarities between small-scale societies and the modern West, or, by contrast, as showing fundamental differences, is in the end a matter of philosophical standpoint and interpretation, depending also on the level and the framework within which the interpretation takes place. What this collection demonstrates, we hope, is that the anthropologists now at work in organizations have a distinctive and valuable set of perspectives to offer, not just on 'tribes' or villages, but on the modern world of organizations as well.

References

Asad, T. (ed.) (1973), *Anthropology and the Colonial Encounter*, London: Ithaca Press.

Bate, S.P. (1997), 'Whatever Happened to Organizational Anthropology? A Review of the Field of Organizational Ethnography and Anthropological Studies', *Human Relations*, **50**(9): 1147–75.

Buchanan, D., Boddy, D., and McCalman, J. (1988), 'Getting in, Getting on, Getting out and Getting back', in A. Bryman (ed.), *Doing Research in Organizations*, London and New York: Routledge.

Chambers, R. (1983), *Rural Development: Putting the Last First*, London: Longman Scientific and Technical.

Clifford, J. (1988), *The Predicament of Culture: Twentieth-Century Ethnography, Literature, and Art*, Cambridge, Mass: Harvard University Press.

—— (1997), *Routes: Travel and Translation in the late Twentieth Century*, Cambridge, Mass: Harvard University Press.

5. See Asad (1973) for an early statement along these lines.

Edwards, J. (1994), 'Idioms of Bureaucracy and Informality in a Local Housing Aid Office', in S. Wright (ed.), *Anthropology of Organizations*, London: Routledge.

Geertz, C. (1988), *Works and Lives: The Anthropologist as Author*, Cambridge: Polity.

Gillespie, R. (1991), *Manufacturing Knowledge: A History of the Hawthorne Experiments*, Cambridge: Cambridge University Press.

Hammersley, M. (1983), *The Ethnography of Schooling: Methodological Issues*, Diffield: Nafferton.

Heine, B. (1985), 'The Mountain People: Some Notes on the Ik of North-Eastern Uganda', *Africa*, **55**(1): 3–16.

Kuper, A. (1994), 'Anthropological Futures', in R. Borofsky (ed.), *Assessing Cultural Anthropology*, New York: McGraw Hill.

Latour, B. (1993), *We Have Never Been Modern*, tr. C. Porter, Cambridge, Mass.: Harvard University Press.

—— and S. Woolgar (1986 [1979]), *Laboratory Life: The Construction of Scientific Facts*, Princeton: Princeton University Press.

Law, J. (1994), *Organizing Modernity*, Oxford: Blackwell.

Le Witta, B. (1994), *French Bourgeois Culture*, Cambridge: Cambridge University Press.

Lienhardt, G. (1961), *Divinity and Experience: The Religion of the Dinka*, Oxford: Clarendon.

Marcus, G.E. (1995), 'Ethnography in/of the World System: The Emergence of Multi-sited Ethnography', *Annual Review of Anthropology*, **24**: 95–117.

Mayer, J.E. and Timms, N. (1970), *The Client Speaks: Working Class Impressions of Casework*, London: Routledge & Kegan Paul.

Miller, D. (1997), *Capitalism: An Ethnographic Approach*, Oxford: Berg.

Mitchell, S.A. (1993), *Hope and Dread in Psychoanalysis*, New York: Basic Books.

Morgan, G. (1990), *Organizations in Society*, Houndmills: Macmillan.

Morley, D. (1988 [1986]), *Family Television: Cultural Power and Domestic Leisure*, London: Routledge.

Naipaul, V.S. (1991), *India: A Million Mutinies Now*, London: Minerva.

Rabinow, P. (1996), *Making PCR: A Story of Biotechnology*, Chicago: University of Chicago Press.

Sanjek, R. (1985), *Fieldnotes: The Makings of Anthropology*, Ithaca: Cornell University Press.

Sinclair, S. (1997), *Making Doctors: An Institutional Apprenticeship*, Oxford: Berg.

Stocking, G. (1992), *The Ethnographer's Magic and Other Essays in the History of Anthropology*, Madison: University of Wisconsin Press.

Strathern, M. (1991), *Partial Connections*, Savage, Maryland: Rowman and Littlefield.

—— (1992), *After Nature: English Kinship in the Late Twentieth Century*, Cambridge: Cambridge University Press.

—— (1996), 'Cutting the Network', *Journal of the Royal Anthropological Institute* (N.S.), 2: 517–35.

—— (n.d.), 'Critique of Good Practice', AAA 1998.

Thornton, R. (1988), 'The Rhetoric of Ethnographic Holism', *Cultural Anthropology*, 3: 285–303.

Turnbull, C. (1972), *The Mountain People*, London: J. Cape.

Van Maanen, J. (1988), *Tales of the Field: On Writing Ethnography*, Chicago: University of Chicago Press.

—— (ed.) (1995), *Representation in Ethnography*, London: Sage.

Wright, S. (ed.) (1994), *Anthropology of Organizations*, London: Routledge.

—— (1998), 'The Politicization of "Culture"', *Anthropology Today*, **14**(1): 7–15.

Young, M. (1991), *An Inside Job: Policing and Police Culture in Britain*, Oxford: Clarendon.

Part I
Business

–1–

Social Anthropology and Business Studies: Some Considerations of Method

Malcolm Chapman

A conference was held at Manchester Metropolitan University in April 1998. It was called 'Managing Global Change'. The conference broadly concerned business and management studies, with particular reference to the economies of East and South-east Asia. The conference was an interesting one, with invited contributions from some well-known figures of local and/or international repute: Patrick Minford (economist; see 1998), Peter Dicken (geographer; see 1998), John Dunning (doyen of scholars of international business), Gerald Kaufman (politician), and Bruno Leblanc. The last of these is a scholar, researcher, consultant, and teacher in the world of management education; he is of long experience, and able to work in English, French, German, and Polish. He gave the final address, in which he looked at issues for the future of management education and research. This involved him in looking at the various disciplines which have contributed to business studies – notably economics and psychology. Here he noted an absence. 'Looking back,' he remarked, 'it amazes me that we have never had anthropologists in our faculties of business and management; we need them and their ideas.'[1]

I was sitting next to Professor Leblanc at the time, having earlier made my contribution to summing up the proceedings. We had not previously conversed during the conference, so I had the heartening experience of being told that I was needed by an entirely disinterested source. Anthropologists will recognize that this is not a particularly common occurrence; not, perhaps, since the days of the Colonial Office have anthropologists had any clear instrumental role in mainstream political and economic activity. Economists, sociologists, and psychologists have, in their different ways, achieved this; anthropology has not. An invitation into the heart of business studies, therefore, where so much busy and expensive pedagogy and research is taking place, is not one to be treated lightly.

---

1. This is a cheat. I pretend to quote verbatim, but am really reconstructing from memory; the reconstruction is not far off, however, and the meaning is faithfully rendered.

Business

I was and am an anthropologist, Oxford-trained from the early 1970s, and particularly influenced by the work and teaching of Edwin Ardener.[2] I studied ethnicity and the Celtic fringe, and have published variously on the subject (1978, 1982, 1992, 1993). I began a move into business studies in 1989 by reading for an MBA at one of the U.K.'s oldest business schools, Bradford University Management Centre. This was not, to judge from the surprised responses of my colleagues, a self-evident career move, and its motivations bear upon the content of this chapter. In the Celtic fringe, I had studied ethnicity and language, and I had studied a fishing village and fishing as a means to this. These were interesting subjects, but there nevertheless seemed to be a great deal of life that I was under no compulsion to study, or that was only at the edges of my vision – very generally, nearly all the things that went on in offices, factories, bureaucracies. Virtually everybody in Brittany had some sort of investment in being (or not being) Breton, but for most this was not something they thought about or cared about very much. What where they doing the rest of the time? I came to the view that my concentration upon a 'traditional' occupation, and upon ethnicity, had in some important ways impeded a study of still more important things. I believe that this was not merely a personal idiosyncrasy, but was built into the subject of social anthropology at the time. The limitation was difficult or impossible to surmount, although with hindsight it is not obvious why that should have been so.

It was, therefore, with a view to overcoming this lingering primitivism in the subject, that I turned to business studies. Social anthropology has a post-war history of concentrating upon primitive societies, of working through the shift from 'function to meaning', of holistic study, of participant observation, and of retreat from numerical analysis. Business and management studies, by contrast, have been late-born aspirants to the positivist social sciences. They have many precedents, and some of the 'founding fathers' (there are no founding mothers) are from the first half of the twentieth century; in general, however, the great explosion in research and teaching was to be in the second half of the century, beginning in the USA in the 1950s and spreading to Europe in the 1960s and 1970s. Business and management academia have been working through their own (as it were indigenous) positivist agenda. For academic resources, in the post-war period, they have looked to social sciences which also aspired to this model: most particularly, to social psychology and to economics (see Buckley and Chapman 1996; Chapman 1996–97). Social anthropology was not an obvious partner, as business and management studies pursued their positivist agenda.

2. For what it is worth as an anthropological credential, I was, I think, the very last to be obliged to endure (or to achieve) the once-classical sequence of degrees (MA, Diploma, B.Litt., D.Phil.), ruinously expensive in both time and money, which Oxford anthropology used to require. Innocent pride to salvage from the wreckage: Evans-Pritchard was similarly qualified.

Researchers within business and management studies eventually started to notice, however, as anthropologists had noticed several decades before in relation to their own preoccupations, that the results were not forthcoming – that the predictive science was being continually postponed, amid ever-repeated calls for further research funding. Faith in the ultimate appearance of a predictive science is still strong, but doubt is growing nevertheless.

In this situation, many authorities are calling for an integration of other social sciences into the weaponry available to management studies – social anthropology is increasingly cited. This is partly driven by the hope that the specialist knowledge provided by social anthropology will allow the positivist agenda to be furthered, as if the obstacle were merely technical. Within cross-cultural management studies, for example, scholars have commonly tried to tease out the variables which might explain differences from one context to another – variables like law, religion, industry structure, organization structure. There has long been an intuition that something like 'culture' might be important as well, and scholars have turned to social anthropology for a definition of 'culture' (vain hope), so that this too can be measured and fed into the multivariate statistical models – one independent variable among others which will help to explain 'behaviour' (see Sekaran 1983; Negandhi 1983; Roberts and Boyacigiller 1984).

We can perhaps predict that nothing much will come from this, for the potential that social anthropology offers is based upon more fundamental features. Social anthropology has already had the experience of being knocked completely off its poise by anti-positivist and anti-behaviourist arguments; it has already had several decades of experience of finding some sort of (fragile) equilibrium in the aftermath of this; it has also, through its own long debate with itself, gained considerable sophistication in constructing arguments aimed at positivist and behaviourist positions. All these features make it a particularly interesting ally for business studies at the present stage: business studies is still predominantly behaviourist and positivist; it is also still predominantly monocultural (and effectively USA-centred). It is, therefore, vulnerable to, and perhaps capable of enrichment from, social anthropological criticism; business studies is currently undergoing something oddly like 'a shift from function to meaning', and social anthropology can offer its own experience and hindsight. So social anthropology and business studies, by their very differences, offer interesting possibilities for cooperation.

I have experienced the meeting of social anthropology and business studies in many ways and many places, in teaching and research. One particularly fruitful context, however, was provided by a research project, funded by the ESRC under a more general programme called 'Contracts and Competition'. This general programme was inspired by a desire to understand how markets work, particularly in the context of attempts to introduce elements of competition and competitive tendering into the National Health Service. The ESRC wanted to know how markets work, so to speak, so that they could be made to work in the British public sector.

The project, 'The Management of Cooperative Strategies', was conceived by Professor Peter Buckley; his background is in economics, and he is one of the world's leading theorists of the activities of multinational companies. The project was therefore phrased in terms of academic economics, but from the first it was looking explicitly at the frontiers of economics, and at innovative approaches. The aim was to understand how companies organize and understand the range of activities which confront them at their own boundaries. Within text-book economics, the boundary between a company and the outside world is often conceived of as one between 'firm' and 'market'. For the great majority of economic analysis, the firm is a black box, around which inputs and outputs, cost-curves and break-even diagrams, are elaborated. What happens inside a firm to lead to these results is not open to debate within this form of argument. Rationality and competition assume away all problems, all idiosyncrasy, all diversity.

Ronald Coase, in his pioneering attempt to theorize the very existence of the firm (1937), brought the issue of transaction costs into view, opening up as problematic the boundary between the firm and its environment. The firm was still conceived, however, as a unitary entity, unproblematically distinguished from other firms, and unproblematically distinguished from the market. From this viewpoint, there were two kinds of organization – those of market, and those of hierarchy (or organization as commonly understood); within themselves, firms were organized through hierarchy; between firms, market principles ruled. The fluctuating boundaries of firms were to be explained by the varying transaction costs which required, or forbade, recourse to one or another organizing principle. This was a very fruitful approach, and it has been pushed forward in many ways (see Buckley and Casson 1976; Williamson 1975).

The Coasian dichotomy between firm and market, however, is an oversimplification. Many years ago Richardson (1972) argued that the simple dichotomy, firm vs market, actually represented two rather unlikely polar opposites, which were in fact rather rare in reality: the reality, by contrast, occupied the whole range of grey area between these two polar opposites, with things like alliances, friendships, networks, relationships of trust, and so on, actually occupying the real empirical ground. The reality, therefore, could not justifiably be analysed on the basis of a polarization which so signally misrepresented it.

The project 'The Management of Cooperative Strategies' was an attempt to find a method, and a mode of argument, which would allow this problem to be researched. This involved a continuous negotiation of the mutual possibilities and powers of social anthropology and economics. It is possible to live a life as a professional economist, working out complicated models based entirely on assumptions about what the world is like, and without the input of any real factual information at all.

When economists look for empirical information, they have a tendency to analyse this using models which are rigorous at the expense of reality: they operate, that is, with assumptions which allow determinate analysis to be carried out, but which are so unrealistic as to preclude any serious tangling with the complexities of real life.

Social anthropology is a kind of polar opposite of this. Anthropologists try to tackle reality head on; they don't necessarily expect it to make unilinear or determinate sense; if there is a clash between theory and reality, then their sympathies – and their responsibilities – are usually with reality. Although anthropology is (at least in my view) a conceptually very sophisticated subject, there is not much within it that could be regarded as 'theory', in the sense in which positivist social science understands the word.

My colleague Peter Buckley's previous research projects had been carried out using either questionnaires or structured interviews. That is to say, his work has always been empirically rather than theoretically based; but the empirical work has been explicitly designed to answer questions arising from theory: it has been, as the research manuals have it, 'hypothetico-deductive'.

My own previous research projects had been carried out using participant observation fieldwork. They were in part related to problems that I wanted to solve, but they were certainly not containable within the framework of positivist research. My main period of fieldwork was spent in Brittany, where I lived in one village for nearly three years; I was interested in fishing and farming, in ethnicity, in bilingualism, and all sorts of other things. I wrote that work up as a doctoral thesis, a 'monograph', which is typically what social anthropologists do. A single case, years of work. No possibilities of comparison, no sampling, no controls, no statistical analysis: a single case.

The result of this is that our attitudes to what counted as evidence, what counted as research, and so on, were very different. To find some sort of compromise of method between the two styles of research to which we were accustomed, we decided to interview managers using what the textbooks call 'unstructured interviews'. (I think my colleague at the time viewed this as a subset of 'interviews'; I regarded it as a subset of 'talking to people'.) To get some idea of the differences that we brought to the exercise, a few illustrations may serve.

When we went to do our first interview, my colleague said that going in without a questionnaire he 'felt naked'. At the time, a questionnaire would have felt to me to be an unwieldy and intrusive burden. In retrospect, and now that I have been for several more years in the field of business research, I can better appreciate his feelings, while still not necessarily sharing them. From his research background, going in without a questionnaire raised unwelcome questions such as 'how are we going to find anything out?' and 'what will we talk about?'; for me, going in without a questionnaire promised this: that we would be able to talk about what was important to the manager whom we were interviewing, in terms of understandings that were his, not ours. Thus, we revealed an aspect of the theoretical fissure which runs right through the social sciences, generating many oppositions: quantitative/ qualitative, positivist/ interpretive, and so on (see Buckley and Chapman 1997c).

Our first interview lasted about four hours, including talk, lunch, and a walk around the factory. After this, my colleague remarked that this was a particularly long period of time to spend in a company; administering a questionnaire usually only took about half an hour, and you were in any case reluctant to trespass further on management time. (In this case, as in all others, we left to the manager in question the decision as to how long the interview should go on.) I was genuinely surprised by this perception, since by my own standards we had done nothing more than poke a head round the door; the 'four hours' contrasted, for me, not with the half-hour that it would have taken to administer a questionnaire, but with the year-long total immersion fieldwork in the company which would have satisfied purist anthropological criteria.

holism

In an early interview, a manager (who was in production) began to talk of the difficulties of his personal relationship with the new people in the marketing department. My ears pricked up. My colleague's attention wandered. In another interview, we were exploring the relationship of a company to its competitors and suppliers. The conversation wandered to the relationship of the company to the regulators, and to the downstream customers (wholesalers, retailers). Again, I continued scribbling, steeped in holism, and not able to suppose that there was such a thing as 'irrelevant information'. Again, my colleague's attention wandered.

These trivial illustrations have behind them some rather important points of difference. For a social anthropologist, there is no end to relevance. Anthropologists try to be 'holistic' in inquiry. They assume, without even necessarily thinking very hard about it on most occasions, that everything is related to everything else: that somebody's personal relationship with another will affect their professional relationship; that friendship will affect arm's-length market dealing; that politics will affect economics, religion will affect morality, language will affect politics; that the life of somebody within a company cannot be divorced from his or her life outside the company; and so on. All of the major thrusts in social anthropological theory in this century – functionalism, structuralism – have confirmed this bent of thought. Social anthropologists also assume, as a matter of course, that truth is socially created, socially relative, and multi-faceted: that what a manager says to you on Tuesday about his relationship with Mr X from finance might be rather different from what he says on Wednesday, and that since his relationship with Company Y is mediated through Mr X, this will have an effect not just upon the reporting of events, but upon the realization of the events themselves.

The decision to conduct unstructured interviews, and to allow those being interviewed to have a strong hand in conducting the research agenda, proved very fruitful. We asked managers being interviewed to talk about problems that they faced across the boundary of their company, at its interface with others; at its simplest, this was asking the classic make or buy decision: if the company needs something, does it make it or buy it, and why, and how is this decision made? This proved to be a potent question, which in virtually all cases provoked a long series of reflections and considerations; we usually needed to do little more than nudge the ball along from time to time. Perhaps I am overstating a case here: we did carry a theory with us into the interviews (a theory about the importance of the definition and realization of the boundaries of the firm, as outlined above); we did hold the view that research into managerial perceptions of how the company boundary was created and crossed was theoretically important. After that, however, we found it very useful to allow managers to formulate their own problems, and their own discussion of these. And they were very willing to do so. My colleague was surprised not only by the quality and depth of the knowledge that we gathered during the interviews, but also by the willingness of those interviewed to carry on talking once the interviews were under way.

There is growing resistance, within business, to continued cooperation with the research procedures of traditional business academia – in particular, there is growing resistance to filling in research questionnaires; return rates are low, and the quality of response must often be very doubtful, even when return is made. Some managers that I have talked to now make it policy to put all questionnaires immediately in the bin. This is partly driven by pressure of work and shortage of time. It is partly in consequence of the constant increase of questionnaires arriving in the mail, itself a consequence of the enormous increase in academic activity in this area (undergraduate dissertations, MBA dissertations, doctoral work, post-doctoral work, consultancies, and so on). It is also, however, to judge from our own work, partly driven by an impatience with questionnaires as a research tool. This impatience is provoked by a sense that the questionnaires are simply asking wrong questions, irrelevant questions, and (perhaps most importantly) questions which (to remember Hocart) 'unite what others divide, and divide what others unite'.

Our own approach, by contrast, allowed managers to formulate and pursue problems in their own terms. From a social anthropological point of view, this is routine. Within business and management studies, it was rather a radical departure (see Buckley and Chapman 1997c). It had the virtue that managers were not dis-affected by the research procedures, and were not anxious to end the interviews as soon as possible; on the contrary, most interviews went on longer than originally scheduled, and some only ended because of mutual exhaustion in telling and listening. Managers, like everybody else, are interested in themselves and in what they do. A long unstructured interview allows them to talk about this, in all its com-plexity, with somebody who is also genuinely interested; we conjectured that perhaps this did not happen very often (who else would listen? Spouse? Fellow manager?).

Even managers who felt that it would be hard for them to find the time, have allowed the interviews to run on for several hours, and have given every appearance of enjoying them. No one has yet said 'don't come back', and in some cases we have been back five or six times. In one interesting case, the manager had stressed that he was very busy at the time of arranging the interview, and had restricted it to half an hour in his diary. At the start of the interview, he repeated this constraint. He was one of a very few who answered our probing questions tersely, and was difficult to launch into a stream of reflection and narrative. We eventually ran out of different ways of attempting to effect this, and conceded defeat; that, we said, was all we had to ask. The clock had gone for about twenty minutes. He looked mildly disconcerted, and rallied by telling us all the interesting things that we should have asked about. The interview eventually went on for over two hours, revealing some highly interesting stories of intercorporate and interpersonal trust.

So, by conducting long, unstructured, and multiply repeated interviews, we have not, in anthropological terms, precisely carried out fieldwork. With such a method, some of the anthropological interest in context, in intimacy, in creative remembering and forgetting, can be satisfied. By interviewing different people within the same company, we get multiple accounts, multiple perspectives. We have presented our method, to the managers we have interviewed, as an attempted alternative to the orthodoxy of structured questionnaires, administered at a single point in time. It is interesting that our approach has been almost unanimously approved by the managers that we have been studying.

Did we replicate some of the sense of continuity that fieldwork produces? Well, yes, to some extent, simply by going back again and again to the same people. We already had, of course, a great deal of contextual knowledge of much of their activity, so we did not have to spend several apprentice years learning about all of their social lives; we knew what they were likely to eat, wear, say, and so on. So repeated unstructured interviews, of an open-ended kind, are perhaps not fully satisfactory, but they can certainly be defended. They can certainly be expected to generate friendship, or at least companionability; they can generate shared experience, which grows, and can then be used as the basis for further reflections. It is much easier to talk to somebody about important things, if you have shared experience to provide a context for expression: 'You remember what I was saying about old so-and-so? Well, only last week . . .', and the like. Our own increasing contextual knowledge, not only of individual companies but of the industry as a whole, was important in this.

Open-ended and unstructured interviews also allowed the expression of all apparently relevant dimensions of thought and action. Social anthropology cannot avoid taking a holistic view, and this is a view that seems to appeal to managers. Companies can only thrive in a holistic sense (it is no good making things if you can't sell them . . .), and management is so protean an activity that it is almost impossible to put boundaries round it; managers recognize this, and appreciate it when academics recognize it as well. The traditional approach of business studies, particularistic and specialist, does not serve this requirement. Anthropologists are interested in social context, without any predetermined limitations, and again this strikes a chord with many managers; they know, from practice and intuition, that the boundaries of relevance are never clear-cut. In long and repeated interviews, they are allowed to tell their story.

What of the results? My colleague's first perception remained valid: our results were rich and detailed. There remained, and remains, the problem of how to write these up, and how to relate the data to the economic theories from which the project originally derived. Here we are still at work. The characteristic approach within business and management studies is to generate numerical results, which can then be subjected to statistical analysis (typically through SPSS). Many conceptual issues which would have troubled a social anthropologist at the start of the research are, by the time the results of statistical analysis emerge, very distant memories, rolled flat and forgotten. It is striking, indeed, that when the results of such research procedures are discussed, attention commonly focuses upon the rectitude of the statistical procedures, rather than upon the often very problematic conceptual issues surrounding the original hypotheses. We are spared these problems, only to be faced with others. Our data is not amenable to statistical analysis, so that route is closed. But the economic theories to whose refinement we hope to contribute have typically accepted only quantitative data as legitimate and valid. One way in which we have tried to get round this is to introduce the idea that managerial *perception* of quantity, and relative quantity, as verbally expressed, is socially real (Buckley and Chapman 1997a).

We have noted that previous studies in this area have typically involved questionnaire responses and published data. The most intimate forms of enquiry have proceeded through one-off in-depth interviews. Such one-off interviews are satisfactory for examining states, moments in time, but not for examining processes, movement through time. Of course, any interview contains an implicit time dimension, in that the interviewee uses past material to make sense of the present, and to predict future events. It is typically present understanding, however, which dictates the structure of recollection, and this present understanding changes over time. The past is not necessarily objectively remembered. This is by now an anthropological commonplace (Tonkin *et al.* 1989), and one which, on the basis of our project, we have explored in the corporate domain (Buckley and Chapman 1997b). By using repeated interviews of the same companies and people, we were able to focus attention not only on successive states, but also on successive recollections of the past. Events that, in prospect, looked catastrophic, can be recollected with tranquillity, as having led to success; events that, in prospect, were scarcely considered significant, can be seen, in retrospect, to have had dire consequences. This is a very fruitful field of inquiry in business studies, and also potentially revolutionary. Business strategists, investors, managers, researchers, are all profoundly interested in being able to predict the future: the potential rewards are colossal, like knowing the result of the next Grand National. In fact, most models that claim to be successfully predictive of the future are little more than slightly disguised models by which the present is successfully predicted by the past. If, in that past and present, managers were continually recreating their past decisions and their expected futures, then the status of models of future prediction looks precarious indeed.

There is not space here to give any full analysis of the materials gathered through our research project. Many different kinds of analysis are in any case possible. In order to give some idea of the advantages that our approach has over questionnaire-based, single-point-of-time-studies, one or two examples may help.

The virtue of continued and ever-deepening acquaintance with our interviewees was manifest in many ways. We had of course promised confidentiality and anonymity, with a guarantee not to disclose corporate or personal names in any of our analyses. Nevertheless, interviewees were sometimes a little guarded at our first meeting, as one might expect. This caution often wore off even during the first interview, so that after an hour or so it was thrown to the winds. Certainly, by the second or third interviews, it was always much reduced. One clear marker of this was the telling phrase, 'I shouldn't be telling you this, but . . .' It sometimes helped, at this critical moment, if the interviewer stopped scribbling notes; the interviewee, helped by the momentary sense that this was *not* going down on paper (though eventually it did), continued with the illicit tale. The point of this is not specifically that we *were* interested in confidential material for its own sake. It is of course true that any full account of corporate life, satisfactory in an anthropological sense, would have to include a great deal of material that was confidential and sensitive, either at the individual, office, or corporate frontier, and we were after as much information as we could get. The significance of the 'I shouldn't be telling you this . . .' moment, was, in part, that it presaged the disclosure of deeper and juicier information, and we were grateful for this. There is no doubt that in most cases, had we been trying to elicit information through the use of a tick-box questionnaire, we would not have been able to access information at this level of sensitivity. One interviewee (already alluded to above) gave us rich information about practices to which he had been a witness that bordered on the corrupt. (The nature of the border is itself an interesting one, since the border is often a grey twilight, rather than a black-and-white line.) Had we asked, from a bald questionnaire, 'have you ever been bribed? If yes, go to section ci, how often?, section cii, how much?, section ciii, who by?', then it is reasonable to suppose that we would have been fobbed off with a negative. (We have a colleague who carried out just such a questionnaire interview among multinational corporations active in sub-Saharan Africa, and found that none of them ever paid or received bribes.)

A more important point about the 'I shouldn't be telling you this . . .' moment, was that it was clear evidence that the narrative necessity gripping the interviewee was overcoming certain kinds of caution and suspicion. The stories that we were told, usually hours long, discursive, multiply recursive through past events and future interpretations, were *whole* stories in an important sense. The people telling them were often as involved in them as it is possible to be. The confidentiality issue – what could and could not be told according to certain conventions – was one that cut across narrative and holistic necessities, and it was generally these necessities that prevailed. If the story needed confidential elements, then the story got them; the narrative drive and integrity, as driven and experienced by the interviewees themselves, demanded this. They wanted to tell their story, and they wanted it to be understood. We were, from many experiences of this kind, confident that our information was indeed richer than anything a questionnaire could have produced. We are not suggesting, of course, that there were no areas of secrecy left undisclosed; only that we got further than most alternative methods (short of full participant observation).

A further example relates to the issue of prediction of possible futures, and the interpretation of realized events. As noted above, the business world is passionately interested in the future. The academic and consultancy discourses surrounding corporate strategy are in many respects exercises in futurology. Every interview we conducted held elements of speculation about forthcoming events, with current action designed to accommodate expected or possible futures. By conducting repeated interviews, we were able to track events in something rather like real time. There is a multi-layered controversy within the economics and strategy literatures about whether corporate strategy is top-down designed, and competent to predict and control the future, or whether strategy is chaotic (perhaps even in a technical sense) and (to use a term made useful by Austrian economics) 'emergent' (that is, you know what you are doing when you find yourself doing it).

We have been able to contribute in this area as well, since we had numerous examples where the futures expected and planned for in interview 1 were confounded and overturned by interview 2 (and so on). One company had an elaborate plan for expanding its sales force, at considerable expense and with some degree of risk. All managers in the company had contributed to the thinking which led to this conclusion, and it was generally accepted, on the basis of available evidence, that this was the right thing to do. Steps were taken towards this. As this was happening, a consultancy was called in to do some in-house management training. As a result of the contacts established through this activity, the same consultancy was asked to look briefly at the corporate decision to engage its own enlarged workforce. The consultancy rapidly came to the conclusion that the right way to move was towards outsourcing of virtually all sales activity, with compelling arguments employed. All this took place over a period during which we conducted eight interviews with the company. Any single interview, however deep, would have failed to track these rapid changes in the wind, with their profound effects on corporate strategy, and on accepted managerial thinking. The implications of such events for the more confident and predictive of strategy models are profound, and we will be exploring these in future publications.

In another company that we interviewed repeatedly, we found ourselves meeting one manager, at the same desk, who was working for a different company, with a different name, and a different strategic rationale, every time we met him. He carried on doing more or less the same thing, with more or less the same people around him, in the same place, while a whirl of corporate acquisition and divestment went on around him. Because his own activity had to make sense within the larger corporate environment within which he worked, and because this larger environment changed its name, structure, and strategic rationale several times during the course of our research, he too had to adopt subtly varying accounts of what he was doing, and why. Again, single-point-of-time studies and questionnaire studies could not have captured the detail and entertainment of this.

There are other problems involved in attempted studies of modern companies, in the social anthropological style, problems that were not fully anticipated when the anthropologist was working on a coral island. We can discuss these under three headings: disclosure, access, and other opportunities.

Disclosure

Anthropologists traditionally came back from exotic fieldwork with a total conviction that the world of their research (coral island, tropical jungle, mountain village) was totally separate from the world of their academic publication. The classic anthropological monograph was about illiterate people speaking another language on the other side of the world. An anthropologist could say what he or she pleased, without any thoughts of confidentiality, libel, ethics, law suits, and the like. An anthropologist could publish photographs of the naked savages, without any fear that the savages, or their children or grandchildren, would turn up demanding reparation. We could take the work of the Oxford Africanists, led by Evans-Pritchard, as an example here.

The security of separation between anthropologist and people is best exemplified, in my own mind at least, by the work of Lawrence Wylie. Wylie was an American anthropologist, who carried out research in the Vaucluse in the south of France, in the late 1950s. His theoretical background was psychosexual, and he devoted considerable attention to how children were reared, the effect of this upon their sexuality and social activity, and so on. He returned to the United States, and wrote what he regarded as a scholarly monograph, directed at serious students of social organization. The work, *Village in the Vaucluse*, is highly respected. However, in the 1960s, it was getting easier and easier to send information back and forth across continents. One of the people from the village got hold of a copy of the book, and it found a home in the village bar, sitting on the bar-top. The book was in English, and most of the people from the village in the Vaucluse were unable to read it with any fluency. They could look up their own and other people's names, however, and they could get some idea that the book seemed to be about sex, and the curious habits and practices of various individuals – filtered through the half-understood foreign language of English. The result was a predictable uproar, a widespread village sense of having been belittled and betrayed.

Wylie was very surprised by this. The conventions of anthropology to that date had required no sensitivity to this kind of problem. Ever since, the problem has grown more intense. An anthropologist must expect that the objects of study will become readers of the monograph. Wylie's response was to translate the book into French, so that at least the villagers would have direct access to what he said, rather than having bawdy and malicious half-translations thrown at them.

Anthropologists today are almost morbidly sensitive about this kind of problem. It is interesting to note, however, that even as late as the early 1960s, no problem was perceived.

A company, unlike a 'primitive society', is potentially a highly sensitive and litigious organization. The researcher can have no illusions that the readership of the published findings will be confined to a small scholarly audience. The information, moreover, is not just morally sensitive, but potentially commercially sensitive as well. This is not an issue with which social anthropologists have commonly had to deal. One can give disguised names to the companies under discussion, but this is not always an effective solution, particularly where the companies are large ones, and their largeness matters. (Consider: 'this data comes from a large UK manufacturer of aero-engines'.) One of the most celebrated single-company studies in business literature was provided by Geert Hofstede (1980); the company was originally disguised as 'Hermes', but it was not long before everybody knew that the company in question was IBM.

Access

In many societies, there are no formal barriers to an anthropologist. Most anthropologists have not needed 'permission' to go and do their study. They have simply moved in with their tent, or rented their flat, and begun making local contacts. Company research is not like that. We might expect that under most circumstances, if an anthropologist wandered vaguely into the Managing Director's office, sat down, and announced that he was going to do three years' fieldwork there, the security men would move briskly in.

Access is always a problem in business research. We have already noted above that many managers and companies feel 'over-researched' already (although this varies from country to country, and from sector to sector). Many business researchers rely upon the exploitation of previous contacts, friendships, and the like, for first access to a company (and it is first access that is most problematic; we always ended interviews by asking if we could come again, and, as noted above, nobody has yet said 'no'). The problem of access is compounded by the disaffection of managers from the practices of business research. That is a major reason why we congratulated ourselves upon having a research method which managers, once into their stride, could almost be said to have enjoyed.

One solution to the problem of access is to *work* for the company under study: true participation, with or without telling the company of one's true intentions. If with, then the problems referred to below (under 'other opportunities') will raise themselves. If without, then there are clearly ethical issues arising. Activity in these areas is not sufficiently deep or widespread for protocols of any strength to arise. People make their own bargains with their conscience.

Other Opportunities

Social anthropologists face a problem that there is nothing for them to do to earn a living but teach other people to be social anthropologists. This is not healthy. This problem seems to have arisen in large part because of the enduring primitivism of the subject. The smaller, the more exotic, and the more materially impoverished the people of your study, the more prestigious was your work in academic circles; that was your reward. The punishment was that nobody outside academia cared: you had no knowledge to sell for which there was large consumer demand. There are many degrees and examples of partial exception to this generalization, but it can be defended from observed social realities.

In business and management studies, this is not necessarily the case. Many people in business and management academia and research have potential alternative careers in business and management. Many successful researchers become successful consultants, and the rewards are very much higher than those in academia (at least as measured in the wallet). If an anthropologist succeeded in doing a long term of participant observation in a single company, he or she would probably, as a result, be in a position to start operating as a consultant in various domains. Such people would stop being anthropologists, and become something else, too busy to go to conferences or to write learned articles, because the opportunity costs would be so high.

References

Ardener, E. (1989), *The Voice of Prophecy, and Other Essays*, Oxford: Blackwell.
Buckley, P. and Casson, M. (1976), *The Future of the Multinational Enterprise*, London: Macmillan.

Buckley, P. and Chapman, M. (1996), 'Economics and Social Anthropology – Reconciling Differences', *Human Relations*, **49**(9): 1123–50.

Buckley, P. and Chapman, M. (1997a), 'The Measurement and Perception of Transaction Costs', *Cambridge Journal of Economics*, **21**(2): 127–45.

Buckley, P. and Chapman, M. (1997b), 'Wise Before the Event: The Creation of Corporate Fulfilment', *Management International Review 1996*, **36**(1): 95–110.

Buckley, P. and Chapman, M. (1997c), 'The Use of Native Categories in Management Research', *British Journal of Management*, **8**: 283–99.

Chapman, M. (1978), *The Gaelic Vision in Scottish Culture*, London: Croom Helm.

—— (1982), 'Semantics and the Celt', in D. Parkin (ed.), *Semantic Anthropology*, London: Academic Press.

—— (1992), *The Celts – The Construction of a Myth*, London: Macmillan.

—— (1993) (ed.), *Social and Biological Aspects of Ethnicity*, Oxford: Oxford University Press.

—— (1996–97), 'Social Anthropology, Business Studies, and Cultural Issues', *International Studies of Management and Organization*, **26**(4): 3–29.

Coase, R. (1937), 'The Nature of the Firm', *Economica* (n.s.), **4**: 386–405.

Dicken, P. (1998), *Global Shift*, London: Paul Chapman Publishing.

Hofstede, G. (1980), *Culture's Consequences*, New York: Sage.

Minford, P. (1998), *Markets not Stakes*, London: Orion.

Negandhi, A. (1983), 'Cross-Cultural Management Research: Trend and Future Directions', *Journal of International Business Studies*, **14**: 17–28.

Richardson, G.B. (1972), 'The Organization of Industry', *Economic Journal*, **82**: 883–96.

Roberts, K. and Boyacigiller, N. (1984), 'Cross-National Organizational Research: The Grasp of the Blind Men', *Research in Organizational Behavior*, **6**: 423–75.

Sekaran, U. (1983), 'Methodological and Theoretical Issues and Advancements in Cross-Cultural Research', *Journal of International Business Studies*, **14**: 61–73.

Tonkin, E., McDonald, M., and Chapman, M. (eds) (1989), *History and Ethnicity*, London: Routledge.

Williamson, O. (1975), *Markets and Hierarchies*, New York: Free Press.

Wylie, L. (1964 [1957]), *Village in the Vaucluse*, Cambridge, Mass.: Harvard University Press.

–2–

What is an Ethnographic Study?
Alexandra Ouroussoff

The reasonableness of institutions, and above all their utility, is the principled [sic] way we explain ourselves to ourselves. Rationality is our rationalization. *Marshall Sahlins (1976: 72)*

When asked to contribute to a volume on ethnographic method with special reference to organizations, I could not help wondering why Western organizations deserved special treatment. There are no books giving similar preferential treatment to, for example, matrilineal societies or the islands of New Guinea. This is not an omission on the part of anthropologists but follows from (a) the success of ethnographic research over the last 100 years and (b) the principle that one does not modify one's methodology without good reason. Moving away from established principles of research in the field of organization studies would suggest that ethnographers had encountered methodological problems specific to this field.

The anthropology of organizations is, however, a new field of theoretical enquiry. I believe this to be true despite the periodic interest within British social anthropology in studying them. With few recent exceptions, ethnographies of organizations have given low priority to interpreting and describing the culture through which organizational reality is constituted; that is, the symbols, metaphors, and emotions through which each organization coheres as a distinct cultural entity.[1,2]

---

1. The best known are the Manchester shop-floor studies: Cunnison (1966), Lupton (1963). In these studies the issue of *cultural* coherence is not a subject for ethnographic investigation but answered *a priori* in terms of the economic function of the organization and/or the political function the organization fulfils in the wider society. They are grounded, in other words, in a functionalist interpretation of liberal or Marxist theories of political economy. There are also many examples of policy-driven ethnographies of organizations. For an excellent discussion of the contradictions between policy-defined paradigms and anthropological aims, see Okely (1987).

2. I take coherence to be a condition of human society. Every ethnography is implicitly an attempt to give an answer to the question: What accounts for social coherence? or: Why is everything not undifferentiated chaos? Indeed, one way of thinking about anthropological theory is as a history of the answers anthropologists have given to this question.

The historic lack of interest in developing a cultural perspective of organizations is a consequence of an assumption implicitly held by anthropologists and others, that in this context the question of cultural cohesion has already been solved. This follows from the culturally given yet false assumption that rationality is the primary agent of organizational coherence. Yet if one not only listens carefully to what the natives say but, in an attempt to get beyond the rhetoric, closely observes what they do, one is drawn to a very different conclusion.

This deeper-level analysis reveals a complex, often contradictory relation between managers' explicit formulations and the ideas which underpin their day-to-day practice. And it is in the midst of this complexity that one realizes that the notion of rationality as a unifying factor has to be abandoned. It simply cannot explain organizations and their culture.

This throws into relief two questions: How do the people who constitute the organization conceive of rationality? And what, in fact, accounts for the organization's coherence? These questions differ fundamentally from those generated by positing rationality as prior to enquiry, and if pursued across a whole range of organizations they would reveal a rich and hitherto unfamiliar picture of contemporary capitalism.

An anthropological approach would, for example, raise fundamental questions about the nature and extent of our dependence on organizations and the implications of this dependence for the way we perceive social life. In contrast with societies traditionally studied by anthropologists, access to the natural resources on which we depend for our livelihood is mediated by the relatively concentrated network of extractive industries, manufacturing corporations, and financial institutions that constitute political economy. As individuals, we do not have direct access to natural resources or the skills to transform them. And whether through our wages, social security, or a return on our investment, we depend on political economy for our survival.[3]

Since Malinowski there has been a high degree of awareness within anthropology of the limitations of the rationalist approach to political economy, in particular its failure to include the question of the cultural significance of rationalist explanations. But these ideas are debated by anthropologists in the abstract, leaving rationalist theoreticians to define its mode of operation. And the question of how real men and women in actual situations constitute the human relations through which the processes of political economy must necessarily proceed remains hidden by their categories. An anthropological approach may well reveal that these categories have as much to do with rationalizing the loss of control that lies at the root of our dependence on political economy as with a genuine attempt to

---

3. A theory of political economy will be found to be implicit in any description of organizational life. I take political economy to be constitutive of hierarchical relations within and between organizations the most significant of which are orientated towards capital expansion and accumulation.

comprehend the nature of its institutions. In any case, the potential of this approach is, as yet, untapped.[4]

Recent changes in government policies in higher education are, sadly, reinforcing the historical trend.[5] In the field of organizational study, anthropology is competing for funding with well-established rationalist frameworks, familiar in social science methodology. These include, for example, positivist sociology, theories of rational choice, and behaviourist psychology (which underpins much of organization theory). These frameworks partly derive their power and prestige from the belief that they have produced powerful results relevant to people who manage the economy, whether civil servants or chief executives. They also have the advantage that they reaffirm commonly held assumptions about the nature of our society. Most importantly, they accept as self-evident that organizations are consciously realized; that is, they assume that people know what their motives are and that these motives are recognizable by certain kinds of social science methods: the extended interview, for example. By definition, rationalist frameworks lack the conceptual tools for identifying the profound discrepancies that can exist between the way people conceive of the organization and their actual practice. Nor are they designed to handle the subtle, imaginative, and symbolic ways people have found to deal with the inconsistencies and contradictions that arise from such discrepancies.

It is against this background that one needs to look carefully at some of the more recent 'ethnographies' of organizations. The tendency is to abandon anthropological conceptions of culture and society in favour of rationalist conceptions associated with more prestigious methodologies.[6]

The question this raises is whether rationalist 'ethnographies' of organizations can contribute to the wider intellectual aims of anthropology. My own view is that this is unlikely. What ultimately distinguishes an ethnographic study of an

4. This dependence may well be the source of our affective experience of the nature/society dichotomy. If this is so, then the prevalence of the dichotomy (Descola 1996) might be better understood through a critique of it as ideology; the way it obliges us to conceal the concrete human relations through which our society creates subsistence wealth and the process of alienation found within these relations. Efforts to dislocate the dichotomy by detailed studies of scientific activity (Latour 1987; Woolgar 1993) implicitly overvalue scientific thinking by positing it as a defining instance of Western thought. Although it is true that scientific thinking has been central to the technological transformation of our society over the past few hundred years, it is easy to exaggerate the pervasiveness of this mode of thinking because of its power and prestige. But it is not the dominant mode, even if it is the most important specialist mode.

5. For a discussion of these changes see Willmott (1995) and Ryan (1998).

6. For an example of a study carried out in this vein, see Harper (1998) and also Chapman (Chapter One of this volume). For an example of one of the few recent ethnographic studies of an organization emerging from the theoretical tradition of anthropology, see Janelli and Yim (1993).

organization from other kinds of studies is its goal: to extend our perception of cultural difference. From a cross-cultural perspective, the rationalist framework constitutes local native theory and forms a part of the *object* of study. As Sahlins says, rationality is how we explain ourselves to ourselves: it is our rationalization. Developing a cultural perspective on political economy involves understanding the relation between this rationalization (our theory of ourselves) and our practice. Failure to explore this relation, far from extending our perception of cultural difference, will only succeed in further reifying an ethnocentric *idée fixe.*

The aim of this chapter is to examine the question of organizational rationality through the prism of anthropological theory. It contrasts the relations between sexual liaisons and corporate ethos in two organizations. While in one of them *symbolic* sexuality is unconsciously tied by managers to the driving logic of corporate success, managers in the other make no such link. I deliberately chose this comparison to give ethnographic prominence to the profound cultural differences that can be found to exist between organizations within British political economy.

The ethnography focuses on the organizations' Head Offices, both located in the southeast of England within 200 miles of one another. Bion International is a highly successful multinational manufacturing corporation, itself forming part of a much larger corporate enterprise, BDC, which holds 55 per cent of its shares. C&R is a non-profit-making service organization. Although managers in both come from all over the British Isles, they share a similar social background in that they are the first generation in their family to have been educated to 'A'-level and/or university and consider their entrance into the managerial class as a significant achievement.

Bion International[7]

During my initial fieldwork in Bion I attributed no great significance to sexual liaisons between managers and their secretaries, regarding their affairs as external to corporate concerns. It was only later, while carrying out fieldwork in C&R where a radically different attitude towards sexual liaisons prevailed, that I began to re-evaluate their significance in Bion. In this chapter I have decided to follow the logic of this re-evaluation to emphasize the remoteness of the link between libidinal desire and economic performance from formal articulations of corporate exigencies and to bring attention to the role of comparison in forcing the appearance of this link.

Bion International, a manufacturing corporation, produces a product with a high international public profile. Unlike a society, a corporation has an explicit

7. All names, both of companies and of individuals, are pseudonyms.

goal. The accumulation of profit is a legal obligation and directors are bound to act in accordance with it (Companies Act 1948). Incorporated in 1949, in terms of both profit and market share, Bion has grown from strength to strength. Managers and directors are proud to be a part of what is regarded as a highly dynamic and successful enterprise. In 1979–80, when I carried out the original fieldwork, the Company employed 7,000 people in the UK.[8]

An atmosphere of urgency pervades Bion's Head Office where eight Directors and 320 managers are responsible for co-ordinating production and distribution between five factories. The managers' orientation is towards the future of the company, a future which depends on their capacity to overcome the problems with which they are confronted daily. On the first of the two occasions on which the Financial Director agreed to let me accompany him through his working day I arrived, as he had requested, at 7 a.m. to find him already at work. As early as 6 a.m. the Chief Executive and other senior managers can be found in their offices preparing for the day ahead.

Even at this time in the morning the Financial Director was under considerable strain. As the day progressed it became apparent that the pressing issue was whether a new overseas advertising campaign would bring a return on capital recently invested. A significant cash investment had been made and he had arrived at work already aware that there was some doubt as to whether initial expectations would be met. By the time his secretary came into his office at 9 a.m., he had a list of tasks for her to carry out. With a constrained 'Good morning', he handed it to her and brusquely (though not rudely) asked her for a cup of coffee.

When she returned, he told her, this time with less courtesy, to set up an urgent meeting with the Overseas Sales Director. She seemed to take his manner entirely in her stride. Speaking on the telephone with the Sales Director, his tone was abrasive as he listed the figures he needed for his meeting with the Chief Executive in two hours' time. His day continued at the same pace and with the same level of underlying impatience. He left his office at 7 p.m., but whether he was able to leave his work is another matter.

Although every day is not equally arduous, the ability to keep pace and accomplish tasks under pressure is an important theme in the working life of managers. Production must keep up with expanding demand, and market share sustained or improved. The ability to move through the day with speed and deliberation, maintaining the offensive, being seen to be in control of events, are all aspects of a temperament considered to be essential to the advancement of Bion's interests.

---

8. I was a participant observer between November 1979 and January 1980 (returning in 1981 as an outside researcher). I made return visits to Head Office in 1988 and 1994 and to the principal manufacturing location in 1999.

From the standpoint of Bion's Head Office, the key to corporate viability lies in selecting managers whose character traits ensure that skills and experience will be properly harnessed to corporate objectives. The competent Bion manager is described as independent and tough-minded, a man of character, who is not afraid of taking tough action.

These attributes shape and guide a manager's general demeanour, making him easy to recognize. Selecting the right kind of manager for Bion is considered to be a fairly straightforward process. Managers scorn the use of personality tests and other 'scientific' procedures designed to improve the quality of new recruits. Their confidence is well placed: they are very successful in selecting men who share their orientation to reality.

An important feature of this orientation is the idea that only men can be responsible for corporate success or failure. The capacity to manage is seen as an exclusively male attribute, though not all men possess it. The ninety-four women who work in Head Office as secretaries occupy the more static administrative sphere. Both managers and secretaries regard secretarial work as peripheral to the central purpose of the company.[9]

By contrast, the most dynamic and challenging work takes place in the manufacturing division, which also carries the highest prestige. Managers and Directors in Bion's eight divisions agree that without the product, there is nothing to sell and therefore no profit to be made. In terms of routine pressures the biggest threat to profit is a decline in productivity. Although far removed from the manufacturing locations, Head Office buzzes with news of events affecting production. Managers are well aware of the personalities in charge of each of the five factory locations, and a great deal of energy is spent on comparing their distinctive approaches to 'controlling production' (their term).

The capacity to control is, in the context of day-to-day management, the most important trait of the tough manager. A critical issue facing the Company at the time of study was the need to cut unit costs in its largest manufacturing location. The factory manager's brief was to improve capital equipment and to maintain costs (including wages) while not lowering output. Success would depend on the 1,360 shop-floor workers accepting the new techniques. Since the company's inception, Head Office and factory managers have held the conviction that male workers in the manufacturing department (as contrasted with men in processing or women in packing) overvalue their contribution to the production process and are prone to lowering output when working conditions do not suit them. From the

---

9. This less essential role is also reflected in the fact that their skills are more easily replaceable and less expensive to purchase. (Literally unseen by managers are 104 Head Office clerical workers. There is, unfortunately, no space here to describe the considerable implications for gender and class relations.)

managers' standpoint, the male workers in the five manufacturing departments have proved the greatest threat to productivity.[10]

Reflecting the perceived volatility of production, the Director of manufacture is informed on a weekly basis of factories' productivity levels and divisional executives are quick to visit a factory manager if productivity falls below target. During declines in productivity tensions can run very high (tough managers can be *temporarily* defeated) but these are nevertheless routine problems, and precisely the reason why tough managers are necessary. Despite the high tension managers also know that the overall pattern of action tends towards the creation of profit.

Although the association between managers' positive masculine traits and the capacity to meet corporate aims is not formally acknowledged as such, it is indirectly expressed in spontaneous discourse. Weak managers are ridiculed for their failure to act, their failure of nerve, and their generally pathetic attempts at control. Regardless of the nature of his experience or the quality of his skills, a weak manager constitutes an economic deficit. His dithering and indecisiveness will mean, for example, that the energies of his subordinates will not be properly directed. Weakness denotes dependency, a susceptibility to being manipulated (particularly by subordinates), and the need to refer to colleagues or superiors for advice. Thus, weak managers involuntarily undermine corporate interests by deflecting substantial amounts of energy from the corporate goal.

The contrasting image of the weak manager highlights the most significant positive masculine trait through which corporate interests are served: the capacity to behave independently. This capacity is seen as intrinsic to the person, summed up in the Director of Sales' quip, 'You either have it or you don't.' There are no training courses designed to instil independence in the weak manager. Needless to say, weak managers are not contenders in the hierarchical bids for promotion.[11]

---

10. The scope these workers have for lowering output is considerable. The process of production is continuous: an interruption caused by, for example, a momentary lack of vigilance by a single worker can, in an instant, lead to thousands of pounds in lost revenue. The line between intentional and unintentional lapses in vigilance is difficult to draw and senior managers – though not always line managers – are predisposed to assume intention. There is unfortunately no room here to explore the basis of this conviction. However, changes in legislation have not affected the fundamental dynamics on the shop floor or managers' perception of the machine operators. Changes in labour law and the reduction of workers' rights (Employment Acts, 1980, 1982, 1988, 1990, and 1993; see Hendy 1993), while increasing managers' control over production, have simultaneously led to an increase in underlying tension between managers and workers in Bion and the issue of control is as pressing as before. The difference is that now workers are less able either to voice their disagreements or act on them collectively .

11. The few managers deemed to be incompetent are explained in terms of external pressures such as constraints in the labour market. A position may need to be filled for which there may only be candidates without relevant skills and experience. A weak manager may then be brought in as a temporary substitute.

Although not all managers aim for the top job, promotion to the Board of Bion is considered the pinnacle of a manager's career, the point at which his abilities become acknowledged within Bion and the industry as a whole. As a manager is promoted his reputation for autonomy is consolidated. Expensive cars, larger offices, and bigger salaries are emblematic of his increased value to the company. Unlike some other companies, particularly in the financial sector, where moving on to another company can be seen as an achievement, in Bion leaving the company, even for a higher salary, is regarded as an admission of defeat.

The board of the holding company lies outside managers' aspirations. BDC is composed of men who inhabit a social sphere far removed from those who direct Bion. The chairman of Bion, John Holmes, is the only chairman of a subsidiary to sit on the board of BDC. This is a consequence of Bion's position in the group as a whole and does not reflect his social standing.[12] Although only one of forty-five businesses in the BDC portfolio and not the largest or the most profitable, Bion is the most important manufacturing business in that, unlike BDC's other acquisitions, it is the only company to manufacture a product with a high public profile. A positive public image is considered by BDC to be vital to the stability of shareholder value.[13]

The relatively closed, comprehensively male domain of Bion is supported and complemented by the presence of women. Relative to the contribution men make in meeting the demands of production and distribution, women have less dynamic significance; but their dependence on men is, nevertheless, deeply significant insofar as it naturalizes male autonomy. Both officially and in practice, secretaries depend for their status on their association with their boss's autonomy. By promoting her boss's interests and carrying out her tasks effectively, she adds to her manager's and therefore to corporate strength.[14] The dependence of women complements the positive predisposition of men to behave autonomously. Despite

12. BDC's twelve directors include a number of titled persons who, with the exception of John Holmes, also sit on the board of at least seven other companies (one is on the board of thirty-five companies). Holmes holds no other directorships, nor does he have an office in BDC's London Head Office. In terms of social background he stands well apart, not having attended public school, nor belonging to a gentleman's club; nor is he listed in either *Who's Who* or *International Who's Who,* as the majority of BDC directors are.

13. Reflecting recent structural changes in the global economy, in the mid-1990s BDC was bought by an American mega-national corporation. (For an analysis of these changes see Luttwak, 1999.) The internal structure of BDC, however, remains unchanged and Lord H**** still presides as chairman.

14. This is not an expression of passive accommodation. Secretaries actively identify with their bosses' power and autonomy, competing with each other to promote their own bosses' interests. Somewhere in *The Second Sex* Simone de Beauvoir makes the elementary but sometimes forgotten point that if women did not internalize male values there would be no need for a feminist movement. Unfortunately there is no room here to include ethnographic material showing how the dominant male perspective is expressed through the secretaries' competitive behaviour.

their peripheral status and the manner in which managers characteristically relate to them, 'secretary' is a positive term.

The positive evaluation of women's dependence extends outward towards wives and their children. There is an unwritten rule in Bion that managers should be married by age 30, and the majority are. There is a close consensus that traditional marriages are to be preferred, in that managers earn enough so that their wives do not have to work and should therefore be able to enjoy what is regarded as a far less arduous life of domestic responsibility.

Gender provides a separation between positive and negative expressions of dependency. The deeply pejorative 'weak' cannot apply to women, for whom dependence is appropriate. The positively valued dependent woman symbolically highlights the defective nature of the dependent man. In a man, dependence denotes emasculation, powerlessness, an inherent inability to live up to the male ideal.

Changes in legislation (e.g. the Sex Discrimination Act, 1975) and the appointment of female managers have had little effect on gender formulations. Because women are predisposed to dependence, any initiatives taken by a female 'manager' are assumed to stem from the manager to whom she reports. The four women appointed into management grades so as to avoid public scrutiny and possible litigation are managers in name only. In practice, female managers are thought of as secretaries.[15]

What is striking about these shared conceptions of proper manhood and womanhood is the way they serve to rationalize both the sexual division of labour and the pursuit of corporate aims. In realizing corporate objectives, managers and secretaries simultaneously realize what they take to be their own natural potential.

This being the case, one might imagine that once a tough manager is recruited his competence would be taken for granted, opening the way for closer assessment of each manager's relative contribution to corporate success. The event described below illustrates, however, that far from being taken for granted, the ability to *demonstrate* toughness is essential to a manager's credibility. Following a slowdown in production in one of the factories in Northern Ireland, Martin, a head-office executive in the Manufacturing division who had been with the company for fifteen years, flew to Belfast to inform the workers that failure to reach production targets could lead to the factory's closure. Arriving unannounced, he went straight onto the shop floor and, according to his own account, finding the workers he 'knew' to be responsible for the slowdown, told them that should they continue to hold up production they would be responsible for the loss of over a thousand jobs. His reasoning, presumably, was that his authority as a head-office executive and the fact that he was one of the men who would be involved in the decision to close a

---

15. It has proved difficult to find statistics showing the ratio of female/male managers in manufacturing; I suspect they have remained relatively static compared with those for other sectors of the economy.

factory would lend weight to his threat. Having said his piece, he went to see the factory manager. His intrusion into factory affairs provoked a row. The factory manager was furious that Martin had undermined his authority and that of his thirty-six factory managers.

Head-Office colleagues spoke about this event with evident admiration for Martin. The story was widely commented upon and elaborated, and the factory manager became the butt of a number of jokes. However, the factory manager's loss of esteem was temporary. He was known to be a tough manager in charge of a very difficult situation, which for the most part colleagues felt he handled well. The row was seen principally as being an altercation between two men of the same calibre. The next round could well go to the factory manager.

From the perspective of head-office managers, the significant details of Martin's visit were that he took the decision to go to Northern Ireland on the spur of the moment without consulting his superiors, that he walked onto the shop floor unannounced, and, finally, that he gave the workers a piece of his mind. They did not discuss the consequences of his actions with regard to production levels or workers' relations with management. A month later I began fieldwork in this factory and had the opportunity to talk to shop-floor workers about Martin's visit. The incident did not appear to have had much impact. No one believed that management would shut down the factory and his attitude, which they saw as offensive, was seen as typical of the way many – but not all – managers in this company behaved.

In the weeks that followed Martin's visit, production levels did improve. However, because so many factors influence production, it would be impossible to assess what sort of effect Martin's action had. But from the point of view of understanding what head-office managers consider to be the significant attributes of a successful Bion manager, the important point is that *they* were not engaged in the question of *effect*. There was no spontaneous debate, no weighing up the possible outcomes of his action. What mattered was the nature of the aim – a threat – and the manner in which it was carried out. Martin's actions clearly demonstrated his autonomy and his determination. He had taken a bold initiative and had not hesitated to see it through. It was taken for granted that the effect was in alignment with the company's economic interests.

Faith in a tie between autonomous behaviour and effective outcome is misplaced. Whether in Head Office or in the factories one can observe on a daily basis how giving primary value to visibility of autonomy over actual effect results in rational, quasi-rational, and irrational outcomes.[16] A calculation of the economic cost of

16. Bion managers skilfully employ the idea of luck to mask discrepancies between the ideal and the reality. I have described elsewhere the striking example of how managers used 'luck' to rationalize the dismissal of a weak factory manager who had produced the best productivity figures in the history of the industry (Ouroussoff 1993).

this prevailing hierarchy of values would have to take into account the amount of energy and time they could have otherwise spent on rational calculation, the cost of failure to assess whether actions have the desired outcome, and the cost of not modifying actions in light of this experience. Calculating managers' failure to realize profit relative to investment in capital equipment and human resources would merit another paper of its own. Here, however, I am concerned with the more fundamental question of the underlying pressures on managers to place visibility of autonomy over and above close examination of outcome. The most significant of these pressures came to light during an episode involving the dismissal of a Director.

During the course of my fieldwork, the Director of Manufacture, Mr Sands, a veteran of twenty-five years, was dismissed by the Chief Executive, a move backed by the board of the holding company. The director, now 59, had worked his way up the Company, having been brought into its oldest factory as a middle manager. This factory was suffering from what the majority of directors considered to be endemic labour-relations problems. The board was in favour of closing the factory down.

Sands decided not to back the closure, at least at this stage. He argued that other possible solutions had not yet been fully explored. The disagreement revolved around the loss of a highly experienced workforce whose value he felt the board was underestimating. Almost 2,000 workers, many of whom had twenty or more years' experience in the industry, would be lost. The time and cost of training new workers had not, according to him, been properly calculated. The Chief Executive took the view that Sands' arguments were based on old loyalties and nostalgia and were indicative of a weakness of character. With the backing of the BDC Board, he was given a fortnight's notice.

Sands had been dismissed because nostalgia had weakened his capacity to make tough decisions. From this it followed that his arguments lacked merit.

For the first week of that fortnight Sands did not appear at Head Office. By the second week rumours began to circulate that he had spent several nights locked in his office refusing sandwiches offered him by his secretary. (Director's offices have showers and WCs.) Whether or not this was true, during the second week I saw him walking down a corridor looking dishevelled and unshaven.

Over the days that followed managers expressed concern for his welfare and suggestions that his evident depression might lead to suicide were taken seriously, though no one ventured to offer him any actual support. Despite their concern, the consensus was that he had brought it on himself. He had flinched from making the tough decision and had paid the price. The obvious contradiction between the inherent nature of toughness and his sudden change in temperament which managers implicitly attributed to an act of will, was ignored. During the months that followed managers deliberated over what he had achieved throughout his career. As the weeks went by these achievements began to look less and less impressive. The final conclusion was that, when seen in the cold light of day, his achievements had been, after all, insubstantial. The slow reinterpretation of old events resulted, in effect, in the rewriting of Sands' history.

For twenty-five years Sands was regarded as a tough manager. For ten of those years, from the standpoint of his colleagues, he had successfully run the largest and most profitable factory, did battle with the unions, and survived at least two Chief Executives. He was then promoted to Head Office and eventually to the Board. He was considered, if not the most, at least one of the most successful managers in the Company. Before his dismissal, managers described him as arrogant and difficult to deal with. Although irritating to some, these characteristics were also evidence of his toughness. Following his dismissal, however, the 'inherent' traits that had been a necessary condition of his success suddenly ceased to exist and twenty-five years' worth of evidence amounted to nothing.

Sands was not the only one to have his history reinvented in this way. During the course of my fieldwork, the same happened with regard to two other managers. One was also dismissed and the other, having been denied a long-sought-after promotion, left of his own accord.

Managers did not reflect on, discuss, or elaborate the reasons for their gross collective misjudgement. From their standpoint, they were correct in their assessment of Sands' 'inherent' qualities then and they are correct now. The contradiction implied by their sudden revision of his 'inherent' traits does not form part of their conscious frame of reference. The fact that this revision invalidates the principles which they claim to be the source of the Company's power and success goes unrecognized. Nevertheless, despite their conscious claims, the process of revising Sands' history not only invalidates his past successes but simultaneously invalidates the principle that success within the company is contingent on a manager's inherent masculine traits.

So, although at a conscious level there is absolutely no doubt that success is contingent on toughness, at an unconscious level managers also know that as circumstances change these 'inherent' qualities can be overturned. Since managers collectively engage in the revision of others, each manager must also unconsciously know that it could happen to him: that is, that the nature of his masculinity may, after all, be open to question, and that the one thing that is supposed to guarantee success – constant demonstration of autonomy – in fact guarantees nothing. Hence it is the threat of his masculine qualities being defective that unconsciously drives each manager continually to re-assert his masculine traits. Contrary to their conscious perceptions, managers are in fact under continual pressure – what must seem like an eternal pressure – to demonstrate to their colleagues and their superiors that they are real men and therefore worthy of the designation 'tough', the designation they falsely and unconsciously assume guarantees their usefulness to the Company.

The need to sustain the illusion that usefulness to the corporation is contingent on inherent masculine traits masks a harsher reality: their economic dependency on an entity with power to dismiss them arbitrarily. Managers and directors live on their wages and have limited personal capital. Even in times of low unemployment, many managers have no guarantee that their skills will transfer. Because managers do not avail themselves of the collective support of a trade union which would offer both financial and legal support in the event of a disagreement with the Company, each manager is dependent on his own material resources.[17]

The powerful emotional investment in the idea of their own autonomy protects them from the reality that however hard a manager works, however successful a manager deems himself to be, the corporation has the power to dismiss him. To avoid legal proceedings, managers who are dismissed are given generous pay-offs but, given the powerful investment in the association between the capacity to meet corporate aims and their self-definition as male, this cannot compensate them for their sense of defeat, humiliation, and failure.[18]

From a conscious perspective, their masculinity is not in need of confirmation, but is seen as a fixed quality from which their ability, their security, and indeed their 'autonomy' ultimately stems. From an unconscious perspective, autonomy is an illusion through which managers come to feel they can control the uncontrollable.

The conscious yet false premise that masculinity is not open to question performs a powerful organizational function. In protecting managers from becoming aware of their own vulnerability, managers are also 'protected' from experiencing the discontinuity between their own personal interests and the interests of the corporation. It is not simply that managers experience their own interests as aligned with the interests of the corporation, an assumption which contains within it the idea of two sets of interests, but that managers experience personal and corporate interests as one and the same, thus increasing the motivational force of their commitment.

Against this backdrop it now seems unsurprising that female sexuality would play an important role in sustaining the illusion of autonomy. But at the time of

---

17. The consensus in Head Office is that to make a case of unfair dismissal gives a manager the reputation of a trouble-maker and lowers his chances of finding work elsewhere.

18. It is only within the limited context of this study that managers' psychological predisposition towards dependency is given priority over material dependence on the corporation. Such priority would fall away were the context to be widened to include the manager's upbringing and the relation of his family to the means of production. This issue of context gives some indication of the potential theoretical complexities involved in comparing an ideology of autonomy held by people wholly dependent on political economy with an ideology of autonomy held by people who have both direct access to natural resources and the skills to transform them (the Hageners of Papua New Guinea, to take one example (Strathern 1981)).

the study, I was as blinded as the managers by our shared assumption that the sphere in which managers exercise their responsibilities for the company is separate from the sphere of personal relations, the one area of social activity seemingly undetermined by corporate aims.

The separation between public and private concerns did also generate a great deal of empirical evidence which further stood in the way of my seeing the underlying logic. Managers, for example, do not talk about their wives or children, or their life outside the Company. To raise such issues in Company time is considered unprofessional. Outside official Company time domestic issues are regarded as tedious subjects for conversation. And unlike in many other companies, wives do not attend pensioners' parties or Christmas dinners, and throughout the course of my fieldwork I had no occasion to meet a manager's wife or engage in discussion about their domestic life.

Similarly, talk of managers' sexual affairs fell into the category of the personal. Despite the professional way managers relate to secretaries, their own as well as those of their colleagues, it had of course occurred to me that some managers might be having extra-marital affairs.[19] It was, however, only as I became better integrated into the managers' world, and found myself in circumstances where managers felt relatively relaxed and not obliged to be seen orienting all of their energies towards corporate goals, that the subject would come up. It was, for example, between 7 and 9 in the morning when managers often visit one another's offices and discuss matters unrelated to work, or on the long train journeys between factories that I began to hear of their affairs.

These revelations did not take the form of malicious gossip but tended to be more in the vein of discussing a bit of Company news. As the months went by it became apparent that, despite the discreet way in which affairs were discussed, public display was very much the point. Who was sleeping with whom was common knowledge. Although managers never spoke about their own affairs, they discussed the affairs of close colleagues when they were not present. Their chat usually revolved around the physical qualities of the women or mistresses (their term).

At the managerial level, having a mistress serves to enhance a manager's image. Managers with mistresses, especially those with particularly attractive mistresses, are spoken of with admiration and there is a vicarious identification with managers who succeed in finding a mistress. Managers also boast about one another's successes; the effect seemed to me to be very much like one's home team winning at football: good for public morale. But what seemed to me to be the more important point was that having a mistress was not an indication of a manager's capacity to manage. A tough manager will continue to be a tough manager even if he has no

---

19. With few exceptions, and in contrast to managers, secretaries are single.

mistress. Conversely, a weak manager with a mistress, no matter how attractive, is still a weak manager. By the same token, being a mistress does not increase or decrease a secretary's prospects for promotion. For both managers and secretaries affairs are regarded as a separate, private matter.[20]

Directors also have mistresses and I knew relatively early on, four or five months into the fieldwork, that six of the eight directors were having affairs with their own or another director's secretary. An exception was one director who was having an affair with a female administrator in the company's largest factory. What took quite a bit longer to grasp was that whereas for managers having a mistress falls into the realm of enhancement, at board level having a mistress is an imperative.

The two board members not having affairs were the Chief Executive and the Director of Manufacture. Holmes had recently married his secretary following his wife's death: a gap of three months did not raise any eyebrows. Since his new wife no longer worked for the Company it was widely speculated that he would soon be looking for a replacement. This speculation was not based on the assumption that Holmes was a womanizer. He had no such reputation. It followed rather from what was taken to be a truism, that Bion Directors have mistresses.

The second Director was the newly promoted Director of Manufacture, the replacement for the unfortunate Mr Sands. About three weeks after his promotion I was in the Company bar after work talking to a colleague of the new director. He mentioned to me that Kevin, the director, was looking for a suitable mistress. I asked him what he meant by 'suitable' and he said, 'Well, you know, not someone from the telephone exchange.' He went on to say that the right sort of girls were few and far between. I asked him to keep me posted. A month later I was travelling by car to one of the factories in the North with this same manager and I asked him how Kevin was getting on. He told me that he hadn't managed to find anyone and was in fact very distressed about it. A director, he said, should not have to find himself in such a position. In other words, it was his status as a Director that was at issue. The colleague then asked if I knew anyone who would be 'willing to help him out of this extremely difficult situation'. The problem was that there were no 'girls' of the appropriate status available.

It was following this conversation that I began to notice that directors' secretaries were better educated,[21] better looking, and dressed in a sexually more provocative manner than managers' secretaries. They were also of a more uniform age (20–26).

---

20. There are, of course, a range of reasons why secretaries should wish to have affairs with managers. Describing these affairs from their perspective would merit a separate discussion and would not affect the relevant point here.

21. Directors' secretaries have 'A'-levels plus secretarial college. Three Directors' secretaries were bilingual (i.e. overqualified for the job). Requirements at the lower levels are GCSE English plus secretarial college and some previous experience.

There was a very particular 'look' to secretaries on the fifth floor to which the other secretaries in the building did not conform.

At the time of the original study the emphasis on having a 'posh' mistress at the level of director seemed to me simply to demonstrate a higher level of aspiration which Directors, with more resources at their disposal, could indulge in. This aspiration was a privilege of status that, like company cars and executive offices, widened the division between Directors and their senior managers, providing them with yet another opportunity to make the distinction manifest. Although I found the whole issue of 'posh' secretaries and mistresses intriguing, relative to the managers' intense preoccupation with production and distribution and the amount of energy they pour into profit accumulation, the issue of mistresses did initially appear to be peripheral to their main concerns.

It took the experience of fieldwork in another organization, one that placed the public/private divide along a very different axis, to break the categorical given profit/not sex. Managers and secretaries in this second organization see a clear link between the private world of sexual affairs and the public life of the organization. This led me to realize that I had too readily accepted certain indigenous categories held by Bion managers, namely, the conceptual separation between female sexuality and corporate success.

C&R

What follows is drawn from an ethnographic study of an organization that occupies a very different sector of the economy.[22] It is non-profit-making and ultimately depends on donations rather than investors for its existence. The organization directly employs 10,000 people, a thousand of them in their London Head Office. It is here referred to as C&R.

I spent the first day of what was to be an eighteen-month study, between 1992 and 1994, sitting in on a number of meetings in the Chief Executive's office. The following morning I wrote up my field notes and at 2 p.m. went along to meet the Chief Executive's number three. I was just getting to the purpose of my visit, which was to ask if I could attend a highly sensitive meeting later that afternoon, when he cut me short and said, 'Are you doing anything right now?' 'No.' (Odd question.) He stood up, picked up his jacket, and walked out of his office. I followed him downstairs, across the road, and into the pub. He ordered a couple of drinks and we sat down. He had brought with him pen and paper and without saying anything began to draw a diagram. It took him several minutes. When he finished it he looked up and said, 'You will never understand the politics of this organization

---

22. No attempt is being made here to draw a correlation between the symbolic function of sex in a particular organization and organizational aims.

gasp 7

if you don't know who is sleeping with whom.' He then talked me through the diagram. The first thing that struck me was that the Bion prescription – wives on the outside, mistresses on the inside – did not apply here. Both wives and mistresses were welcome to work for the organization. He explained that some of the long-standing affairs had produced offspring who could be found playing along side their legitimate brothers and sisters in the company crèche. A year's fieldwork proved his diagram to be faultless. This manager's candour also turned out to reflect an intense and explicit – certainly compared with the circumstances at Bion – preoccupation with colleagues' sexual affairs. It is considered perfectly acceptable to discuss one's own affairs, the affairs of others as well as all the complications that follow from having to work in the same organization as one's wife and mistress, or, significantly, lover and husband. In C&R organizational politics are rarely discussed without reference to sexual politics. In contrast to Bion, the two domains are not regarded as separate.[23]

During the second week of fieldwork in C&R I went to see a secretary in one of the planning departments to discuss the forthcoming restructuring of secretarial work. This was the first time we had met. She opened the discussion by saying, 'You may have already heard that I am having a relationship with C&R's most senior Executive . . . well, it's true.' She went on to say they had being seeing each other for seven years. I was surprised at the open and matter-of-fact way she told me this. Guessing what type of response she was expecting, I asked her whether her relationship with the executive had created difficulties with her colleagues. She said that it had. It made people both envious and anxious because they knew she had the ear of the Director and was in a position to tell him anything she might see or overhear. She was very keen to get across to me that she did not in fact do so.

In C&R, affairs were openly recognized as morally problematic. Not only the implications for work relations but also the emotional effects on wives and husbands are openly discussed. In one department, for example, a number of people were concerned about a forthcoming promotion that would place a woman who was having an affair with a married manager next to his wife. Given the size of Head Office, this kind of coincidence happened infrequently. But what was significant was the response the coincidence generated among the men and women who were 'in the know'. They were concerned to find a way of protecting the feelings and reputations of all three. In C&R to say an issue was not public means that it would not be raised in a departmental meeting but would have to be resolved by other, non-institutional means. In other words, a private matter could also be recognized as a collective concern.

23. In C&R profound, unconscious contradictions revolve around the relation between managers and those on whom they rely for contributions.

This followed from the assumption that the quality of working relations underwrites a manager's capacity to carry out his or her tasks effectively. Whether working relations within a department are conducive to eliciting the best from people will to some extent depend on the relations between individual personalities as well as on their personal circumstances, which are seen as subject to change. High tension between two managers within the same department, for example, was initially put down to a disagreement over strategy. Several days later, when the disagreement was still unresolved, a wider range of explanations came into play. The personalities of the two managers were discussed as well as the personal circumstances of one of the managers, which it was felt were hampering his ability to respond sensibly to a difficult situation.

This is not to imply that some people are neither critical of decisions nor judgemental when it comes to the way others may be managing their personal lives. The point is rather that the range of possible causes of tension brought into the discussion by members of the department assume emotionally constituted persons, each with his or her own distinct history. People are deemed to have complex lives that involve spouses and children as well as colleagues. Work and home lives are seen as to some extent interdependent. Referring to domestic problems in work time, and even occasionally allowing domestic needs to take priority, are just part of life. It is, for example, perfectly acceptable for a manager to say he has to leave a meeting early in order to collect his child from school; it would be assumed that he had done his best to make alternative arrangements. When scheduling meetings, it was not uncommon for managers to give domestic reasons for preferring one time to another: attending a child's school play, for example. When I had to miss an important group of meetings because my own son was ill, the reaction was sympathetic. And when I returned I was surprised to find myself in more than one discussion with male managers, comparing the particular strains of flu our respective children had suffered from that winter. Showing responsibility towards one's own family enhances a manager's reputation. My own relations with managers improved once they learned that I also had to negotiate complicated domestic/work arrangements. Because people are expected to be open about domestic matters, a great deal of information about the personal lives of colleagues accumulates over the years. A manager's success, or lack of it, in his job is seen in the light of the person's particular history, that is, as relating to a given set of conditions which differ from manager to manager.

Institutional arrangements for selection and promotion reflected this conception of success. Committees composed of departmental members from each rank – that is, colleagues with whom one has worked, often for many years – follow procedures well known not just to the members of the committee, but to everyone in the organization. There are varying ways in which a manager might be assessed, taking into account his or her skills in relation to the needs of a given department, his or her relations with colleagues, and his or her personal circumstances. The priority given to any of these would depend on the particular department and the constitution of its committee. Although formal procedures are only one aspect of a far more complex reality which can include intense, and sometimes vicious, behind-the-scenes politicking, nevertheless it is the committee as a body that recruits, promotes, demotes, and very infrequently dismisses a manager.

The ubiquitous threat to livelihood that in Bion is connected to the criteria for success in terms of a single rigid ideal finds no parallel in C&R. If, for example, a manager is not considered to be working effectively, a series of procedures are in place to help him identify and overcome his failing. He is given ample opportunity for reform and dismissals are therefore extremely rare. In the previous ten years, only one person had been dismissed: a manager quite low in the hierarchy who had literally been 'caught with his fingers in the till'. It is openly acknowledged that in C&R there are quite a high percentage of incompetent managers incapable of reform. This is a cause of some frustration for those having to work with them: 'having to pull another manager's weight' was a complaint I often heard. In C&R, tolerance of dependence is an institutional imperative. In contrast to Bion, where the managers' assumption of autonomy and the will to be tough causes them to overlook their dependency on the company, at C&R hierarchy is seen as constitutive of relations between unique persons. The social dynamic is experienced as inhering in relations of interdependence rather than driven by the need to demonstrate self-sufficiency.

It is worth stressing that the distinct ways of constituting relations are not simply the effects of the organizations in question. When recruiting, managers explicitly state that they look for not only a candidate with the right skills and qualifications, but for the kind of person who will 'fit in' to the organization. The capacity to fit in, however, refers both to the characteristics managers consciously seek and to a more complex emotional schema to which they do not necessarily have conscious access. In Bion, for example, managers are concerned to discover whether their unconscious assumptions about masculinity – assumptions that play such a critical role in determining how they perceive and experience the organization – are shared by the potential recruit.

As long as a degree of choice exists, on the part of both the applicant and the Corporation, there is likely to be a deep homology between the character of the person and the culture of the organization. It is just as much a case of managers seeking candidates whose internal reality matches the needs of the organization as of candidates seeking external 'objective' confirmation of their own internalized reality.[24] In creating a synthesis an important function of the process of selection

24. This deep-rooted internalized reality is a product of the experiences of childhood. For a discussion of the process of internalization, see Laing (1967).

is fulfilled which is to provide the shared subjective experience through which the organization is able to cohere as an entity.

Although there is obviously enough cultural overlap between some organizations to allow managers to function effectively in more than one, as it happens the cultural differences between Bion and C&R are so profound as to make it extremely difficult, if not impossible, to imagine a Bion manager working effectively in C&R. This point is perhaps most clearly illustrated by the differences in gender formulations.

In C&R gender identity is not rigidly tied to the capacity to meet organizational aims. There are two female heads of department and two female deputy heads. In contrast to Bion, all four are accepted as full social persons and expected to take full responsibility for their decisions. This is not to say that promotion into the senior grades has been plain sailing. Male C&R managers openly discussed their reluctance to promote women, arguing that it is disruptive to what to them is a cosy, club-like atmosphere. They are, they say, used to working in a male environment and it is unsettling and therefore inconvenient to have to learn how to work effectively with women at this stage in their careers. Managers who had not yet experienced working closely with women in senior positions thought it would take time to become accustomed to it. Those who were already working with them confirmed such concern. But senior managers also said, with no prompting from me, that this reluctance, which they think perfectly understandable, is ultimately indefensible both on ethical grounds and in terms of the needs of the organization. The capacity of women to manage is not at issue.

For their part, female managers in C&R found the going very hard. Being accepted as full social persons does not mean they are treated as equals. They feel the standards set for them are higher than for their male counterparts, which they resent. Whether or not this is the case is extremely difficult to assess, but all four of the senior women did feel they were succeeding in meeting these standards.

Unsurprisingly, there is no pressure in C&R for male managers to have either wives or mistresses. And, although some senior managers have both wives and mistresses, possessing a mistress is not, in itself, given a positive value: it does not form part of a collective ideal towards which managers at any level of the organization strive. The lack of identification between having the capacity to manage and being a man means that female managers (and for that matter, mistresses) are considered full social persons, wholly implicated in the world of power. In contrast to what happens at Bion, the 'private' sphere of personal relations is not identified with the domain of women and thus split off from the central needs of the organization.

In C&R, then, a manager's manhood is not contingent on his achievements for the organization. It derives from a much wider moral universe that includes more of his human relations to the world. His qualities as a father, as well as the way he orders relations with his wife and mistress, form a conscious part of the frame of reference through which his manhood is constituted. In C&R it is possible for a man to be a moral person – a full social person – and an indifferent manager. His manhood, his very being, is not at the service of the organization and as a consequence he is not driven by the need to act for something outside himself in order to reconfirm his own sense of self.

It was the experience of doing fieldwork in an organization where female sexuality is neither central to, nor excluded from, the organization's main concerns that shot into relief the symbolic centrality of female sexuality in Bion: more specifically, the way in which female sexuality is covertly brought in to serve Bion's corporate aims. The deep hierarchical motive underpinning the requirement to have a mistress had been obscured by the absolute nature of the conceptual separation between the dynamic universe of the male corporation and the peripheral domain of women.

Bion managers are driven by the desire to demonstrate toughness. Each 'bold action' proves (once again) that they qualify as tough men. Achievements are explicitly addressed to one's peers and subordinates, and they emphasize a manager's ability to determine, and therefore control, the world around him. But displays of toughness are at the same time, though less consciously, addressed to the audience above, to the men who hold their future in their hands.

Here we begin to see the real extent and nature of their alienation. Although not all managers are equally ambitious, there is a powerful consensus that ultimate success of a manager's career is the appointment to the Board of Directors. And for many, over a number of years, the continuing display of their worth and significance has been orientated towards this goal, a goal which holds out the promise of control and security. It is difficult to exaggerate the significance of actually reaching the Board of Directors. Not only is this the top of the British division, it is considered the most prestigious of all the divisions worldwide. Although managers can, and sometimes do, take transfers abroad this is seen as a form of defeat. The real prize is to be appointed to the board of Bion. And managers who have achieved this goal have years of confirmation that their criterion of success works.

But the reality at the end turns out to be very different from the ideal. A manager finally reaches the top, but the top of what? The cars, chauffeurs, and offices that symbolize the final attainment of absolute control are no protection against the arbitrary power of those who actually control the Company. The concrete end that held reality at bay vanishes. They are now directly beholden to BDC, men whom they do not know and have barely met. The nature of their relation to their superiors has changed. They are beholden to men who will not bear witness to their 'tough acts', who are interested in results per se, not in the manner in which they are achieved. Their strategy for survival is redundant yet the responsibilities and the pressures to achieve are greater than ever before. The reality they cannot confront is that the source of their power (proof of their masculinity) is illusory; that, after all, they are mere proletarians: they are, and have always been, expendable commodities.

The problem for Bion Directors is how to get the threat under control. The solution emerges from the internal cultural logic. They must confront reality by the roundabout route of known symbols, in this case by means of performance and the explicit production of achievements. Proof of real manhood fends off threats. The problem is to find a way of presenting the evidence to their invisible audience.

At the managerial level there is no institutional imperative to take a mistress in order to succeed. Having a mistress at this level of the hierarchy is merely one of a number of possible enhancements, like wearing expensive suits. It does not in itself make a manager tough. Nevertheless, a mistress is an admirable possession and many highly esteemed managers have them. From the standpoint of the manager, display is very much the point. But what is being displayed if not the soundness of his performance? The collective ideal contains an implicit symbolic association between achievement and potency. But while, for many managers, achievements alone are enough to indicate potency, others (arguably those with the deepest concern with their own insignificance) turn the symbolic representation into reality. The important point, however, is that the symbolic association exists prior to managers being appointed to the board. It forms part of a more complex range of unconscious motivations that can be drawn upon as external conditions create new demands on unconscious life.[25]

Proof of potency takes on added urgency when the vital belief in the efficacy of toughness finds no other means of being sustained. 'Posh' women, that is, women the directors imagine could occupy the social domain of their superiors, represent a symbolic communication with the men above. And through what is in effect an unconsciously held mystical association, directors attempt to display their potency, their managerial competence, to those who have ultimate power over their labour.

In contrast with the way I had originally understood sexual liaisons, in terms of the indigenous distinction between public and private, I now began to see a complex symbolic organization of shared experience whereby libidinal desire and economic performance are unconsciously experienced as integral to one another. Profit as a symbol of potency, a notion that until this fieldwork had, for me, been no more than a cliché, turned out to be a concretely held creative illusion through which 'privately experienced' sexual desire is fused with the structure and function of the enterprise.

---

25. For a discussion of how sexuality operates as symbol in social hierarchy, see Burke (1969).

Conclusion

The powerful pressures on Bion managers and Directors to accord a higher value to demonstrating toughness than to assessing the consequences of their tough actions are deeply rooted in unconscious self-definitions of masculinity. They do not result either from inadequate information or from a straightforward misunderstanding of the facts. The temptation of rationalist theoreticians is to assume that because conscious thought determines action, a change in the hierarchy of values and a subsequent increase in the rate of profit could be achieved by 'rational' means.[26] But to think in these terms is to entirely miss the point; namely, that such an increase in the rate of profit will depend on the outcomes the *culture* of each specific corporation can yield. In the case of Bion, these outcomes are determined by managers interpreting and defining corporate aims through conceptions of masculinity that limit their capacity to act on the basis of purely economic calculation. Such deep-seated conceptions, whether in Bion or C&R, are not themselves created by pressures imposed on managers by the organization. They have developed historically within each individual manager and are a product of the society into which he was born.

A more fundamental understanding of the underlying cultural process through which these managers' orientation to reality emerges would entail overcoming the very considerable practical difficulties created by the profound separation between domestic and productive life characteristic of capitalist society. To develop an anthropological approach to political economy we would need also to observe these men as husbands, sons, fathers, and grandsons; that is, in the context of family relations as well as the relation of the family to the means of production. Taken together we would then have an ethnographic account of the relations which comprise their universe.

Acknowledgements

I would like to thank Adrian Haddock, Christina Toren, Michael Garnett and Keith Hart for their ideas, criticisms, and encouragement.

References

Burke, K. (1969), *A Rhetoric of Motives*, Berkeley: University of California Press.
de Beauvoir, S. (1984), *The Second Sex*, Harmondsworth: Penguin.
Cunnison, S. (1966), *Wages and Work Allocation*, London: Tavistock.

---

26. This is already to grant them too much. Rationalist paradigms do not have the tools to identify the deep-seated, shared assumptions that underpin organizational life.

Descola, P. (1996), 'Constructing Natures: Symbolic Ecology and Social Practice', in P. Descola and G. Palsson (eds), *Nature and Society: Anthropological Perspectives*, London: Routledge.

Harper, R. (1998), *Inside the IMF: An Ethnography of Documents, Technology and Organizational Action*, San Diego: Academic Press.

Hendy, J. (1993), *A Law unto Themselves: Conservative Employment Laws: A National and International Assessment* (3rd edn), London: The Institute of Employment Rights.

Janelli, R. and Yim, D. (1993), *Making Capitalism: The Social and Cultural Construction of a South Korean Conglomerate*, Stanford: Stanford University Press.

Laing, R.D. (1967), 'Family and Individual Structure', in P. Lomas (ed.), *The Predicament of the Family*, London: Hogarth Press.

Latour, B. (1987), *Science in Action: How to Follow Scientists and Engineers through Society*, Cambridge, Mass.: Harvard University Press.

Lupton, T. (1963), *On the Shop Floor: Two Studies of Workshop Organization and Output*, Oxford: Pergamon.

Luttwak, E. (1999), *Turbo Capitalism: Winners and Losers in the Global Economy*, London: Orion Business Books.

Okely, J. (1987), 'Fieldwork up the M1: Policy and Political Aspects', in A. Jackson (ed.), *Anthropology at Home*, London: Tavistock.

Ouroussoff, A. (1993), 'Illusions of Rationality: False Premises of the Liberal Tradition', *Man* **28**: 281–98.

Ryan, D. (1998), 'The Thatcher Government's Attack on Higher Education in Historical Perspective', *The New Left Review* 227: 3–32.

Sahlins, M. (1976), *Culture and Practical Reason*, Chicago: University of Chicago Press.

Strathern, M. (1981), 'Self-Interest and the Social Good: Some Implications of Hagen Gender Imagery', in S. Ortner and H. Whitehead (eds), *Sexual Meanings: The Cultural Construction of Gender and Sexuality*, Cambridge: Cambridge University Press.

Willmott, H. (1995), 'Managing the Academics: Commodification and Control in the Development of University Education in the U.K.', *Human Relations* **48**(9): 993–1027.

Woolgar, S. (1993 [1988]), *Science, The Very Idea*, London: Routledge.

Part II
Science

–3–

Ethnography in the Laboratory
Christine Hine

Introduction

This chapter aims to illustrate the possibilities and problems of conducting an ethnographic study within a laboratory. The first section introduces the grounds for thinking of the laboratory as an organization open to ethnographic study. The rest of the chapter then focuses on the study which I conducted within a mouse-genetics laboratory, first introducing the project of which the study formed a part, then describing the role which I adopted, before introducing a brief summary of the methods which I used and the results which I gained. The final section of the chapter maps the work in sociology of scientific knowledge which forms the basis for the approach taken in this study and draws together some issues arising from the study which might be relevant in other studies of organizations where knowledge and expertise are highly specialized.

Laboratories and Organizations

This collection of articles is about ethnography in organizations. At first glance, a laboratory might seem quite an esoteric field site for an organizational ethnography. It therefore seems appropriate to consider first what is special about the particular type of organization discussed in this chapter, the laboratory. That laboratories are organizations might not be apparent at first sight, looking from within a culture which gives a very special status to science. The work of scientists is often treated with a deference that suggests it is far too complex for outsiders to understand, and ethnographers might well be deterred from trying to enter a laboratory on the grounds that they would not understand what was going on. It might also seem that the work of scientists offered little for an ethnographer to study. We tend not to think about the work of scientists and the facts that they produce as being cultural artefacts. We generally think of science when it is done properly as being objective, by which we mean outside culture. At the end of the chapter I return to the background which supports a view of science as a thoroughly social practice. For now, it is probably sufficient to say that there is much to be gained by suspending a culturally specific awe about science. Thinking of the laboratory as a kind of organization is one way of demystifying it.

In what ways, then, is a laboratory an organization? As we might expect of an organization, it is a very orderly place. It is a task-oriented setting in which people are employed to do a job. It has, like many organizations, a bounded location. Its membership is quite stable, and there is little difficulty in distinguishing insiders from outsiders. There are definite procedures by which new members are trained, and a status hierarchy with distinct ranks through which members may rise. There are no obvious clients, customers, or users of the organization, but there is a distinct peer community (other laboratories) to which members orient their work. The products of the organization are made available to this peer community by publishing papers and giving talks at conferences. The organization relies heavily on routinized working practices and on documentation. Records of what is done are kept with an almost bureaucratic obsessiveness. The orderliness and purposiveness of the laboratory, as with any organization, are created and sustained through explicit rules, but also through the working practices and embodied culture of the members. On these grounds there is much to occupy the ethnographer.

There is, moreover, the intriguing possibility that the kind of science which the laboratory produces might be shaped by the ways in which it is ordered and by the ways of seeing the world which members share. The laboratory then becomes a vital institution to study if one wants to know how science is shaped. The laboratory is reliant on orderly working practices. It also relies to a great extent on recording and measuring devices which make scientific phenomena visible. Some devices, such as microscopes, literally make things visible (although it takes effort to learn to see them). Other laboratory technologies make things visible in less literal but nonetheless important ways, by producing measurements, traces, and statistical analyses. These devices too, and the working practices which surround them, can be seen as constitutive of scientific knowledge rather than as neutral tools which scientists simply use. Ethnographers in technological settings need to pay close attention to the ways in which the technology, its effects, and its success or failure are interpreted (Pfaffenberger 1988). The rest of this chapter attempts to provide some ideas about how this can be done.

The Study: Information Technology in Science

The study I will be describing was part of a project that set out to examine the use of Information Technology (IT) in human genetics research. The original plan was to provide a counter to some of the hype that surrounded the potential of IT to transform science generally (Denning 1991, Maxwell 1990) and specifically to examine the way in which developments in IT had formed part of the drive for major funding of an international initiative to map and sequence the human genome

(Hine 1993). Pre-sensitized as I was by work in the sociology of scientific knowledge and the sociology of technology, I was aware that the choices made in the production and use of laboratory instruments might play a role in shaping the scientific knowledge which resulted from their use. Also, it seemed possible that there might be a gap between public stories about the benefits of IT and the more private accounts of IT in use. Ethnography provided a means of studying the use of IT in context without prejudging any ways of using it as right or wrong.

The project involved a series of interviews with developers and users of IT in genetics research around the UK. These interviews were semi-structured and aimed to map the range of approaches to the use of IT, capturing the words and meanings of participants in relation to their use of technology and its role in their work. These interviews provided a background to the primary part of the project which comprised two periods of ethnography. The first of these involved a group of computer developers producing IT systems for the UK genetics community. The second involved a mouse-genetics laboratory where the systems were in use. For now, I will focus on the ways in which the first ethnography prefigured and shaped the second.

As a member of the computer developers' tight-knit community, I became well-versed in both the capabilities of the system and their aspirations for it. My role within the team was to rewrite the user manual for the system, bringing it up to date and incorporating changes intended to make it more 'user-friendly'. The work of writing documentation is often a low-status and unpopular task: an ideal role, therefore, for an ethnographer! In addition, it provided a perfect opportunity to interrogate ideas about who the users were who were to benefit from the system and become the readers of the manual. The computer-systems developers spent much time discussing what it was that users wanted from the programs they were developing (and also talking about the ways in which users should be using what they had been given). However, many of the working practices which I observed acted to exclude users from involvement in the development process. Through my role as manual writer I became a part of the separate professional sphere around the development of IT. From these experiences I had a picture of the assumptions and practices that shaped the technologies which were developed and a not inconsiderable although sketchily acquired technical knowledge about how to use the system. In addition, I had a very strong moral picture of the appropriate ways in which the computer-systems developers considered their systems should be used.

In the spirit of 'follow the thing' (Marcus 1995), I set out to find a laboratory where the information systems I had seen being developed were in use. One of the series of interviews I was conducting took me to a mouse-genetics laboratory attached to a large teaching hospital in the UK. The head of the laboratory was friendly and informative at the interview, and expressed strong views on what genetics needed from IT and where it could be improved. The laboratory looked lively, genetics research was going on, and IT was certainly being used. Geographically, the laboratory was ideally placed for me. After the interview, I contacted the head of the laboratory again, asking whether his laboratory might be prepared to host me for a longer period of time. Some faxes and letters later, he agreed.

I was surprised how easy it was to negotiate access. Organizational studies are notoriously difficult to secure, and 'getting in, getting on, getting out and getting back' (Buchanan, Boddy, and McCalman 1988) can be fraught with politics. In this case several factors were on my side. IT was already a problem which occupied the head of the laboratory: he thought that it was not being used as effectively as it should have been. The ways in which I presented the problem had some resonance with the ways in which he already saw it. It is also possible that I was seen as a source of technical assistance, to solve some of the problems more directly, since I had told him about my time with the system developers. Finally, having visitors was, I came to realize, a routine event in the laboratory anyway. This being a prominent laboratory in its field, people would come for varying periods of time to learn techniques and the members of the laboratory were able (until my behaviour became particularly strange and un-visitor-like) to fit me in to that general model of being there to learn how things are done.

So, poised to enter my second field site, I explained to my own project leader where I was going. On hearing that I was off to join a mouse-genetics laboratory he expressed dismay: we had after all gained funding for the project on the basis that we were to study the use of IT in *human* genetics. The answer I gave to his questions raises a more general point about ethnography: the chosen ethnographic site needs to be rendered as an adequate place in which to study a particular problem (Rachel and Woolgar 1995). Given that in these times of funding proposals and dissertation outlines we are rarely free to enter the field and study the problems which arise from the ground, the issue is not how a problem is to be rendered appropriate to a particular field site, but how a field site is to be rendered in advance an appropriate place to study a particular problem.

In the case of human and mouse genetics, the answer depends on a routine piece of transformation work, which my informant had produced at our first meeting. The rationale is that it is difficult to carry out certain kinds of genetic study on humans. Humans do not breed fast enough, and in general you cannot control with whom they breed. Many of the techniques used in genetics depend on being able to control breeding and have access to several generations. Meanwhile, mice do breed fast, and their breeding can be controlled. Mice also share a lot of genetic characteristics with humans, and some portions of genetic material are highly conserved between the two. So, having taken a problem (a potentially faulty gene) in humans, we find a similar problem in mice. We then study the problem in mice to try to find the gene responsible. We then go back to humans, and look for the same genetic trait in affected humans. So, knowledge is translated back and forth from human to mouse and back again. The mouse becomes a 'tool' in human genetics, or an 'honorary human', to use my informant's term. The setting therefore has no necessary and inherent link to the problem being studied. It is rendered adequate to the problem by demonstrating links: in this case, using the informants' understandings to show that a mouse-genetics laboratory can be an appropriate place in which to study human-genetics research.

In this instance the link was considered convincing and so I joined the laboratory. I was scheduled to go to the laboratory four days a week for a period of several months. My plans at that stage went little beyond get there, hang out, watch what goes on, and try not to break anything!

The Role

On my first day, I experienced a routine which I later found was common for visitors on their first day in the laboratory. On arrival I was handed a timetable, which showed the sub-groups within the laboratory, each with a time when a designated person would explain to me what work they were engaged in. A further member of the laboratory was detailed to take me out to lunch at the Chinese restaurant across the road. This structured and informative reception was far more comforting than most ethnographers may have to face. However, by the end of the day I was a mass of confusions. It was fast becoming apparent that I was no geneticist. I do have a Botany degree, which might be expected to give me some of the necessary background: but as an undergraduate I had found genetics difficult and incomprehensible, and it was clear that nothing had changed. Some of the words and concepts were familiar, but I was unable to follow many of the narrative links between techniques and outcomes which seemed self-evident to the people who were explaining their work to me. People were careful to position what they said in relation to my level of knowledge: they would pause in an explanation to check whether a word or concept made sense and took my possession of a scientific degree as some guarantee that I would understand a scientific but not specialist explanation. I was glad to be treated in some degree as an insider, but, ultimately, I was confused.

Over time in the laboratory, with repeated explanations and illustrations of particular procedures and analytic techniques, I became much more comfortable in that I understood the sense of the stories which people told me about their work. Without these stories, about the search for a particular gene, or the construction of a map of a specific region for a specific purpose, the day-to-day activities in the laboratory would have seemed a meaningless jumble. To the untrained eye many of the activities look very mundane: moving between laboratory bench and computer, incubator and dark room, with trays of tiny plastic tubes or fragile slabs of gel, poring over computer printouts or smudgy photographs, and endless waiting for tubes to incubate or gels to 'run'. It was only by coming to understand the wider narratives into which the work fitted that I could begin to see how the difference between something boring, something disastrous, and a major break-through was forged. My understanding of these genetic narratives was hard-won and fleeting: now that I have been away from the laboratory for some time, I can remember that they did make sense, but I would be unable to reproduce those self-evident links. My aim, rather than becoming a genetics expert myself, was to understand how the mundane events in the laboratory became meaningful to the participants, and that involved an appreciation of the wider narratives, the research careers, and the competition with other laboratories within which they made sense.

Some understanding of the procedures being carried out was therefore, for me, crucial to gaining a feel for the life of the laboratory. I had to become, briefly, adept at understanding explanations grudgingly or gladly provided over coffee, overheard in the office, and detailed in scientific papers. However, I was never practically competent in a way that would have allowed me a full part in the work. Precision in genetic techniques is highly valued and results matter: one mistake can mean a week's work wasted. The work is a race against competing laboratories, PhD deadlines, and the end of funding. In this environment, where participants have a highly specialized technical knowledge, there is little that the unskilled ethnographer can offer. As far as the scientific work was concerned, I was very much an observer. Some people who became friends and key informants would take me on for a few days to shadow them or to teach me how to carry out a technique, although there was no expectation that I would ever carry out that technique alone. A lot of my time was therefore spent rather uncomfortably hanging out, trying to look as though I was doing something. I interviewed everyone I could, and spent a lot of time in the office attached to the laboratory where the computers were. I checked my email frequently, and absorbed what I could of the activity going on around me.

As time went on confusion (both mine and my informants') grew about my role. It was apparent that I was not like the other visitors. I found myself gradually becoming constituted as the IT expert. People knew that I was there with an interest in IT and the perception that I must therefore know what I was doing stuck, even though I had not mentioned my experiences with the computer systems developers in my previous ethnography out of a wish not to be aligned with them and not to be placed in a position of carrying tales from one field to another. At first, I was highly uncomfortable with the idea of becoming the local IT expert: after all, I was there to study their use of IT, not to shape it myself. The last thing I wanted to do was to set myself up as an expert and to solve people's problems.

Despite these anxieties I can see, looking back over my field notes, that I did change my role over time and I did accept more and more the role of IT expert.

The day when I showed a few people how their computer could be used to access the World Wide Web stood out as the first time I did anything that seemed to impress people! After this, several people asked me to fix problems with computer programs or to help them in finding information on the World Wide Web and I tried to oblige. Part of this, no doubt, is due to my uneasiness about being a person without a useful role in the midst of a busy environment, and the sense that at least here was something that I could do. Also, by the time I was more familiar with the way in which the laboratory worked, I felt much more comfortable with initiating conversations and making suggestions. By demonstrating a new technique or offering a different way of doing something, I was showing my competence not only with the technology, but also with the culture of the laboratory. By then, I knew how important sharing of skills was, and how to teach someone a new technique. I was also more ready to take a proactive role once I had formed some preliminary observations, and introducing new topics and techniques allowed me to test these ideas with my informants.

Paradoxically, much of what I learned about IT in the laboratory came from not looking at IT at all, if by that is meant sitting next to a computer seeing how it is used. By looking at the work of the laboratory in its entirety I learned things which I would not have done had I taken a narrow view of my problem. In the next section of this chapter I give a brief summary of some observations which trade on the comparison between laboratory practices in general and the use of IT in particular.

Learning from Looking Elsewhere

Learning Practices

I have mentioned earlier the kindness of my informants in taking me on for a day or two to explain to me a technique which they were carrying out, and to teach me to do it. These techniques would typically involve a series of procedures at different locations, moving from one piece of equipment to another, from fume cupboard to laboratory bench to incubator to dark room, with solutions and tubes and gels. I would be given a running narrative of the procedure being carried out, how long it would take, whether we could fit in lunch or coffee at this stage, and explanations of what the various solutions and gels contained in terms of the mice who provided the DNA or the chemical name of the constituents. At key stages, I would be allowed to carry out a procedure and would watch my informant nervously and try to mimic precisely what he did, not clear at any stage which moves might be crucial to our success and which might be trivial. My informant bore patiently with my constant questioning of 'Why are we doing this? Why did you do that?' Finally, when I asked why we had carefully washed a slab of glass down twice with a particularly (so he warned me) hazardous solution, he said, 'Because that's what the person who showed me did, and it works, so I'm not going to mess with it.'

Further experience in the laboratory showed that this account was not unusual. There was a strong preference for being shown a technique by someone for whom it worked. Written protocols giving step-by-step instructions for carrying out techniques were freely available, but these were seen as needing interpretation and as leaving out vital information necessary to make the technique work. Techniques were fragile and prone to stop working for no reason, so it made sense to get as close as possible to the way of carrying them out of someone who had had previous success with them.

Observation and interaction with members of the laboratory using the computers showed strong parallels with the learning practices used for laboratory techniques. New computer skills were often learned by watching someone who already had success with them, and people spoke nostalgically of a time when there were some people in the laboratory who liked computers and knew a lot about them and were able to give a lot of help. In the office I tried and failed to locate a copy of the user manual on which I had spent so much time when with the computer systems developers. Written instructions were treated with suspicion or disregard.

Myth and Magic

Looking at laboratory techniques also exposes the extent to which these procedures are seen as being outside rational explanation. A technique may suddenly stop working for no apparent reason, and, without the researchers being aware of what has changed, they may fail to obtain useful results for days, even weeks, at a time. When this occurs, changes to particular stages of the procedure or new batches of solutions may be suggested, but in the end the advice may consist of a shrug of the shoulders and a suggestion to 'Keep trying'.

A similar event occurred one day at the computer. A researcher sat down in front of the workstation in the corner of the office, and typed in his user name and password. He was refused access. He tried again, and the same happened. Noticing his problem, and taking on my new role of IT expert, I leaned across and asked what was wrong. He explained that the computer would not let him log in. As I started to launch into a potential diagnosis, 'I think you've got Caps Lock on . . .' he cut me off. 'It's OK, it's playing up, it does that with mine from time to time for some reason.' He looked out of the office and called to another researcher who was passing to come and log in for him on her password, because his was not working today.

For this researcher, the computer was not a logical, knowable machine whose problems required a rational explanation. Rather, it was a complex, almost organic being which could 'play up' without warning just like the laboratory techniques.

This perception of computers was not necessarily shared throughout the laboratory. However, the output of the computer programs was often interpreted in a behaviourist way: rather than a logical interpretation based on known processes being carried out, the interpretation of computer results was often discussed in terms of what looked or felt right, and the underlying processes inferred from that. One informant told me of a sequence-matching program: 'I kind of looked at the results and worked out what it must be doing from that.' From the computer systems developers I had gathered that scientists were, or should be, deeply interested in and knowledgeable about the algorithms used by the programs which they used. In the laboratory this turned out to be far from true.

Common Property

According to computer systems developers, users are distinct bounded entities, each of whom has and uses his or her own user name and password. The anecdote I tell above gives the lie to this assumption. Sharing of computer space was common in the laboratory. On PCs in the shared office, files tended to be stored on the hard disc drive where anyone could, and did, access them. Researchers tended to use their own electronic mail accounts, and not to read each other's electronic mail, but for access to external computer systems, including the system whose developers I had spent time with, they all shared the same account in the name of the head of the laboratory. Inspired by these observations, I decided to explore how this view of computer space as shared fitted into ideas of space and property within the laboratory more generally.

In order to discuss the notion of sharing and the use of space within the laboratory, I used a collaboratively produced map. I drew a rough sketch of the laboratory and office space and, during a lunch break, I asked the people who were eating their sandwiches in the office to help me complete it. We shaded and labelled all the places which were thought of as belonging to one person or another. Each researcher had a portion of the laboratory bench which was held to be his or hers, and a place where he or she habitually sat in the offices. This led to a discussion on what was and was not shared. Resources, such as enzymes and solutions, were in short supply at the time. It was generally accepted that these were not yours: rather they belonged to the laboratory and you could not reasonably (morally) keep them to yourself. Similarly, labelling a piece of equipment did not make it someone's exclusive possession, although it did make it more likely that you would return it if you borrowed it. Very little in the laboratory was held to be private inviolable space or property, and even apparent ownership implied respect rather than exclusive rights.

Only in relation to time did it seem that computer usage was viewed differently. Some members of the laboratory told me that they preferred to keep computer work for quieter times: outside normal working hours, when the system might be running more quickly, they were less likely to be disturbed. These were the researchers who were more confident with IT: more likely to be happy working alone, and more likely to resent the communal approach which the less confident members of the laboratory took for using the computer. During the day, computer time was likely to be snatched between stages of a procedure which took a defined time, in just the same way as coffee and lunch would be fitted in with a procedure which would not wait. Laboratory work was seen as the most important feature of the work, and computing work as a subsidiary which could be fitted in at odd moments. I was, however, told by one researcher that she regretted not having done more computing earlier in her project because 'it would have been giving me feedback and telling me where I was going wrong.' Generally, the priority of laboratory techniques over other uses of time went unchallenged.

Looking at time and space tends therefore to reinforce a view of the computer as something which is fitted into the routines of laboratory work, and which is incorporated into pre-existing assumptions about the sharing of space and property. The computer tends to become just another piece of laboratory equipment, less exacting in its demands on time than some other procedures.

Transformations of Representations

The results of computer analysis of data were part of a chain of transformations of representations within the laboratory. On a major scale was the transformation from humans to mice and back to humans which I described earlier. On a smaller scale, laboratory work is about moving from one kind of representation to another, with the adequacy of the transformation in principle questionable at every stage (Latour and Woolgar 1986).

To illustrate this point, I need to return to the experience of learning a new technique. The day, for me, started with the tubes which contained mouse DNA held in solution. (I never saw a live mouse during my time at the laboratory.) To these tubes enzymes were added to cleave the DNA, the tubes were incubated to induce cleavage, and then markers were added. Gel was poured between glass plates to form channels for separation of the DNA, and the DNA samples were injected into the channels. These stages called for steady hands and high manual dexterity so as not to lose several hours of work by breaking the gel or contaminating between channels. An electric current was run across the gel to separate out the differently sized strands of DNA, and the gel was stained, washed, and finally taken to a dark room to be photographed. At this stage, my teacher leaned across the gel eager to see if the day's work had been worthwhile, and I too leaned across, watching his face, anxious that my ineptitude might have inadvertently ruined the results. As I watched he smiled, then swept his hand across the gel, crumpling it into several pieces. I was horrified at seeing our hard work so casually destroyed. I had made the mistake of viewing the gel as an end result, rather than as a stage in a process of transformations.

On returning to the laboratory bench with the photograph of the gel, the interpretation began. My informant sat and studied the photograph, interpreting it for me in the light of what he expected to see, and what would be sensible to see. He said, 'Either I did something wrong, or something interesting is happening.' There then followed a process of preparing a diagram to show the implications of this result for the genetic map, and comparison with other people's results obtained from published papers or databases. The process involves the construction of plausible stories to account for the observed results, and the results from databases provide one part of the backdrop against which the decision as to what makes sense is made.

Plausible stories involve the alignment of different kinds of evidence. Matching of DNA sequences identified in the laboratory with those sequenced by others around the world and stored in computer databases forms one kind of evidence in leading to the identification of a gene. While the laboratory techniques are used to identify 'candidate genes', matches with similar sequences in databases are used to discuss what would be a sensible candidate, and what could plausibly be implicated in the genetic disorder being investigated. Judgements of the reliability of database information are based on who did the work and where, and how sensible they seem in the light of other stories.

A published paper which announces a new genetic map, or identifies the gene for a genetic disorder, therefore represents the end point of a series of transformations of representations, and of judgements about what is a plausible story and what makes sense. The end point requires an alignment of different kinds of evidence, and no one source of data or information is necessarily privileged. The results of computerized data analysis and database matching are judged on the degree to which they contribute to the construction of these plausible stories. My account foregrounds IT as a specific concern. In the work of the laboratory, IT is only foregrounded at particular times, when there are debates about the working of a particular package, or the applicability or reliability of results. At other times, IT is effectively invisible in the work of the laboratory, and the talk is of pulling out genes and reading sequences. In the published papers of the laboratory, the transformations of representations which lead up to the results being reported are all but absent.

Conclusions

Ethnography was first notably used in scientific laboratories in the 1970s and 1980s. Up to this point, sociologists of science had tended to be preoccupied with accounting for bad science, where results were believed which later came to be seen as untrue. It seemed that the task of sociology of science was confined to accounting for what went wrong in these aberrant cases. 'True' science was assumed to be beyond social accounting and to be adequately explained by the appropriate application of scientific method. Sociologists and anthropologists began to study the everyday working practices of laboratories, as part of a move to claim the content of (both 'true' and 'false') science for social analysis (Knorr-Cetina and Mulkay 1983).

Establishing the content of science as open to social analysis entails questioning some taken-for-granted assumptions: that laboratory instruments provide transparent windows on reality (Latour and Woolgar 1986); that experiments can be replicated (Collins 1985); that facts can be readily distinguished from artefacts of the experimental process (Lynch 1985); that facts speak for themselves (Latour and Woolgar 1986); that scientific papers straightforwardly report on the process of fact discovery (Knorr-Cetina 1981); and that discoveries are recognized as such at the time that they are made (Woolgar 1976). Ethnographic studies of scientific practice and scientific discourse (Gilbert and Mulkay 1984) aimed to give accounts of what scientists do and how they do it the same status as the accounts of any other culture. In other words, the work of the early ethnographers was to make taken-for-granted features of our own culture seem strange. Scientific 'truths' were to be seen as embedded in and subject to the cultures which produced them (Traweek 1988). Among these broadly ethnographic studies there is considerable disciplinary and methodological diversity (Traweek 1992).

Viewing the content of science as social in this way opens up a whole range of potential questions for discussion. Once the 'sacred' status of scientific truth is removed (at least for the purposes of analysis, if not for everyday life), ethnographers can also begin to track the complex connections between the knowledge-producing practices of the laboratory and the culture which surrounds and permeates the boundaries of the laboratory. Attempts have been made to trace the sociology of scientific knowledge between laboratories (Fujimura 1992), to consider the implications of the apparent boundedness of the laboratory (Knorr-Cetina 1992; Latour 1987), and to make connections between the products of the laboratory and wider social, political, and economic concerns (Charlesworth *et al.* 1989). Recently, the proposal of multi-sited ethnography (Marcus 1995) has been taken up by anthropologists of science who seek to trace the ways in which scientific knowledge travels beyond the boundaries of the laboratory and is rearticulated and reproduced in its new settings (Layne 1998; Heath 1998).

The sociology of scientific knowledge provides a rich supply of experiences on which to draw in conducting an ethnographic study in a laboratory. In my own work I drew on approaches which open the everyday practices of science to inquiry and see them as crucial in the construction of scientific knowledge. I also drew heavily on a sceptical analytic approach which did not give a priori privilege to any accounts of what was going on in laboratory work. My question, however, in common with that of many current ethnographies of scientific practice, was rather different from that of the earlier ethnographers. Rather than making a strong point about the social construction of scientific facts, I was concerned to trace the role of one particular laboratory technology and the ways in which its design and use were shaped by local experience.

The brief results which I have described here show how, within a short, focused period of ethnographic observation, I was able to gain a rich sense of the practices of laboratory work, and the ways in which IT fitted in as a piece of laboratory equipment. The application of an ethnographic sensitivity, combined with the specific insights of the sociology of scientific knowledge, allowed me to approach the use of IT in the laboratory as a locally meaningful part of the process of scientific work, without making judgements about the truth or otherwise of the knowledge being produced. By focusing on laboratory work as a whole, rather than narrowly focusing on situations in which a computer was being used, I was able to show the ways in which IT fits into and is transformed by the laboratory setting.

The computer system became incorporated into and transformed by laboratory culture, to become a piece of technology almost unrecognizable to the computer-systems developers who designed it. The dual-site ethnography which I conducted allowed me to contrast the perspective of the designers of the system with the perspective of its eventual users. The different beliefs and practices which prevailed in the laboratory allowed a completely different view of the technology to exist from the one which the systems developers would have advocated. Possibly the greatest irony is that the 'users' in the laboratory were highly satisfied with the system.

In common with many other organizational field sites, the laboratory is a site of specialized expertise. This raises some specific problems and issues for the ethnographer setting out to enter and gain analytic purchase in such a field. The foremost of these issues is that of specialized knowledge: how much is needed before entering the setting, and how much needs to be acquired as an ethnographer? Understanding the technical content of the work, and learning to understand technical content are both very useful ethnographically: not in themselves, but because of the purchase they offer on the meanings which participants give to events and for the access which they provide to the details of working practices. At the same time, however, not being a scientist provides the crucial ethnographic purchase which comes from questioning taken-for-granted practices.

Without a high starting level of scientific expertise, it is unlikely that in a short space of time an ethnographer in the laboratory will acquire enough competence to take a full part in the work. Roles are therefore likely to be limited, and without being a full participant it is easy to feel useless or self-conscious. In my own case I tackled this anxiety through a combination of strategies: accepting the discomfort as a price to be paid for being there; adopting an apprentice role where possible; and drawing on alternative skills in IT to contribute to the work. This latter strategy I drew upon only in the later stages and reluctantly, but it proved to be useful in foregrounding IT for discussion at stages when I was keen to explore some of my earlier observations with my informants.

Any ethnography, particularly one in such a setting, is necessarily partial. There will be locations and aspects unexplored. In particular, I felt that I was missing some aspects by not being in the laboratory at weekends, when I was told some people did a lot of their computer work. In addition, many of the researchers had computers at home, and I was unable (or unwilling) to follow them to their homes and see what work they did there. The laboratory is only a small portion of the lives of the people who work there. Strategic decisions have to be made about what is practical and what is likely to be the most efficient use of limited time. In my case, I chose to focus on the physically bounded location of the laboratory and the normal working hours. My ethnography was extended outside that space and time only insofar as my informants told me about their lives outside.

Finally, reporting on an ethnography within a highly specialized technical setting can also be problematic: readers need to be given enough insight in order to interpret the analysis, without subjecting them to a science lesson combined with an ethnography. In part, I hope I have achieved this by allowing enough time to elapse before telling the tale that many of the technical details have been forgotten: what remain are the crucial elements in telling the ethnographic stories at the heart of the analysis.

References

Buchanan, D., Boddy, D., and McCalman, J. (1988), 'Getting in, Getting on, Getting out and Getting back', in A. Bryman (ed.), *Doing Research in Organizations*, London and New York: Routledge, 53–67.

Charlesworth, M., Farrall, L., Stokes, T., and Turnbull, D. (1989), *Life Among the Scientists: an Anthropological Study of an Australian Scientific Community*, Melbourne: Oxford University Press.

Collins, H.M. (1985), *Changing Order: Replication and Induction in Scientific Practice*, London: Sage.

Denning, P.J. (1991), 'A new paradigm for science' in C. Dunlop and R. Kling (eds.), *Computerization and Controversy: Value Conflicts and Social Choices*, Boston: Academic Press, 379–82.

Fujimura, J. (1992), 'Crafting Science: Standardized Packages, Boundary Objects and "Translation"' in A. Pickering (ed.), *Science as Practice and Culture*, Chicago: University of Chicago Press, 168–211.

Gilbert, G.N. and Mulkay, M. (1984), *Opening Pandora's Box: a Sociological Analysis of Scientists' Discourse*, Cambridge: Cambridge University Press.

Heath, D. (1998), 'Locating Genetic Knowledge: Picturing Marfan Syndrome and its Travelling Constituencies', *Science, Technology and Human Values* 23(1): 71–97.

Hine, C. (1993), 'Possibility and Necessity: Science, Ethics and the Technological Imperative', paper presented at BSA Annual Conference (Research Imaginations), 5–8 April, Essex.

Knorr-Cetina, K. (1981), *The Manufacture of Knowledge: an Essay on the Constructivist and Contextual Nature of Science*, Oxford: Pergamon Press.

—— (1992), 'The Couch, the Cathedral and the Laboratory: On the Relationship between Experiment and Laboratory in Science' in A. Pickering (ed.), *Science as Practice and Culture*, Chicago: University of Chicago Press, 113–38.

—— and Mulkay, M. (eds.) (1983), *Science Observed: Perspectives on the Social Study of Science*, London: Sage.

Latour, B. (1987), *Science in Action: How to follow Scientists and Engineers through Society*, Cambridge, Mass.: Harvard University Press; Milton Keynes: Open University Press.

—— and Woolgar, S. (1986 [1979]), *Laboratory Life: the Construction of Scientific Facts* (2nd edn), Princeton: Princeton University Press.

Layne, L.L. (1998), 'Introduction to Special Issue: Anthropological Approaches in Science and Technology Studies', *Science, Technology and Human Values* 23(1): 4–23.

Lynch, M. (1985), *Art and Artifact in Laboratory Science: a Study of Shop Work and Shop Talk in a Research Laboratory*, London: Routledge & Kegan Paul.

Marcus, G.E. (1995), 'Ethnography in/of the World System: the Emergence of Multi-sited Ethnography', *Annual Review of Anthropology* 24: 95–117.

Maxwell, R. (1990), *Information Technology as a way of Reducing the Costs and Time in Dissemination of Scientific and Technical Information*, The British Library Dainton Lecture, 5 March, London: The British Library Science Technology and Industry Section.

Pfaffenberger, B. (1988), 'Fetishised Objects and Humanised Nature: Towards an Anthropology of Technology', *Man* 23(2): 236–52.

Rachel, J. and Woolgar, S. (1995), 'The Discursive Structure of the Socio-Technical Divide: The Example of Information Systems Development', *Sociological Review* 43(2): 251–73.

Traweek, S. (1988), *Beamtimes and Lifetime: The World of High Energy Physicists*, Cambridge, Mass.: Harvard University Press.

—— (1992), 'Border Crossings: Narrative Strategies in Science Studies and among Physicists in Tsukuba Science City, Japan' in A. Pickering (ed.), *Science as Practice and Culture*, Chicago: University of Chicago Press, 429–65.

Woolgar, S. (1976), 'Writing an Intellectual History of Scientific Developments: the Use of Discovery Accounts', *Social Studies of Science* **6**: 395–422.

Ethnography in the Science Museum, London

Sharon Macdonald

Why carry out an ethnographic study of an institution? What can be gained from an ethnographic and anthropological approach? And what kinds of problems and issues is the researcher likely to encounter? In the following account I attempt to give some answers to these questions through providing a case study based on ethnographic research which I have carried out in the Science Museum, London. My aim is to highlight some of the information and insights an ethnographic and anthropological approach is able to provide, and to discuss some of the difficulties of trying to analyse and write about such research.

The Science Museum is itself, of course, a specific kind of institution and therein lies some of its interest to an anthropologist: Why gather up all these artefacts? Why put 'science' on public display? How do those working in the Science Museum see their task? At the same time it has parallels with many other kinds of institution in which ethnographers of organizations might work. In its creation of exhibitions, it is part of the culture industry – those institutions involved in creating cultural products (including film, television, newspapers, advertisements). It is also part of the leisure and tourist industry; it has a research and educational function; and it establishes links with universities, schools, and scientific and industrial establishments. Furthermore, many museum staff themselves are technically civil servants and members of public service trade unions. Moreover, as a large public institution, it is also subject to many of the same managerial structures, difficulties, and fashions as are other (especially large and public) organizations. And, like many organizations, it has well-educated staff, many of whom are actively engaged in reflecting upon the organization in which they work and who are well able to give accounts of it. This latter raises a question about what an *ethnographic* approach can add. Why not just ask the staff for their account? To address this question, I begin first with a discussion of the ambitions of ethnography. This is followed by some general background to my Science Museum research, its aims and context; and then I offer a more detailed discussion of how these 'ethnographic commitments' were fulfilled (or otherwise) in this research.

Ethnographic Commitments

Ethnographic research is sometimes seen simply as meaning 'participant observation': 'participant observation' entailing the ethnographer participating in, and observing, daily life. While 'participant observation' is generally a key dimension of ethnographic research, most anthropologists understand the term more broadly. This is well expressed by Daniel Miller, an anthropologist who has used an ethnographic approach to subjects such as 'capitalism' and 'consumption' in industrialized and multicultural contexts including Trinidad (1997). He suggests that ethnography is characterized by a 'series of commitments that together constitute a particular perspective' (1997: 16). These are:

1. To be in the presence of the people one is studying, not just the texts or objects they produce.
2. To 'evaluate people in terms of what they actually do, i.e. as material agents working in a material world, and not merely of what they say they do' (1997: 16-17).
3. To 'long-term commitment to an investigation that allows people to return to a daily life that one hopes goes beyond what is performed for the ethnographer' (1997: 17).
4. To holistic analysis 'which insists that . . . behaviours be considered within the larger framework of people's lives and cosmologies' (1997: 17).

In other words, ethnography is not a 'mere method' (1997: 16) but is a broader 'approach' and may itself incorporate other 'methods' besides participant observation. For example, ethnographers may also carry out interviews, undertake historical and survey research, and analyse texts and other representations produced by those they are studying. The aim is to bring together whichever methods seem appropriate to try to understand the social life and cultural assumptions of those being studied. For anthropologists, this is also coupled, implicitly or explicitly, with a 'relativizing' perspective – i.e. trying not to take features of the group being studied for granted but attempting to see what it is that is specific about them through thinking about how they might be otherwise. This may be done, implicitly or explicitly, through cross-cultural examples. By thinking about how people in another part of the world do things differently, anthropologists can raise questions about aspects of social life and local knowledge that might more usually be taken as given and not questioned. In so doing, anthropological ethnographers generally accept that they may find their research moving into areas that they had not originally expected because these turn out to be significant in the worlds which they are investigating. This open-ended flexibility is also an important feature of an ethnographic approach.

Below, I take each of Miller's 'commitments' in turn and discuss each more fully in relation to my research in the Science Museum. My aim is to try to show why each is important and how each can contribute to an understanding of a particular organizational culture, in this case that of the Science Museum. First, however, I give some background to the research.

Ethnography in the Science Museum: Background

The research was funded under the ESRC's 'Public Understanding of Science' programme; and its aim was to look at the kinds of explicit, implicit, and practical definitions that museum staff made about science, how this was reflected in the exhibitions that they produced, and what visitors made of this.[1] The ethnography focused on the making of one exhibition in particular, an exhibition which opened in October 1989 as *Food for Thought: The Sainsbury Gallery.* This is a large exhibition on the subject of food – particularly changes in food availability and choice in Britain in the twentieth century – which at the time of writing is still in place. Ethnographic research on the making of the exhibition took place for the year leading up to the opening; and further research on the wider Science Museum context and on visitors to the exhibition continued after this, with funding for the project coming to an end in September 1990.

Six members of the museum staff were the 'Exhibition Team'. They were primarily responsible for defining the content of the exhibition and for organizing it into being. In doing so, however, they were in turn 'managed' by their superiors in the Museum (the 'Head of Public Services' being their 'line manager', he in turn being managed by the Museum Director), and they were involved with many others who also played a part in the making of the exhibition. These included exhibition designers, nutritional advisers (university professors), industrialists (from whom various food-processing machinery exhibited in the exhibition was acquired), educational advisers, experts on creating interactive exhibits, picture researchers, and many others. Because all decisions about what would finally be included would have to go through the Team, it made sense to be based with them. However, although Team members were based in two adjacent offices and had many collective meetings, there were many days when different team members were meeting different consultants or carrying out different activities. Decisions on whom I would accompany were generally made on the basis of either who was willing to let me go with them (a willingness which was generally shaped by how inappropriate they thought it might appear to those they were meeting to have an ethnographer

---

1. The research was directed by Roger Silverstone and it was based in the Centre for Research into Innovation, Culture, and Technology (CRICT) at Brunel University.

accompanying them)[2] or how interesting I thought it might prove to be. As all Team members reported back on their excursions at regular Team meetings as well as often discussing them informally in the Team offices, I was generally able to keep a reasonable track of the different activities of members, even where I had not observed them directly, though obviously this was less satisfactory than in those cases where I was able to 'I-witness' (Geertz 1988: 73ff.). The same was the case for telephone calls, an important means of communication in the construction of the exhibition. Lacking phone-tapping equipment, I necessarily relied on accounts related. Nevertheless, at the point where all events had to be 'translated' into becoming part of the exhibition itself – an 'obligatory passage point', as Bruno Latour (1987) calls it – I was able to observe that process.

This direct observational work generally involved me in sitting in a corner of the offices or other location (e.g. conference room, gallery, stall in Hyde Park) with a pen and notebook. This was not just being 'a fly on the wall', however: I took my turn making tea and coffee, accompanied Team members to lunch or to pick up faxes or to check on various exhibits, and sometimes joined in discussion (mostly by asking questions). In the Team offices, I would also use time when not much easily observable was going on – e.g. when all were at work on their own word-processors – to go through the filing cabinets of documents related to the exhibition. I tape-recorded Team meetings and most other formal meetings, such as those with designers. I also kept copies of as much relevant paperwork as possible (e.g. the various 'drafts' of the exhibition 'storyline'); and took numerous photographs of, and many notes on, the actual construction of the exhibition itself. In addition, I also carried out recorded semi-structured interviews with Team members at various stages through the process and after its completion; and with other Science Museum staff (in order to get a broader sense of key debates and issues on the subject of the representation of science and other relevant matters) and various other personnel involved in the construction of the exhibition (e.g. the Education officer, the Divisional line manager, the Museum Director). The study of visitors to the exhibition entailed a somewhat different approach and to some extent, as I have discussed elsewhere, raises rather different questions and, therefore, I do not consider it here.[3]

2. Where they thought it inappropriate it was generally because they had had difficulty negotiating their own access (e.g. to a particular food company headquarters). In some cases, they specifically thought that a person being contacted (e.g. graphic designers) would be interested to know of a study being undertaken and therefore encouraged me to attend.

3. See Macdonald (1993) and (1995).

Commitment 1: Being There

The great majority of analyses of museums focus on finished exhibitions, and generally provide a 'reading' based on the content and form of that which is represented. Such 'readings' tend to assume that finished exhibitions are rather unproblematically the product of dominant class, race, and gender interests. In recent years, such studies have been accompanied by a growing, though still small, number of studies of the consumption of museums and exhibitions. These have served to highlight the possible variety in visitors' own readings as well as, in some cases, particular cultural patterns and readings positioned in terms of class, race, and gender. As yet, however, there has been very little work on the *production* of exhibitions, and that which there has been has mostly been historical – based primarily on documentation – rather than on participant-observation ethnography. The question for ethnography, then, is: What can this give us that we couldn't get from an analysis of the finished exhibition?

For me, one of the interesting and surprising things about the *Food for Thought* exhibition when it opened was the extent to which it did not entirely 'feel' like the kind of exhibition which those making it had envisaged. During the making of the exhibition, a lot of the discussion in meetings as well as informal talk in the offices and over lunch had described the exhibition with adjectives such as 'lively', 'exciting', 'busy', 'buzzy', 'fun'; it had particularly emphasized the idea that there would be 'lots going on', 'lots of hands-on', 'it won't be boring'. The large flip-chart sheets produced during the early 'brainstorming' sessions show bubbles and words –food mountains', 'cosmetics (food for the face)', 'eating out (multi-ethnic/ethos of the chef)', 'hydroponics' – jostling together; and the early sketches produced by the designers have what was described to me as 'a market-stall kind of feel', with lots of different well-occupied and even over-flowing areas and cascading potted plants. In the brainstorming charts, in some of the ideas suggested, in others that circulated during the making of the exhibition, and in some of the suggestions for names for the exhibition, there was plenty of humour. One exhibit planned (and described in a press release) was intended to give visitors the 'experience of being a frozen pea'; there were early ideas for a robot for hamburger-making and an area for tasting foods; and the exhibition includes exhibits such as a giant pot of chocolate mousse, mirrors to make you look fatter and thinner, and a (non-functioning) McDonald's food outlet. Names suggested – many never really intended, of course – included 'Bread and Butter Show', 'Nosh', 'Grub Up', and 'Feeders Digest'. In the Museum the Team itself was often referred to, and sometimes referred to itself, as 'Fruit and Nut'; and Team members enjoyed a sense of 'winding up' more 'traditional' members of the Museum staff with suggestions of 'wacky' exhibits such as a giant cup of tea to be hung over the Museum's central atrium. There was also a sense of willingness to address controversial and politically difficult subjects: world food distribution and famine, industrial food production, food poisoning, diet, including consumption of fat and sugar. In all of this, the sense of 'difference' from previous exhibitions was frequently expressed by the Team during the making, a sense of difference that they articulated to their gender – an all-woman Team being unprecedented and frequently commented upon – and to their relatively 'non-scientific' backgrounds – most having degrees in subjects such as history and archaeology – and to their 'in-touchness' with popular culture and lay people, which they tended to see many other Museum staff as not having.

Given this sense of difference, of controversy, and of fun, that infused so many of the projections of the exhibition, the finished product felt 'rather flat' or 'a bit disappointing in some ways', as Team members themselves said to me afterwards. This shouldn't be exaggerated, of course; many visitors, for example, commented positively on the number of 'hands-on' exhibits and made favourable contrasts with other Science Museum exhibitions; and some reviewers did likewise. However, others also commented negatively on the extensive text ('too much reading'); the amount of text also surprised Team members when they saw the finished exhibition. There was also negative comment both from some visitors and from some reviewers on what they saw as a lack of proper engagement with the politics of food production, particularly with the role of supermarkets (something which they sometimes linked to the fact that Sainsbury's was the main sponsor for the exhibition).

One interesting question, then, which arose from the study of *Food for Thought* – a question that I had not anticipated – was why there was a disjunction between the process that in cultural studies is sometimes referred to as 'encoding' (Hall 1980) (i.e. the production of the exhibition), on the one hand, and the 'text' (i.e. finished exhibition) and at least some of its 'decodings' (i.e. interpretations by visitors), on the other. What was clearly evident was that just to 'read back' from the finished exhibition would have missed this disjunction and its accompanying complexity. For example, the exhibition could readily be interpreted – in a manner which is consistent with many text-based readings of museum exhibitions (and indeed other cultural 'texts') – as a product of dominant cultural interests, in this case those of food companies and market-led politics. The point is not that such readings are 'wrong' or, more generally, that there is no relation between production and product. Rather, what is interesting is *how* an exhibition envisaged in a particular way might end up being open to other kinds of interpretations. It is here that an ethnography of production – direct observation of the processes of exhibition-making in this case – can help to provide answers. More generally, this can also highlight the *complexity* of production, moving us beyond the rather simplistic, deterministic models typical of much cultural studies (see Du Gay 1997 for a summary).[4]

4. For an excellent, more general analysis of the difference between much cultural studies' and anthropological research, see Werbner (1997). She argues that the former retells an 'allegory of resistance' in which 'class, race, gender, nation' are 'treated as analytic terms . . . [which] become stop words which block analysis' (Werbner 1997: 41, 45).

So, in the case of the making of the *Food for Thought* exhibition, when and how did it happen that the exhibition became 'readable' in the ways that it did?[5] To give a full answer to this question would take more space than I have here, and would involve a large number of different features and events, some relatively unpredictable (e.g. the failure of the frozen-pea experience to be completed on time), others somewhat unexpected outcomes of decisions about other matters (e.g. the 'invisibility' of the giant chocolate mousse pot to many visitors because of its size and position within the exhibition – so big one couldn't easily get far enough away to see what it was); others a sometimes unanticipated consequence of the way in which exhibition-making was undertaken (e.g. the primacy of the 'storyline' and the aim to 'convey messages'); and others a function of particular museological assumptions at the time (e.g. that visitors could learn better from 'interactive' than from static exhibits). 'Being there' certainly highlighted the numerous events and decisions that played a part in shaping the final outcome of the exhibition, and the variety of 'routes' – or 'biographies' (Kopytoff 1986) – by which different exhibits might have 'made it' to the finished exhibition. It also, of course, made visible the *exclusions* that happen during the making – artefacts, dimensions, and styles of representation which were once contemplated and perhaps even included until a relatively late stage, but which do not reach the finished exhibition. These 'dead ends', of course, are generally quite invisible to analysts who only read the finished text. Yet, as historians of science have argued of 'scientific failures' (e.g. Gooday 1997), that which doesn't 'make it' is no less interesting for that, and can be highly revealing of the implicit local knowledge and cultural assumptions involved.

To illustrate these points, let me give an example of a particular 'exclusion' or 'dead end', for by following this (as sociologists of science, such as Bruno Latour suggest, 1987) we can see some of the more general processes and tensions at work in exhibition creation. The example concerns a set of exhibits which in some

5. Of course, we might simply say that any exhibition (or other cultural 'text') is readable in infinitely variable ways and that these do not necessarily bear any relation to the text anyway. (This is a perspective sometimes voiced in museum studies and some cultural studies.) This seems to me to be not only analytically unhelpful – all we can do is list the variations – but also misguided. While there is, of course, individual variety in interpretations, and while some bear little relation to the 'text' itself, there are also identifiable patterns and commonalities in 'readings', and it is also possible to identify where a 'reading' is of a different text altogether. (Anthropology is helpful here in making us aware of how people from a different cultural background might interpret an exhibition rather differently, as Errington and Gewertz, for example, describe of readings of *Wuthering Heights* by an American and a Chambri teenager (1987: 128).) Some of the 'commonality' is derived from the common experience of those making the readings (e.g. experience of other media representations, shared cultural assumptions about food) but it also relates to particular features of the exhibition. The task is to identify these and to see how, when, and why the exhibition became readable in these ways.

of the early planning documents is listed as 'Superstition or fad in each area (carrots and seeing in the dark/garlic and Dracula/salt and the Devil/Shrove Tuesday/Ginger Bread men)'. Many Team members were extremely enthusiastic about these themes and one commented to me that this was part of the exhibition that she was especially looking forward to as she found this 'more beliefs and superstitions' aspect of more interest than 'some of the, you know, more production, sciency bits'.[6] So why did it not 'make it?' Looking back, we can see that some of the seeds of its exclusion were sown early on in the exhibition, though at the time this was not evident. Originally, the Team had begun to plan the gallery by using particular foods, or groups of foods, as the focus for different areas of the exhibition. Thus, peas and fruit, say, or bread and sugar, would be linked to particular production processes (e.g. freezing, canning, and jam-making; bread-making, sugar production; pasteurization, and bottling), to particular nutritional components (e.g. vitamins, carbohydrate, protein), and to the 'superstitions and fads'. However, when the Team presented these ideas to a panel of nutritional experts, the latter objected to the idea that foods be associated with particular nutrients. This, they said, was an outdated idea which nutritionists found unhelpful: the public should instead be encouraged to think in terms of foods as containing a mix of different nutritional components. Following this intervention from science (an intervention which we should note shows that exhibition-making was not a linear process of taking scientific ideas and packaging them, even though this is likely to be how at least some of those involved would describe it), the Team decided to reorganize the exhibition to remove the sections on nutrition and to bring these together in their own section of the exhibition, later to be named 'Food and the Body'.

Even at this point, however, the superstitions remained, and indeed, in some cases these sections seemed to be expanding as Team members found more that might be of interest to include in them. Of significance here was an elision which Team members frequently made between themselves and visitors or 'ordinary lay people'. This, in turn, was associated with their sense of difference from other Museum staff, and articulated to their gender and relatively low place in the Museum hierarchy to be allocated the 'jammy job' of exhibition-making. So, if Team members found a subject interesting, they would extrapolate that the general public was likely to do so also. In doing so, they tended also to regard 'science' as likely to be relatively uninteresting to visitors: 'science' needed to be 'dressed up', 'packaged', and enlivened by linkage with 'more interesting', 'history and culture' topics. This too created a rationale for including the superstitions and fads.

6. That identification of 'superstitions' and 'fads' as separate from other dimensions of the exhibition – dimensions which by contrast might be thought to be not a matter of 'incorrect belief' – is itself of anthropological interest here.

Their inclusion was overdetermined by another feature too: a desire to include 'objects' in the exhibition. 'Objects' to museum staff are not simply 'things', they are, in the definitions given to me by two curators, 'things to be put on a pedestal and worshipped' or 'anything with an inventory number'. That is, they are specially selected objects, worthy of becoming part of a museum collection. This does not mean that they necessarily have to be especially valuable or rare: the Science Museum collects many examples of 'everyday' items (e.g. domestic technologies, or artefacts which illustrate the use of a particular plastic or metal) as well as more unusual or historically singular items. *Food for Thought* was not, however, an exhibition with many objects, and indeed those working on it were given job titles of 'interpreters' rather than 'curators' (even though all had been curators previously). This had a good deal of significance within the overall politics and managerial structuring of the Museum for it meant that, in theory at least, this exhibition was not to managed by 'curators', whose primary affiliation would be to the objects (the term 'curator' being derived from the Latin for to 'care for'), but by 'interpreters', whose primary affiliation was to be to 'the public'. In keeping with this, *Food for Thought* was a 'message-led' exhibition defined by the 'messages' to be conveyed to the public, with 'objects' only being included where necessary to illustrate these messages. In practice, however, things did not always work like this for often those working on the exhibition would become attracted to – or even infatuated with (the language of 'love' and 'irrationality' was often used here) – particular artefacts or ideas. Moreover, in response to criticisms from some in the Museum over the likely paucity of 'objects' in *Food for Thought,* there was a desire by some Team members to try to include more objects in order to prove the critics wrong. 'Superstitions' was a dimension which had originally been thought likely to include objects. However, objects proved not to be quite so easily forthcoming or prolific as had been anticipated, and this too was to be a seed towards its later exclusion.

The demise of superstitions came in a particular intervention which was to prove crucial to transforming the 'feel' of the exhibition. A year before the exhibition opened, the Team gave a presentation of their plans to the Museum's Director and their line manager. The outcome of this was that a consultant was employed to work with the Team to help them 'clarify the messages of the exhibition'. 'Clear unambiguous messages' were to become the central determinant of all that was included in the exhibition: anything extraneous was to be removed. Moreover, messages were not to be a set of separate points, but were to be tightly linked together in a pyramid structure, such that more specific messages were to be subsumed under more general ones, and all were to fit neatly under what became the exhibition's 'central message': 'To help people understand the impact of science and technology on our food'. Every exhibit was to be justified by this 'rigorous logic' – a phrase that echoed repeatedly in the offices at that time, enough to become the subject of self-conscious humour (we even drank 'rigorous' coffee on occasion). Moreover, in this period of 'rigorous' editing, 'science and technology' (as in the newly defined aim) was given a renewed prominence in a falling back on readily identifiable institutional status in times of difficulty (a phenomenon which is probably quite frequent in organizations and which we might call 'organizational regression'). Superstitions and fads had no place in this redefined exhibition space.

Following through this 'exclusion' – a following-through based on being there – shows us, then, some of the processes and assumptions at work during exhibition-making: e.g. the consequences of the thematic model and the drive for 'clarity'; the separation of 'science' from 'superstition'. It also helps show at least something of when, how, and why the exhibition became less effusive and challenging than it had once seemed that it would be. But could I not have identified this just from interviewing staff? This brings us to the second commitment.

Commitment 2: People as Material Agents

The second ethnographic 'commitment' – to 'evaluate people in terms of what they actually do, i.e. as material agents working in a material world, and not merely of what they say they do' (Miller 1997: 16–17) – is clearly related to the first commitment. 'Being there', spending months carrying out participant observation, is premised on the notion that researchers can get 'more' this way than by relying on people's accounts of what they do. There are a number of reasons why this is so. First, which takes us directly to commitment 3 ('Beyond performance'), those we are studying may actually wish to dissemble or at least to 'tidy up' an account. In other words, what they say may be shaped through their own expectations of what they think we want to hear, or what they think we should not hear, or what they want us to hear. Erving Goffman has famously written about social life in terms of 'impression management' (1971) and as consisting of a 'front stage', where impressions are relatively managed and polished for an (outside) audience, and of a 'back stage' with more relaxed codes for 'insiders'. While the idea that social life can be neatly divided into two distinct realms, analogous to the difference between a restaurant and its kitchen, is obviously too simple, Goffman's account is useful in helping us to perceive the way in which participants may act differently in different contexts. The ethnographer is interested in both the front stage and the back stage and the interplay between them; whereas an account explicitly related by a participant would be likely to focus on the front stage. One of the points of ethnography is that the ethnographer should become able to understand how those being studied are likely to present themselves in particular contexts and why. In other words, through fieldwork the ethnographer is learning not just what people say and do but also what particular utterances and actions mean. I discuss these further in relation to commitment 3.

Another reason for looking at what participants actually *do* is that it may be very difficult for participants to describe this themselves because they take it so much for granted. They are likely to miss out things which an observer might find highly relevant, e.g. the layout of an office, the physical separation of particular tasks within an organization, the way in which people dress, or how they talk to one another. Moreover, participants may simply be too busy getting on with their tasks to be able to make note of what they are doing, and later they may either still be too busy to spend much time trying to recount what actually happened or there may be too much for them to remember in any detail. Certainly, for those involved in the *Food for Thought* exhibition, it would have been difficult to give a detailed verbal account in retrospect, given that so much actually went on. Any such offered description, as I discuss further below, would likely be framed within a culturally standardized account of the process: it would privilege conscious decision-making and clearly formulated plans over the contingent and messy.

Furthermore, *action* or *practice* is not necessarily readily translatable into words for participants (Hastrup 1995). Although it is easy to assume that all actions are preceded by clear cognitive 'decisions', and indeed this is entirely assumed by much management theory and by the notions of organizational process that operate in institutions such as the Science Museum, this is not necessarily the case (cf. Alvesson 1993). Material actions may be simply *performed* or *done*; processes set in motion may seem to have their own momentum. (For example, when I once asked a carpenter in the museum workshops how he would set about turning the plans by designers into a finished product, he looked at me in surprise and made an expansive, opening movement of his arms which I took to mean that you simply got on with it. He then showed me around the workshops, pointing out exhibits at various stages of construction and explained to me aspects of craftsmanship involved. The direct 'seeing' and *in situ* accounts of particular instances were the way in which he felt my question could be answered.) Moreover, as some sociologists of science have suggested (e.g. Latour 1987), we might want to attribute agency to non-human actors also (see also Chapters Three and Nine, this volume): in other words, in the case of the making of an exhibition, we might see the outcome as a result not just of human decisions and actions, but of those of the artefacts and exhibits themselves. Again, this runs counter to taken-for-granted ways of seeing the matter both for those involved and for the ways in which most social sciences conceptualize 'agency'. Doing so, however, can enable us to attend to aspects of exhibition-making and the outcome of the process that we might otherwise ignore: for example, we might note the weight-bearing demands made by some exhibits which meant that they could be positioned only at certain locations in the exhibition, so infringing on plans drawn up earlier; or the refusal of the pea experience to complete itself on time; or the obstreperousness of the chocolate mousse pot and exhibits nearby in making its very enormity a hindrance to its visibility.

In the case of the making of the *Food for Thought* exhibition, there was a constant attempt by the Museum to make explicit the processes and structures involved through plans and managerial restructuring, mission statements, aims and objectives, and the use of management consultants. Some of this could be seen as part of an attempt to lessen the agency of objects: in particular to create exhibitions which would be much more the result of visible, calculable 'decisions' than as flowing from collections and the relatively closed, esoteric knowledge and practice of a curator. Nevertheless, this 'making explicit' was its own particular kind of cultural account, containing its own selections, assumptions, and omissions. As such, there were aspects of material practice that such an account would be unlikely to note. For example, the 'love' of particular objects that I mentioned above would have no place in the 'rigorous' 'message-based' model that was being worked with. Nor, to take another example, would it be likely to include the numerous adjustments made as the exhibition was being physically installed. Yet all of these aspects would have material consequences in the finished exhibition and in its 'readability'.

Commitment 3: Beyond Performance

The third commitment is to 'long-term . . . investigation that allows people to return to a daily life that one hopes goes beyond what is performed for the ethnographer' (Miller 1997: 17). In our interest in what people actually do, anthropologists aim not to rely on the kind of performances that may be carried out specially for us. Again, this can be expressed in terms of an interest in the 'back stage' as well as the 'front stage': a full picture means trying to get both (and their variations).[7] This is a major reason for spending a considerable amount of time carrying out participant observation. Even though the ethnographer's presence is likely to be something of which those studied remain well aware, it is difficult to maintain a performance for outsiders over a long period. I certainly found during my fieldwork in the Science Museum that some staff, on hearing how long I was likely to be there, said that as this was for such a long time then they might as well tell me things which I would 'find out anyway'. I could also 'feel' the difference in the ease with which those around me talked and behaved as I settled into daily routines in the offices with them: gossip and jokes, and displays of frustration and anger, flowing more freely once I had spent more time there. Moreover, by being present over time the ethnographer should become better able to judge the kinds of shifts in presentation made for different kinds of audiences and so be more aware of the

7. For an excellent discussion of 'front stage', 'back stage', and impression management – and the ethical problems raised by the ethnographer's interest in the backstage – see Berreman (1994: introduction).

way in which he or she might be related to in different contexts within the institution. This 'reflexivity' – the attempt to understand how one is oneself perceived and how this may shape the research – is an important component of what is otherwise a rather 'naturalistic' ambition of trying to observe social life as far as possible in the contexts in which it generally takes place.[8]

Returning to the example that I have already described above, it was evident to me that the disjunction between expectation and the finished exhibition was in many ways surprising to the participants. This in itself suggests that their accounts, ethnographically interesting as they certainly were, would not be enough to provide an explanation. Moreover, when Team members talked about the exhibition after it was completed, the way in which they did so shifted depending on whom they were talking to. For the most part, the accounts that they gave were decidedly 'up-beat': they said how pleased they were with the finished product, how they thought it had a good mix of interactives and traditional objects as they had hoped. They also responded robustly to criticism of the exhibition. For example, when one review said that the exhibition was just what Sainsbury's would have wanted, Team members recalled examples which they felt indicated the contrary; and when they heard that it had been said that the exhibition 'did nothing for the representation of gender', they argued fiercely that just the fact of having some images of women in the exhibition was different from many Science Museum exhibitions but also that 'just because we're women', people should not expect the exhibition necessarily to be about gender politics. The point here is not that these positive and defensive accounts by the Team were in any way 'inauthentic' or even 'not what they really felt'. There was much that Team members were pleased with about the exhibition and for good reason. However, their positive accounting was also part of a more general cultural phenomenon within the Museum: exhibitions and persons were regarded as inextricably intertwined, with exhibitions seen not just as having been put together by particular curators, but as being a revelation of their personalities.[9] Because of this, and because, of course, exhibitions like any cultural product are framed and read in terms of the accounts that circulate about them, Team members worked hard to manage the impressions of the exhibition both during making and afterwards (at least until sufficient time had passed for personalities to be disentangled from products, for exhibitions to be consigned to an earlier 'childhood').[10]

8. For further discussion of naturalism and reflexivity, see Hammersley and Atkinson (1995). See also Okely (1996, esp. chs 1 and 2) and Hastrup (1995) for relevant discussion.

9. This is in interesting contrast to the formal public presentation of exhibitions which is as the work not of individuals but of the institution as a whole. The names of the curators/interpreters who work on them is not mentioned in the 'credits' at the entrance to exhibitions.

10. The notion of 'impression management', and its importance for institutions, has been elaborated by Goffman (1961, 1971). For some particularly interesting and insightful use of it, see Berreman (1994) and Law (1994), the latter dealing with managerial practice in an organization.

The point, then, was just that there was another dimension too which could only really be admitted in private, among Team members themselves and to those who they felt were sympathetic to them. I was privileged to have access to this more 'back-stage' dimension because I had accompanied them through the ups and downs of the making process and because I was there alongside as we tidied up, sorted out loose ends, and mulled over the adventure afterwards.

Ethnography, then, seeks to go 'beyond performance' not because performance is somehow 'inauthentic' but because the ethnographer strives to contextualize performance in order to understand the factors that made it possible. This cannot be done if we have only a single account to go on. How then would we be able to identify an 'extraordinary' event (Cohen 1983)? It is here that commitment 4 – to holistic analysis – is also crucial.

Commitment 4: Holistic Analysis

Holistic analysis, as Daniel Miller explains, 'insists that . . . behaviours be considered within the larger framework of people's lives and cosmologies' (1997: 17). Rather than focusing on particular behaviours or isolated views, the aim of the ethnographer is to try to understand what these mean to people and how they relate to other aspects of their experience. One aspect of this concerns the categories with which we begin our analysis. Although ethnographers today generally set out not simply to look at a particular people but to investigate a specific problem or domain of life, they nevertheless attempt to explore it within the terms and relationships which seem important to those they are studying. This may mean that they find themselves drawn into all kinds of concerns that they had not anticipated.

For example, although the main aim of the research which I carried out in the Science Museum was to focus on ideas about 'science' and how it was constructed in exhibition-making, I kept finding myself drawn into other matters that did not always feel as if they were much about 'science'. The politics of the institution itself, and more specifically the managerial restructuring, was one of these. It was the subject of considerable discussion among Museum staff. As I came to realize, however, it was also crucial to the way in which 'science' was being represented in the Museum. For one thing, the managerial restructuring was largely concerned with changing the priorities involved in exhibition-making, placing visitors rather than collections at number one. This had consequences for 'science', for it led to it being defined not so much as an objectifiable practice, located in particular tangible products, but as a more abstract 'message-based' conceptual matter. This latter, being defined primarily in relation to the visitor, was also often directed not so much at general scientific principles as at more individual experiential matters (e.g. giving visitors the experience of being a frozen pea, inviting them with 'trick' mirrors to see how they might look a little fatter or a little thinner). Moreover, the very clear-cut hierarchical managerial structures, in which the different museum functions became more precisely defined and separated off from one another (each 'division' in the new managerial scheme being intended to have its own clearly stated aims and remit), was precisely replicated in the editing process which led to 'superstitions and fads' being eliminated from the exhibition and, more generally, to the 'flatness' of the finished exhibition. Just as the rigorous exhibition editing process resulted in eliminating anything which did not fit clearly into the newly defined structure, however much those involved may have thought certain topics or objects interesting or valuable, so too the larger scale 'editing' of the museum staff – through restructuring, redeployment, and sometimes redundancy – meant that only tasks and personnel which had a clear aim and place within the overall structure would remain.[11] The emphasis on 'accessibility' and 'clarity', like the emphasis on 'experience' and 'messages' and the broader matters of managerial restructuring and, beyond that, Thatcherite politics, then, were not somehow separate from science, but were part of the means through which it was constituted for the public.

This is not to say, however, that ethnographers must necessarily delve into every nook and cranny of the lives of those they are studying. It is, rather, a case of attempting to understand the context in which whatever we are exploring operates. Ethnographers do not necessarily, therefore, have to follow those they are studying home (cf. Hine, p. 74). Although one might certainly learn some interesting matters about those who work in an organization by doing so, not only is access likely to be difficult but also, especially if those studied make a distinction in their lives between 'home' and 'work', it may not reveal much about the organization itself. More useful than details of individual lives might be going beyond those who are the direct focus of the study to try to understand other similar or related contexts.[12]

11. I should note that while I have identified a close correlation between the processes involved in exhibition making, the wider managerial restructuring, and wider still processes of a cultural emphasis on 'the public' as 'consumers' rather than 'citizens', I would not wish to give the impression that these would always map neatly on to one another. If this were the case, it would be possible to just 'read off' a finished exhibition in relation to broader cultural politics. However, there always are exhibitions and museums which are critical of, or out of keeping with, the dominant political directions of the time. It is more useful, I think, to see each of the junctures between these 'levels' as a site of potential contest or struggle for definition. Thus, the Museum was not entirely putting Thatcherite principles to work; and nor were those creating the exhibition simply going along with this. This is why the Museum and the exhibition are more complex than the deterministic account would expect. What is interesting in this case, it seems to me, is that in many ways it was the organizational/editing model – something which was regarded as somehow 'neutral' or 'objective' – which was responsible for the 'flattening' of the exhibition.

12. For another example in relation to 'science' which takes a still wider approach than my own, see Emily Martin's *Flexible Bodies* in which she explores ideas about the immune system as far afield as 'outward bound'-style management training courses (Martin 1994).

Thus I found that visiting other museums and heritage sites and talking to staff there, and attending museological conferences, and reading newspaper coverage of museum matters, helped me to understand more about the 'museum world' (as it was sometimes referred to), its cosmologies, and its contests. This in turn helped me to 'situate' assumptions, processes, and contradictions involved in the exhibition which I was looking at in detail.

Anthropological Expertise?

Commitments, of course, are not as easy to keep to as to state and they can raise their own particular difficulties. Being allowed 'back stage' and witnessing 'beyond performance' raises problems of confidentiality, privacy, and trust. Confidentiality and privacy of respondents are likely to be hard to maintain in the case of a singular institution which cannot easily be disguised (cf. Chapman, p. 31). The ethnographer's crossing into domains usually restricted to outsiders can create difficulties over what can and should be revealed. Berreman (1994) describes this as an ethnographic dilemma of trust: being allowed 'back stage' may implicitly entail being trusted not to divulge that which is kept back stage. Institutional conventions, as in the Science Museum, making a sharp distinction between critical reports produced for internal consumption, and impression management – 'good PR' – for external, can lead to difficulties over forms of writing and publication. Such difficulties can be compounded by a specific version of the trust dilemma which is also an ethnographic version of curatorial 'object love': having been deeply entwined in the lives and views of those with whom I spent so much time, I felt a sense of protectiveness towards them. Yet at the same time I also felt critical of some of the things that they had done. These different impulses were not easy to marry; and all made writing an especially awkward process of negotiation and expression. The negotiation was both with myself – between my analytical and protective sides – and with museum staff. Having agreed to host the study, naturally they were keen to read its outcomes.

I have written about some of the reception of, and negotiation over, my accounts of the Science Museum elsewhere (Macdonald 1997). Here, I want to look at the writing problem slightly differently and to ask, as many in the Science Museum did, especially in the face of some of my work, what was in it for them? Being aware of, and highlighting, complexity, or pointing to the commonality with broader cultural changes, may be all very well, and it may well help move beyond certain academic simplifications (e.g. deterministic readings of exhibitions) as I hope to have shown, but is it in any way *useful*? Much though I think that we should resist judging knowledge predominantly in terms of its utility, the question is a legitimate one from the perspective of those who have hosted an ethnographic study. Why should they agree to let somebody hang around for months on end, taking notes, asking questions, and tape-recording?

Of course, this goes back to issues of access. Few organizations are likely to grant this without some expectation of results which may prove useful to them. In the case of the Science Museum research this was implied through the title of the ESRC programme – 'the public understanding of science' – under whose auspices the research was conducted rather than through any particular promised piece of writing, though from early on I said that I hoped to write a report for them and I did so. The reception of this, however, reveals some of the potential problems with an ethnographic approach from the point of view of managers within an organization. Having, through the fieldwork, become well aware of the format of management reports, I attempted to set my own report out as clearly as possible, using numbered sections and short paragraphs; and on the advice of one member of staff who read a draft, I included a bullet-pointed summary of the key points which, my advisor said, was all that would be read by senior museum staff. When I was told by the Exhibition Team manager that she had been told to 'implement all [my] points', I realized my advisor had been rather optimistic even on this score (on that occasion at least), for very few of my points could be turned into improvements to the now finished exhibition. But did this make the research 'useless' to the museum?

The problem here, I think, is a particular version of an old anthropological chestnut: the generalizability of anthropological findings or, as Hastrup (1995) puts it, translation of ethnographic experience into a form which can 'travel' (cf. Clifford 1997). The line manager who instructed the 'implementation' of my report saw a title and research on a particular exhibition and, logically enough, suggested that the outcome be applied to that exhibition. But my account was mainly of its production; and such generalizability as there was concerned *processes* of production. Most of my report was set out in terms of the innovations that the Team saw themselves to be making, how each was implemented, why, and how it turned out. Insofar as such innovations (e.g. the use of the pyramid organizational structure discussed here, or of a multimedia approach) were ones in which many in the museum world were interested, I saw this as offering concrete information on what can happen when you try to put them into practice, together with my own anthropologically informed discussion of some of the possible pitfalls. This was where its generalizability lay as I saw it – as a kind of cautionary, and sometimes inspirational, tale for future exhibition-makers. And this indeed is how it has been taken up by some at least. By comparison with the prescriptive recipes offered by many museum consultants – 'This is how you should do it!' – mine is, however, a fairly modest and even cautious form of travelling. Perhaps I should have been bolder? Perhaps. In some ways that is an attractive proposition. However, the kind of complexity that ethnography highlights also gives good reason to be cautious of simple prescriptive recipes; and, rather than aping much current practice, I think that anthropologists should be bolder in arguing for the potential helpfulness of their perspectives. The museum story that I have told in this chapter is, after all, about problems with simple or 'rigorous' models whose full implications (in this case for the politics and poetics of the finished exhibition) are screened out by the very 'single-focus perspective' that such approaches produce.[13] It is to just such matters that anthropologists can usefully draw attention. And just as Malcolm Chapman argues from his experiences with the business world (Chapter One above), this is something to which many of those working in organizations are likely to be sympathetic, aware as they are from their own first-hand experience that practice is rarely (if ever) as described in textbooks.

But merely to recount a general story of complexity, of actions having all kinds of implications other than those expected, is not enough. As with any anthropological account, we need to be able to 'lift out' more general patterns, connections, and dilemmas from direct ethnographic experience. The ethnographically based text needs not just to recount managers' own experiences back to them but to try to highlight the way in which certain implicit models (e.g. the 'direct through-put' knowledge model inherent in the way in which this exhibition was organized) or cultural assumptions (e.g. that 'messages' need to be expressed in words) lead to unanticipated effects (e.g. the 'screening out' of certain, and in some cases politically important, knowledges or an unexpected predominance of writing in the finished exhibition). It needs to show how highlighting those models and assumptions in future can help avoid such effects. This entails *analytical reflexivity*: a process of careful reflection upon the cultural context and processes examined with a view to identifying the particular formations of knowledge and practice operating within that organization. This is something for which anthropologists are well trained, used as they are to looking and listening carefully, to following their respondents where they lead them (often literally as well as metaphorically), to gathering multiple perspectives and contextualizations, to recognizing that apparent minutiae and mundane activities may be highly significant, and to 'relativizing' that which is observed, i.e. conveying how it might easily be otherwise. All those ethnographies which anthropologists read in training and continuing anthropological engagement provide not only possible models of ethnographic practice and anthropological theorizing, but also intellectually provocative examples of how some of our most basic cultural assumptions – about, say, the nature of personhood, material culture, time, or what is judged valuable in life – are far from universal. They help to highlight not just 'how things are' (or appear to be) but also, crucially, 'how they might be otherwise'. This, I suggest, is what the 'anthropological imagination' (cf. Mills 1959) can, and should, offer.

---

13. Marilyn Strathern makes a similar point when she writes, 'Anthropologists have no need to aggrandise their own accounts; in any case, to do so runs the risk of failing to see the work that aggrandisement does in human affairs' (1995: 180).

References

Alvesson, M. (1993), *Cultural Perspectives on Organizations*, Cambridge: Cambridge University Press.

Berreman, G. (1994 [1972]), *Hindus of the Himalayas: Ethnography and Change*, Oxford: Oxford University Press.

Clifford, J. (1997), 'Traveling Cultures', in J. Clifford, *Routes: Travel and Translation in the Late Twentieth Century*, Cambridge, Mass.: Harvard University Press.

Cohen, A.P. (1983), 'Blockade: A Case Study in Local Consciousness in an extra-local event' in A.P. Cohen (ed.), *Belonging: Identity and Social Organisation in British Rural Cultures*, Manchester: Manchester University Press.

Du Gay, P. (ed.) (1997), *Production of Culture/Cultures of Production*, London: Sage, in association with the Open University.

Errington, F. and Gewertz, D. (1987), *Cultural Alternatives and a Feminist Anthropology: An Analysis of Culturally Constructed Gender Interests in Papua New Guinea*, Cambridge: Cambridge University Press.

Geertz, C. (1988), *Works and Lives: The Anthropologist as Author*, Cambridge: Polity.

Goffman, E. (1971 [1956]), *The Presentation of Self in Everyday Life*, Harmondsworth: Penguin.

Goffman, E. (1961), *Asylums: Essays on the Social Situation of Mental Patients and Other Inmates*, New York: Anchor.

Gooday, G. (1997), 'Instrumentation and Interpretation: Managing and Representing the Working Environments of Victorian Experimental Science', in B. Lightman (ed.) *Contexts of Victorian Science*, Chicago: University of Chicago Press.

Hall, S. (1980), 'Encoding/Decoding', in S. Hall, D. Hobson, A. Lowe, and P. Willis (eds), *Culture, Media, Language*, London: Hutchinson.

Hammersley, M. and Atkinson, P. (1995 [1983]), *Ethnography: Principles in Practice*, London: Routledge.

Hastrup, K. (1995), *A Passage to Anthropology: Between Experience and Theory*, London: Routledge.

Kopytoff, I. (1986), 'The Cultural Biography of Things: Commoditization as Process', in A. Appadurai (ed.), *The Social Life of Things: Commodities in Cultural Perspective*, Cambridge: Cambridge University Press.

Latour, B. (1987), *Science in Action: How to Follow Scientists and Engineers through Society*, Milton Keynes: Open University Press.

Law, J. (1994), *Organizing Modernity*, Oxford: Blackwell.

Macdonald, S. (1993), *Museum Visiting: A Science Exhibition Case Study*, Keele: Keele University, Department of Sociology and Social Anthropology working papers.

—— (1995), 'Consuming Science: Public Knowledge and the Dispersed Politics of Reception among Museum Visitors', *Media, Culture and Society* **17**(1): 13–29.

—— (1997), 'The Museum as Mirror: Ethnographic Reflections', in A. James, J. Hockey and A. Dawson (eds), *After Writing Culture: Epistemology and Praxis in Contemporary Anthropology*, London: Routledge.

Martin, E. (1994), *Flexible Bodies: Tracking Immunity in American Culture from the Days of Polio to the Days of AIDS*, Boston: Beacon Press.

Miller, D. (1997), *Capitalism: An Ethnographic Approach*, Oxford: Berg.

Mills, C. Wright (1959), *The Sociological Imagination*, New York: Oxford University Press.

Okely, J. (1996), *Own or Other Culture*, London: Routledge.

Strathern, M. (1995), 'Afterword', in M. Strathern (ed.), *Shifting Contexts: Transformations in Anthropological Knowledge*, London: Routledge.

Werbner, P. (1997), '"The Lion of Lahore": Anthropology, Cultural Performance and Imran Khan', in S. Nugent and C. Shore (eds), *Anthropology and Cultural Studies*, London: Pluto Press.

Part III
Family, Health, and Welfare

–5–

Swords into Ploughshares: Manipulating Metaphor in the Divorce Process
Bob Simpson

Introduction

This chapter aims to show how an ethnographic approach can be used to understand the ways in which complex life transitions are generated and experienced in contemporary Britain. The case in point is that of divorce and separation. Out of the complex tangle of legal, economic, and social threads which make up this increasingly common transition in the life course, it is the day-to-day use of metaphor on which I have focused. More precisely, I demonstrate how an ethnographic approach illuminates different metaphorical complexes at work shaping the experience of divorcing couples as they move between different institutional contexts. Such an approach is important because the experience of divorce and separation is not so much an event as an extremely complex organizational process which effects a significant re-arrangement of emotional, economic, and legal ties and attachments. In recent decades this process and its longer-term consequences have become a common feature of family life but it is one which, in anthropological terms, is under-researched and under-theorized (Simpson 1998).

The particular aspect of this process which I would like to discuss here concerns the legal and welfare mechanisms encountered by couples when they formally end their marriage by means of divorce. When the divorce process is set in train a number of organizations, agencies, and professionals come into play to adjudicate, arbitrate, mediate, or advise upon the difficult and painful conflicts which arise when couples begin to dismantle their joint investment in family and home. Furthermore, the organizational back-drop is far from static. Organizational and institutional configurations change as legislation is adapted and reformed. This was evident, for example, in the ideological shift from 'parental rights to responsibilities' which underpins the 1989 Children Act, and in the move away from conflicted and adversarial divorce, which the 1996 Family Law Act seeks to foster. Change is also evident as different professional groups compete for ascendancy in the growth of occupations stimulated in response to rising divorce rates (McCarthy 1996).

At a time of serious personal disorientation a couple may thus find themselves being dealt with, both as a couple and as individuals, by a plethora of professionals each with their distinctive legal and bureaucratic domains and discourses. In a conflicted divorce a couple may find themselves at different times in discussions with solicitors, judges, barristers, probation officers, mediators, social workers, doctors, counsellors, benefits officers, housing officers, estate agents, and many others. In organizational and bureaucratic terms, the divorce process is not a clearly defined transition. For the couple, it entails passing through a kaleidoscope of organizational cultures which interlink and overlap and which are apt to leave those passing through confused and disempowered regarding their objectives, purpose, and procedures (Simpson, Corlyon, McCarthy, and Walker 1990; cf. Collins 1994). As one man I interviewed put it when being asked about the role of the Court Welfare Officer in his case: 'You'll appreciate, I've been to see so many people in the last three years . . . I didn't know where they fitted into the network and I didn't really know in what order one should be seeing anyone like them in similar circumstances.' At a time of profound personal disruption, men, women, and, on occasion, their children find themselves passing through some unfamiliar organizational contexts each of which shapes, directs, and gives meaning to this complex transition. The sphere of family life, which is usually taken to be private and discrete, is apt to be made uncomfortably public in the pursuit of justice, welfare, and the 'best interests of children' after divorce.

On the face of it, the organizational management of divorce is an unlikely context for an anthropologist to explore and it is my aim in this chapter to illustrate some of the analytical possibilities that open up once the stuff of ethnography begins to accumulate in notebooks, tapes, and the memory of experience. The first part of the essay considers the novel methodological strategies that might be used to conceptualize 'the field' in studies such as this. In the second part, a series of illustrations are given of the way that metaphors are used by professionals and their clients to make sense of conflicts arising from divorce. These illustrations demonstrate that the mechanisms available to deal with conflict are not linear but are themselves the subject of change and contention; the adversarial paradigms which previously underpinned family law have been progressively supplanted by ideologies which promote private ordering and the privatization of domestic life. Careful attention to the language of divorce as recorded in the various contexts and encounters that make up the divorce process enables one to move from the fine-grained reality of, say, an exchange between a husband and wife in the context of a conciliation appointment, to the broader ideological landscape within which divorce is situated. The final section presents a short case study which shows how in one particular divorce case different metaphors were used in different organizational settings. However, before considering metaphor in detail it is necessary to place this research into a broader context.

Ethnography: Process versus Place?

My involvement with the study of divorce and separation began in 1985 when I joined a multidisciplinary team of researchers engaged in a major divorce-related project. On the team were lawyers, economists, and social policy experts. I, a recent anthropology PhD, was brought in to work with another researcher on the qualitative dimensions of client satisfaction with the divorce process in general and dispute-resolution procedures in particular. Earlier research in this field had been criticized because it failed to examine the 'client perspective'. In other words, attention had been paid to professionals, processes, and outcomes, rather than to the fact that there were people being passed through these systems and, furthermore, that they might have things to say about the experience (Walker 1989). The project on which I was employed would be different from earlier ones in that considerable resources had been committed to eliciting and understanding the views of those who were directly experiencing the processes the project was seeking to evaluate. A cohort of couples would be identified as they entered courts and conciliation services and 'followed' as they passed through the domains of judges, registrars, solicitors, welfare officers, and conciliators. In this endeavour an anthropologist was deemed a useful addition to the disciplinary mosaic because it was assumed I would be (a) 'good' with the natives, (b) able to deal with the sensitive situations they would be experiencing, and (c) in possession of knowledge of kinship, and therefore might have something interesting to say about the changing shape of the nuclear family which was ultimately what the project was all about.

As it turned out, what I thought was going to be a brief sojourn in the world of social policy turned into a rather longer stay. Over a seven-year period and under the auspices of a variety of research centres I was engaged in a number of projects related to divorce and spent many hours in discussion with divorcing and divorced men, women, and (occasionally) their children. I attended court hearings and appointments, observed conciliation appointments, and interviewed conciliators and court welfare officers. Research projects undertaken covered post-divorce issues such as custody and child contact, use of welfare and legal services, housing, conflicts and dispute resolution, and most recently a study of post-divorce fatherhood (see for example Ogus *et al.* 1989; McCarthy and Simpson 1991; McCarthy *et al.* 1991; Corlyon *et al.* 1991; Simpson, McCarthy, and Walker 1995).

The research projects undertaken during this period were, to a large extent, driven by the policy agenda of the time. High on this agenda, then as now, were the unprecedented levels of divorce in England and Wales and the substantial costs engendered by changes in the way that families are structured and resourced after divorce. Of particular interest to those responsible for dealing with divorce and its consequences was the question of conflict: 'Who catches the fall-out when the nuclear family explodes?' as one writer pithily expressed it. The social and economic costs of dealing with divorce-related conflicts had risen inexorably and looked set to continue doing so. Disputes over children, finances, and property were finding their way in increasing numbers to the doors of the courts and of welfare agencies. These disputes were seen to create direct costs in the form of legal-aid expenditure to fund the pursuit of settlement through litigation and indirect costs such as rising welfare dependency and increased health provision. Longer-term costs were believed to arise from supposed links between family breakdown, crime, and poor school attainment.

Much of the debate triggered by these developments in the 1980s and early 1990s focused on reform of the legal machinery to process divorce and, in particular, on the theory and practice of conciliation (now more generally referred to as mediation). Drawing upon a broad tradition of dispute resolution which combined elements of interests-based negotiation, community justice, and traditional methods of dispute resolution, the emerging conciliation movement in the UK offered an attractive alternative to conventional adversarial models of conflict management. Its appeal was based on two sets of claims. The first was that conciliation would provide benefits to divorcing couples and their children by reducing conflict, focusing on children, and empowering parents. The second, rather more pragmatic attraction, was that this method of dealing with disputes could save considerably on legal costs and also increase administrative efficiency.

The original conciliation-project research developed out of government concern to evaluate such claims. The two questions which the research team set out to answer were: first, did conciliation save money by making the resolution of divorce-related disputes cheaper to manage and, second, did it improve the quality of the process by generating more effective agreements and relationships after divorce? The latter issue was deemed to be particularly significant in mitigating the impacts of divorce on children.

Throughout this period I was part of a loose network of researchers, academics, and practitioners engaged in the production, promotion, and dissemination of empirical research and its findings. The relationship between the producers and consumers of this type of research is a complex one. The model of the policy machine lubricated and adjusted with the benefit of research input is idealistic to say the least. An apparent hunger for information to service the policy process is contradicted by the fact that government is highly selective and discriminating in what is appropriate material when it comes to policy considerations (Weiss 1986: 221–3). Inevitably, attempts to formulate research agenda with these possibilities and constraints in mind shape the form and content of the research undertaken. For example, research must address clearly identifiable questions, it has to be turned around quickly, its methodologies have to be crisp, and its results easily condensed. Divorce as a complex, contingent, situated process must necessarily be recast as a simple mechanistic one for which it is possible to assume clear commonalities from case to case. As an anthropologist I was clearly expected to lean in the direction of 'extensive' data and away from 'intensive' data (Geertz 1983; cf. Leach 1967).

Indeed, as an anthropologist working in a multidisciplinary team addressing such questions, I felt as though I was on a steep learning curve which often ran counter to my intuitions about the ways that people, communities, and organizations operate. Stimulating though the experience was, I felt that many of the strengths of an anthropological perspective were at best diluted and at worst rendered completely redundant in this setting. Take, for example, the notion of community. Community is central to any notion of participant observation as typically conceived within the methodological canon of social anthropology. There has to be some ongoing collectivity in which the anthropologist can locate her- or himself; without this it is difficult to develop a holistic picture of how that collectivity is given form and meaning by those who are committed in some sense or other to its continuity. However, as I soon found out, there is no community of the divorced, or at least not in the conventional sense of the term. Entry into marriage is marked by ritual and witnessed by representatives of state and the wider community of family members. What is being celebrated, to a greater or lesser extent, is the induction of a couple into the normative categories of Western domestic, social organization. Divorce, however, is quite the reverse: it is the movement out of these categories into unpredictable social terrains which on the face of it suggest fragmentation, isolation, and finality vis-à-vis the collectivities which went before. The 'kinscripts', to borrow Carol Stack's term (Stack and Burton 1994), available to those who formally exit nuclear family arrangements are still in the process of being written in Britain today. From a research perspective the problem would thus appear to be twofold: on the one hand the emergent collectivities of family life after divorce are difficult to study using 'extensive' research methodologies, but on the other hand their fragmented nature means that they are also difficult to study using conventional participant-observation approaches. In short, an altogether different conceptualization of the issue needed to be considered.

My own work in this field led me to explore ways of studying divorce and its aftermath as an expression of kinship which is not so much 'after nature' (Strathern 1992) as after affinity (Simpson 1998). The co-resident, heterosexual, nuclear family which is stable through time and made up of recognizable and predictable roles and relationships can no longer be taken as the blueprint for domestic life in the West. On the contrary, the life-course as it is centred on family and parenthood is increasingly fragmented and dispersed. The boundaries between public and private, market and household, interest and emotion are redrawn to accommodate individualism and democratization into the cultural and social fabric of family life (Beck and Beck-Gernsheim 1995). The conduct of family life is no longer discretely separated off from a 'heartless world' (Lasch 1977) but is in many respects shot through with it. An important dimension of this shift is the changing role of organizations and institutions in the re-structuring of family life, especially after divorce. Indeed, it would appear that in future the extent to which civil and market institutions will mediate the experience of family and domestic life will increase significantly (Robertson 1991).

In order to capture these fundamental changes in domestic and family life in the late twentieth century, novel methodological strategies needed to be considered. One which carries considerable appeal in this context is the idea of multi-sited ethnography (Marcus 1995). The idea of a multi-sited ethnography has developed out of a recognition that traditional ethnography – typically associated with the intensive study of a single place or context – fails to capture crucial connections, associations, and relationships that transcend particular localities. Failure to incorporate these wider connections into research obscures crucial dimensions of social and cultural life. For example, Hastrup and Olwig (1997) demonstrate the importance of this theme in relation to migration, identity, and the connections which are sustained between migrants across space and time. As many of the articles in their collection reveal, the impact of migration can only be understood by following people, sometimes literally, in order to track their connections. Other multi-sited ethnographic researches do not just present new ways of study but also posit new objects of study, such as in Ginsburg and Rapp's ethnography of reproduction and new reproductive technologies (Ginsburg and Rapp 1996) or Haraway's account of how recent developments in science and technology impact upon ideas of nature and woman (Haraway 1991). I would suggest that many contemporary Western family arrangements might usefully benefit from a multi-sited ethnographic approach. In recent decades the family has become less part of 'the essentialistically based architecture of unambiguous identity' (Beck 1997: 159) and increasingly dispersed, individualistic, voluntaristic, and public in character. As a consequence it is only partially accessible to approaches which presume discrete families and households.

It perhaps ought to be stressed at this point that at no time during the researches which I undertook did I think of what I was doing as a multi-sited ethnography. On the contrary, for much of the time I yearned for a single site within which I could be anthropologically at home. I consistently failed to find such a niche and, like some jobbing social scientist, turned my hand to all manner of methodologies and strategies for data collection as I played my part in actualizing the grand plan known as the 'research design'. Playing my part involved exploring different perspectives on the divorce process: interviewing a parent here, a solicitor there, observing a couple's appointment in a court one day and another's session with a conciliator the next. Throughout my immersion in the burgeoning services to cater for the growing number of divorced and separated couples I continued to note conversations and contexts, and I tape-recorded interviews and conversations for later transcription. It was only with hindsight that the mass of interviews, observations, and encounters began to take some sort of ethnographic shape.

The principal direction in which I have taken my analyses to date has been to focus on the continuities established at divorce. In other words it is not just about endings, but also about the beginnings of new kinds of social relation (Simpson 1998). Here I touch on a different aspect of this process, namely the role that organizations have begun to play in shaping and reinforcing certain kinds of relations after divorce. In the next section, I present an illustration of the analytical possibilities when data is gathered from a variety of institutional contexts all of which contribute to the creation of transition and passage. The data I rely upon is primarily language-based and focuses upon the way metaphors are used in different institutional contexts. The data is the kind which is culled from notes and transcripts of meetings and interviews during the course of prolonged fieldwork which is then sifted through in order to try to answer the question 'What is going on here?' One rarely knows the significance of particular conversations or dialogues at the time they occur and careful recording, both of what was said and of one's immediate and often intuitive commentary on it, is of the essence.

Close attention to the use of language in context, that is, not just what is said but how it is said, provides the means to access broader landscapes of culture, ideology, meaning, and identity. For example, I was able to sit in with a judge during his day-long processing of Children's Appointments (also known at that time as Section 41 Appointments). Such meetings normally took place in his chambers; there were no wigs and no oaths, just a few minutes' avuncular chat in which he elicited information from a sad and often fearful parade of mothers and fathers about their proposed arrangements for their children after the divorce. In the absence of a more rigorous divination, the arrangements so described are quickly rubber-stamped and one case ushered out as the next is ushered in. However, this judge ended each of his meetings with his own particular incantation: 'You may not be husband and wife any more but you are mum and dad for the rest of your lives.' For some reason this simple statement struck me as being particularly poignant and meaningful: the enactment of a special kind of knowledge which produces for the ethnographer what Strathern has recently referred to as the 'dazzle' effect (Strathern 1999: 6–11). Indeed, in my subsequent attempts to theorize kinship relations after divorce, the phrase proved to be an important encapsulation of the problem which divorce poses for the categories of Western kinship and the 'official' solution to this problem. In effect, the judge was asking parents to ponder on the verities of Western kinship: ties made by means of law (that is, being a husband and wife) are reversible whereas ties in nature (that is, being a mother and a father) are not (cf. Schneider 1968). Although divorce re-arranges and terminates the conjugal relationship, parental and, more specifically, paternal rights and responsibilities are expected to continue. In other words, mothers generally live with their children after divorce whereas fathers are expected to maintain economic and emotional links to them. Or, putting this opposition into social-structural terms, notions of patrifiliation are increasingly separated from and brought into conflict with the facts of matrifocality, a conflict which the state is keen to resolve or at least ameliorate.

Metaphors of Conflict and a Conflict of Metaphors

The example of the judge given in the previous section illustrates how, by unravelling a small snippet of linguistic and observational data, it is possible to oscillate between the particular contexts of people's experiences and the broader ideological and cultural frameworks within which these are suspended. Ethnography, as process and as product, is the device whereby events and structures are read one from another and conveyed in written form. In this section I want to take this notion further by paying attention to the way metaphors are used in different contexts within the divorce process. Again, the method relies on recording people's talk in formal settings such as interviews as well as in more informal conversations without necessarily being able to predict what data is likely to become meaningful and informative. Paying attention to these exchanges as discursive talk and narrative rather than as sources of factual information opens up the possibility of exploring 'experience near' concepts, that is, ones which are used 'naturally and effortlessly' by an informant to make sense of experience (Geertz 1983: 57). Paying attention to metaphor is particularly useful in this regard because not only does it reveal how people make sense of experience but also how in different institutional settings different metaphorical uses nudge participants towards different kinds of experience. First, however, a word about metaphor.

Metaphor is often taken to be the preserve of the poet and the writer for whom it provides a means to heightened forms of expressivity. In this sense, metaphors in language are performing a sort of meta-activity. However, there is a more prosaic approach to metaphor which locates it at the very heart of human experience. Following a tradition which includes Ricoeur and Lévi-Strauss, metaphor is taken as a linguistic device which uses experience from one realm in order to make sense of experience from another (the Greek *metapherein* means to transfer). Often the way that metaphor works is to take a difficult concept which is not easily articulated, described, or understood and to render it concrete, tangible, solid, and thereby comprehensible and communicable. For example, from aboriginal clans (Foxes and Bears) to crowds of football supporters (Magpies and Canaries) people make sense of their relationships to one another and to other similar groupings by analogy with natural species and their apparent differences (Lévi-Strauss 1962, 1966). In this sense, metaphor is not simply a linguistic ornament, but is the result of a creative act fundamental to human consciousness and understanding. Metaphors are not simply individual creative acts, however. They also belong to a community of experience and are, therefore, in a sense shared and maintained by the people who use them on a regular basis. This process is a highly dynamic and generative one with metaphors not merely suggesting passive similarity but actively making connections and asserting similarity. For the researcher, being alert to the way that different contexts are brought together and in particular to the role of metaphor in this process is to glimpse the work of culture. Metaphors thus provide important paradigms for the organization of experience and as such are deeply political; they are an integral part of the power structures prevalent in a society, community, or institution. As Lakoff and Johnson point out, 'Whether in national politics or everyday interaction, people in power get to impose their metaphors' (Lakoff and Johnson 1980: 57). This point is particularly important when it comes to under-standing the way marital breakdown is managed within systems of adversarial justice and the current quest for alternatives (Collins 1994). Understanding the role of metaphors in these different settings is thus just one way in which access can be gained to the underlying organizational and institutional cultures which currently structure the divorce process.

In the context of divorce, the important role played by metaphor becomes particularly evident when professionals and clients try to articulate the pain and complexity of post-marital conflict. However, the point I wish to make here is not just about metaphors of conflict, but about how a multi-sited ethnographic approach brings out a conflict of metaphors. Let me illustrate this point by beginning with Lakoff and Johnson's elaboration of the 'argument is war' metaphor (Lakoff and Johnson 1980: 4–5). In the West, they contend, there is a powerful metaphorical complex which pervades everyday language when it comes to thinking and talking about conflict. Quite simply, in talking about arguments, conflicts, and disagreements we slip easily into the metaphors derived from warfare and armed conflict. The language of war thus provides a handy and powerful device to make sense of rather less dramatic processes of argumentation. This metaphorical complex shows a high degree of 'coherence' (Lakoff and Johnson 1980) and, in Schön's terms, constitutes a 'deep' metaphor, that is, one that determines 'the centrally important features' of the system being considered (Schön 1993:149).

My own experience of people talking about divorce does not contradict Lakoff and Johnson's general proposition. Unsurprisingly, professionals and their clients draw upon the service of metaphor extensively as they try to make sense of the conflicts which swirl around the breakdown of intimacy, domestic interdependency, mutuality of parenting, and economic cooperation. For example, probation officers, judges, social workers, and even couples themselves will talk of divorce in terms of 'combat', 'fight', the 'rough and tumble of family work', and 'battle'. The outcomes of such encounters result in 'wounding', 'injury', 'pain', and even 'blood on the floor'. Divorcing parents will become 'entrenched' in their positions and, as one man said in grim assessment of the state of a dispute over access to his son, 'the battle lines are drawn'. In any war there are 'innocent victims' and 'casualties' and in divorce these are often identified as the children. As such, one mother expressed the need to keep her children 'shielded from the flak', that is, protected from the arguments which raged between her and the children's father. However, in the brutality of marital warfare it is not uncommon to find allegations that children themselves are being 'used as a weapon'. In a further elaboration of this metaphorical complex, a recent television documentary talked about how some parents in disputes over contact and residence were opting to use the 'ultimate weapon', that is, making allegations of child abuse against their partners.

The nitty gritty of divorce is enacted in a number of different spaces and these too are understood in metaphorical terms as places of competition and combat. Thus, the space set aside for the purpose of confrontation may be described relatively benignly as a 'playing field' which somebody might feel the need to 'level' or carried out in rather more ominous settings such as an 'arena', 'ring', or 'battle-field'. The professionals involved with divorce may also carry and reinforce these metaphorical usages. One judge commented how a particularly belligerent client had 'opened up the batting' with a question about a social worker's qualifications and competence. Another judge commented: 'It is not the task of the judge to jump into the arena and act as a sort of untrained, amateur, Court Welfare Officer.' In another telling example, an informant spoke of needing his 'gladiator' (i.e. his solicitor) with him in the arena (i.e. the court) for a forthcoming hearing over disputed access.

A particularly rich vein of violent and conflictual metaphors is drawn from interpersonal combat sports such as boxing. Men in particular slip easily into the extensive repertoire of metaphors generated by this sport and its variants. I have heard men complain that in trying to resolve conflict their partners are 'not playing by the rules' or are doing things that are 'below the belt'; they then feel that 'it's time to take the gloves off'. When things become particularly difficult, there may be a realization that 'we're just going to have to slug it out' and when that becomes too much, it may be time to 'throw in the towel'. Finally, the idea of divorce as some kind of pugilistic contest is given state reinforcement by the tendency of courts to report divorces publicly in the same way as all other civil disputes, that is, as a one-to-one encounter of the 'Smith v Smith' variety.

In the following example, several metaphors are brought together in one informant's attempt to explain to me the differences and similarities between going through the courts and going through conciliation meetings to settle a dispute over child access. In a discussion about the role of the conciliator operating in the court the man was critical of what had happened because the conciliator had not been a good 'referee' and he went on to comment: 'It was the difference between a street brawl and a boxing match: same end result, you end up with black eyes and bloodied noses. Same end result, just a different way of doing it.'

The above metaphors were all noted in conversations about a legal system which is essentially adversarial, that is, one which deals with divorce as a kind of contest or dispute which is governed by rules of legal procedure and which is presided over by a judge whose role is that of ultimate arbiter. However, few cases ever reach adjudication by a judge and they are in fact resolved by a combination of private agreement between parties and negotiation on their behalf between solicitors and, on occasion, barristers (Davis 1988, Mnookin and Kornhauser 1979). In most cases the law provides a remote backdrop against which the day-to-day business of adversarial negotiation and contestation between husbands and wives and their legal representatives is carried out. Nonetheless, it is at this level that we encounter the extensive systematicity of metaphors among professionals and their clients. As I have indicated, the dominant metaphorical complex which occurred in general conversation about the divorce process was one which tends to see divorce in terms of battles to be fought and victories to be won, and the majority of disputants would seem to have little problem in casting the process in these terms.

One of the major claims of advocates of conciliation in the UK has been that it provides an alternative to the above system (Parkinson 1986: 67; Walker 1991: 262). Many such advocates took their cue from the Finer Report of 1974 (Report of the Committee on One-Parent Families) which was acclaimed at the time as bold and farsighted in identifying ways that the legal process might impact negatively on the lives of divorced people and in particular those of their children. The Report advocated radical alternatives for dealing with family matters in the courts. It was in the Finer Report that the seed was sown for conciliation as an appropriate way of 'assisting the parties to deal with the consequences of the established breakdown of their marriage' (Finer 1974: para. 4.288) and thereby 'civilising the consequences of the breakdown' (ibid. 4.311).

However, as King and Piper have argued (1990: 83–6), much of the energy which has gone into establishing the legitimacy of conciliation has involved a denigration of the law, or at the very least an attempt to displace legal discourse with ones imported from psychology, psychotherapy and other 'psy' discourses. These discourses operate with relative rather than absolute notions of truth and seek to reframe conflict by focusing on interests rather than rights. Parents are advised that court procedures are slow, unhelpful, disempowering, and likely to be bad for children (King and Piper 1990: 85). By contrast, conciliation offers the opportunity for parents to retain control of their disputes and to discuss their differences rationally in ways that will minimize damage to their children. High on the conciliation agenda is joint decision-making and joint responsibility for the future welfare of children.

Not surprisingly, the 'argument is war' metaphor is not particularly compatible with this approach to dispute resolution. Indeed, attention to the metaphors used in mediation settings reveals a subtle but significant shift in language use. Mediators endeavour to introduce a different metaphorical repertoire to describe the disputes presented to them and, furthermore, will try to challenge their clients when they slip into the 'divorce is war' complex. The metaphors preferred in mediation settings are consistent with an ideology that draws upon ideas of freedom and personal expression rather than the regulation and direction which informs the legal management of marital disputes. Mediators will seek to undermine and discredit clients' use of warlike metaphors and replace them with metaphors of organic growth and movement. As one mediator pointed out, 'We try to use the experience of divorce as an opportunity for personal growth, not defeat.'

Whereas the divorce is war metaphor is apt to leave people 'stuck', 'entrenched' in 'a war of attrition', the mediation intervention draws heavily on the image of divorce as part of a journey. The primary objective of those dealing with divorce in this way is to keep their clients moving. As one judge put it: 'The right word at the right time might set the wheels of conciliation turning.' The idea of motion is very important because it is itself a metaphor for inner states of growth and change. Such metaphors flow thick and fast in mediators' descriptions of their practice: 'We moved quite quickly', 'We were going too quickly', 'I went as far as I could go with . . .', 'I felt we had reached a milestone', 'We were on the right lines', 'To do real work with her she would have had to knock down those barriers', and so on. Parents themselves are apt to realize the switch in the dominant metaphor. One man commented regarding the inappropriateness of an adversarial stance in a conciliation appointment, 'It was as if we were trying to score points off one another.'

The shift in metaphorical usage identifiable in the move between different contexts is readily apparent in the practice of mediators. However, it was evident that in some contexts different metaphors were brought together like immiscible liquids. Conciliation is ideally a voluntary and non-coercive process. However, when practised in a court setting or non-court setting by people strongly associated with authority and adversarial proceedings, it is apt to acquire some of the baggage of those processes. For example, I have heard judges talk of welfare officers adopting a 'conciliation stance' or referring to the 'deployment of conciliation'. The militaristic and hierarchical feel of the process is further reinforced in court settings by referring to those involved in this process as 'conciliation officers'.

Finally, the conflict of metaphors is something that mediators themselves are increasingly alert to. John Haynes, a leading trainer of mediators, incorporates an awareness of metaphor into his writings on mediation theory and practice. His training materials (Haynes 1996) provide direction on the way that mediators might consciously manipulate metaphors to manage and resolve conflict. He provides examples of how in a mediation session a mediator might move towards the resolution of a dispute by continually re-framing client metaphors, that is, turning their swords into ploughshares.

The Case of Mr and Mrs Tate

Mr Tate left his wife and two children (8 and 11) suddenly and without warning. There followed a difficult period during which communication between the couple was almost non-existent and his contact with the children was infrequent and irregular. After three and a half years Mrs Tate applied for a judicial separation because she wished to formalize arrangements for the children's residence and their contact with their father. Both Mr and Mrs Tate were keen to pursue their different griev- ances over one another's behaviour through the courts. Although initially reluctant to go down the judicial route each had come to the conclusion that getting clearly defined orders made was the only way to deal with what each perceived as the other's recalcitrance and unreasonableness. He wanted to bring under public scrutiny her vindictiveness in preventing the children from having contact with him. She wanted to highlight her deep concerns about his long-running problems of alcoholism and the parental irresponsibility that this engendered. In court, neither of these issues was aired. At the Children's Appointment (S.41) the judge quickly identified the couple's lack of communication as an impediment to any agreement over arrangements for the children. He referred the case to the Court Welfare Officer (CWO) who spoke to the couple outside the court. He suggested that they should find a way of arriving at an agreed solution or run the risk of the judge making directions that neither of them would find acceptable. This rather ominous threat was presented alongside suggestions that the couple might benefit from the use of the local conciliation service. This view appeared to be reinforced in the couple's subsequent discussions with their solicitors. Mr Tate's solicitor had phrased it to him as follows: 'If you bounce ahead and get an order, it'll be against a backcloth of bitterness and resentment so you might as well try to get where you have to be through agreement rather than forcing it on your wife.' The whole court episode caused a good deal of frustration to the couple neither of whom felt they had been heard. Mrs Tate in particular felt that the judge and the CWO had 'taken sides' with her husband.

Mr and Mrs Tate each approached the idea of conciliation with suspicion and some trepidation. Indeed, Mrs Tate refused point blank to enter into a joint meeting with her husband. She was concerned that whenever they presented as a couple he always seemed to appear the more plausible and reasonable of the two and therefore gained the upper hand in negotiations. Two single appointments were thus set up which were, despite Mrs Tate's apprehensions, followed by a third joint appointment. Following this appointment, and a good deal of careful shuttle diplomacy by the mediator, regular contact between the father and the children resumed and the relationship between Mr and Mrs Tate improved significantly. In interviews some five years after the appointments the couple each spoke highly of the importance of the mediator's intervention (Mrs Tate described it as a 'turning point').

What the mediator appears to have achieved in this case was twofold. First, a context was provided for the couple to air (particularly in the individual appointments) all the issues which they felt had been overlooked and made to appear irrelevant, unreasonable, or silly in the court setting. However, as is invariably the case in such conflicts, major personal issues were blocking the possibility of resolution. He had grievances about finance and property, had acquired a new partner, and was coming to terms with the end of a long-running alcohol addiction. She had lost both her parents around the time of the separation. She was also angry that due to him she and the children now found themselves living in poverty which had a serious impact on the children. Both parties were nursing substantial levels of pain and anger following the ending of the relationship. The mediator had some success in getting each of the parties 'o acknowledge the other's feelings and to understand that their actions were not borne of irrational and unthinking malice; as Mrs Tate put it, 'she took both sides equally'. Second, the mediator had been able to bring the focus onto the children as the object of their shared rather than their competing concerns.

The dominant metaphor used throughout the accounts of Mr and Mrs Tate and of their mediator is one of movement. There is recognition that in the court they were 'in deadlock', 'at loggerheads', and 'going round in circles'. The move into the conciliation process saw them 'coming through the tunnel', 'moving towards agreements', and 'breaking the deadlock'. As Mrs Tate commented, 'It's been a slow journey to where I can chat with him.' In the mediator's account the image of a journey also appears frequently. The mediator described herself as having had to 'make a lot of the running' and in reflecting on the case drew together a cluster of metaphors of movement and direction:

> It would be very easy to get, you know, totally bogged down . . [] . . and in the end we might not have got anywhere with it. And I felt I had to keep on being quite persistent and I felt that with both of them. Certainly the husband, his instinct was to back off and she tended to side-track all the other issues . . [] . . . it was difficult to keep her on track, I mean I couldn't do it at all . . . [but] . . . because there were such big issues between them and yet at the same time I had to keep her on the main track of things and deal only with bits I could actually deal with.

Conclusion

In this chapter I have drawn attention to the role of institutions and organizations and their role in shaping the experience of divorcing couples who come into contact with them. Thus, what I have presented has been not so much an ethnography of organizations – that is, one that focuses on the spatial and bureaucratic existence of organizations – but an ethnographic account of organizational effects. In other words, organizations are made up of rules, values, ideologies, strategies, and objectives which are enacted in practice on a daily basis and which have varying degrees of impact upon those who come into contact with them. In methodological terms, I have highlighted how careful attention to linguistic usage in different settings shows how couples going through the divorce process may be predisposed to see their conflicts in different ways. The notion of a multi-sited ethnography is presented as one possible way of capturing this aspect of complex life transitions in contemporary society. My analysis reveals a tension between constructions of the divorce process as enshrined in traditional, adversarial legal processes on the one hand and alternatives to that process such as conciliation/mediation. The latter are informed by an amalgam of ideas drawn from negotiation theory and various 'psy' discourses; they direct their users toward self-conscious revision rather than acceptance of normative prescriptions (Giddens 1991, 1994; see also Rose 1990). The shift to 'deep' metaphors of growth and movement in the management of post-marital disputes is thus pedagogic and not merely instrumental; the process not only resolves disputes but educates 'clients' in how to individualize and democratize the arrangements which increasingly characterize contemporary family life.

The processes I have described here have been in train for well over a decade and continue to be worked through in present-day legislation. One of the most recent manifestations of the shift towards private ordering and privatization of the domestic sphere and away from state regulation of the family is to be seen in the Family Law Act 1996. This Act has as one its major objectives an aspiration first mapped out in the 1974 Finer Report, namely, burying dead marriages decently rather than subjecting men, women, and children to processes likely to exacerbate already painful situations. The way in which this is to be achieved is by seeking to minimize distress to the parties and their children should separation occur, and by promoting continuing relationships, particularly between parents and children. The emphasis throughout the legislation is on a conciliatory approach to marital breakdown and its aftermath. The Act seeks to formalize and clarify the networks of professionals identified in the earlier parts of this chapter. In future, parties to a divorce will experience a combination of information giving, marital counselling, and mediation through which the pain of divorce will be assuaged, and its unpleasantness sanitized. Under this legislation, parties will be steered away from traditional, adversarial legal forums and encouraged to seek out the kinds of expert discourse which will enable them to fashion their personal and family relationships anew. Legislative developments of this kind pose new challenges for understanding the way law and policy shape family life. As Donnan and MacFarlane suggest, anthropology should be concerned with 'cultures of the policy professional, in penetrating and uncovering the perceptions and work practices of those who seek to make their definition of the world stick' (1989: 6). An ethnographic approach which can incorporate the dispersed networks and partial connections which characterize the working of modern legal and welfare institutions is an important step in understanding not only how definitions stick but how these definitions are contested and subject to change.

References

Beck, U. (1997), 'Democratization of the Family', *Childhood*, **4**(2): 151–68.
—— and Beck-Gernsheim, E. (1995), *The Normal Chaos of Love*, Cambridge: Polity.
Collins, J. (1994), 'Disempowerment and Marginalization of Clients in Divorce Court Cases', in S. Wright (ed.), *Anthropology of Organizations*, London: Routledge.
Corlyon, J., Simpson, R., McCarthy, P. and Walker, J. (1991), *The Links Between Behaviour in Marriage, the Settlement of Ancillary Disputes, Arrangements for Children and Post-Divorce Relationships*, Report to the Nuffield Foundation, Newcastle.
Davis, G. (1988), 'The Halls of Justice and the Justice in the Halls', in Dingwall, R. and Eekelaar, J. (eds), *Divorce Mediation and the Legal Process*, Oxford: Clarendon.
Donnan, H. and MacFarlane, G. (eds) (1989*), Social Anthropology and Public Policy in Northern Ireland*, Aldershot: Avebury.
Finer, A. (1974), *Report of the Committee on One Parent Families*, Cmnd 5629, London: HMSO.
Geertz, C. (1983), *Local Knowledge: Further Essays in Interpretative Anthropology*, New York: Basic Books.
Giddens, A. (1991), *Modernity and Self-identity: Self and Society in the late Modern Age*, Cambridge: Polity.
—— (1994), 'Living in a Post-traditional Society', in U. Beck (ed.), *Reflexive Modernity: Politics, Tradition and Aesthetics in the Modern Social Order*, Cambridge: Polity.
Ginsburg, F. and Rapp, R. (eds) (1996) *Conceiving the New World Order: The Global Stratification of Reproduction*, Berkeley: University of California Press.
Haraway, D. (1991) 'A Cyborg Manifesto: Science, Technology and Socialist-Feminism in the Late Twentieth Century', in D. Haraway, *Symians, Cyborgs and Women: The Re-Invention of Nature*', New York: Routledge.
Hastrup, K. and Olwig, K.F. (eds) (1996) *Siting Culture: The Shifting Anthropological Object*, London: Routledge.
Haynes, J. (1996), *Metaphor and Mediation (Parts 1, 2, and 3)*, Mediation Information and Resource Centre at http://www.mediate.com/articles/metaphor.cfm
King, M. and Piper, C. (1990), *How the Law Thinks about Children*, Aldershot: Gower.

Lakoff, G. and Johnson, M. (1980), *Metaphors we Live by*, London: University of Chicago Press.

Lasch, C. (1977), *Haven in a Heartless World: The Family Besieged*, New York: Basic Books.

Leach, E.R. (1967), 'An Anthropologist's Reflections on a Social Survey', in D.C. Jongmans and P.C. Gutkind (eds), *Anthropologists in the Field*, Assen, Netherlands: Van Gorcum and Co.

Lévi-Strauss, C. (1962), *Totemism*, Harmondsworth: Penguin.

—— (1966), *The Savage Mind*, London: Weidenfeld & Nicolson.

McCarthy, P. (1996), 'Marital Breakdown: Professional Shakedown', in R. Humphries (ed.), *Families behind the Headlines*, Newcastle: British Association for the Advancement of Science/Department of Social Policy, University of Newcastle upon Tyne.

—— and Simpson, B. (1991), *Issues in Post-divorce Housing: Family Policy or Housing Policy?*, Aldershot: Avebury.

——, Simpson, B., Walker, J., and Corlyon, J. (1991), *A Longitudinal Study of the Impact of Different Dispute Resolution Processes on Post-divorce Relationships Between Parents and Children*, Report to the Ford Foundation (Fund for Research in Dispute Resolution), Newcastle.

Marcus, G.E. (1995), 'Ethnography In/Of the World System: The Emergence of Multi-Sited Ethnography', *Annual Review of Anthropology*, **24**: 95–117.

Mnookin, R. and Kornhauser, L. (1979), 'Bargaining in the Shadow of the Law: The Case of Divorce', *Yale Law Journal*, **88**: 950–70.

Ogus, A., Walker, J., Jones-Lee, M., Cole, W., Corlyon, J., McCarthy, P., Simpson, R., and Wray, S. (1989), *Report to the Lord Chancellor's Department on the Costs and Effectiveness of Conciliation in England and Wales*, London: Lord Chancellor's Department.

Parkinson, L. (1986), *Conciliation in Separation and Divorce*, London: Croom Helm.

Robertson, A.F. (1991), *Beyond the Family: The Social Organization of Human Reproduction*, Berkeley: University of California Press.

Rose, N. (1990), *Governing the Soul: The Shaping of the Private Self*, London: Routledge.

Schneider, D.M. (1968), *American Kinship: A Cultural Account*, Englewood Cliffs: Prentice-Hall.

Schön, D. (1993), Generative Metaphor: A Perspective on Problem Setting in Social Policy', in A. Ortony (ed.) *Metaphor and Thought*, Cambridge: Cambridge University Press.

Simpson, B. (1998), *Changing Families: An Ethnography of Divorce and Separation*, Oxford: Berg.

——, Corlyon, J., McCarthy, P., and Walker, J. (1990), 'Client Responses to Family Conciliation: Achieving Clarity in the Midst of Confusion', *British Journal of Social Work*, **20**: 557–74.

——, McCarthy, P., and Walker, J. (1995), *Being There: Fathers after Divorce*, Newcastle: Relate Centre for Family Studies.

Stack, C.B. and Burton, L.B. (1994), 'Kinscripts: Reflections on Family, Generation and Culture', in E.N. Glen, G. Chang, and L.R. Forcey (eds), *Mothering: Ideology, Experience and Agency*, New York and London: Routledge.

Strathern, M. (1992), *After Nature: English Kinship in the late Twentieth Century*, Cambridge: Cambridge University Press.

—— (1999), *Property, Substance and Effect: Anthropological Essays on Persons and Things*, London: Athlone.

Walker, J. (1989), 'Family Conciliation in Great Britain: From Research to Practice to Research', *Mediation Quarterly*, [number] 24: 29–54.

—— (1991), 'Family Mediation in England: Strategies for Gaining Acceptance' *Mediation Quarterly*, **8**: 253–64.

Weiss, C. (1986), 'Research and Policy-making: A Limited Partnership', in F. Heler (ed.), *The Use and Abuse of Social Science*, London: Sage.

– 6 –

Observing other Observers: Anthropological Fieldwork in a Unit for Children with Chronic Emotional and Behavioural Problems

Simon Pulman-Jones

Introduction

This chapter discusses the opportunities presented by some similarities between the practice of ethnography and the life of organizations. It is likely that the ethnographer of organizations will share much, if not most, of the social and cultural background of the people being studied in the organizational context. The question of such broad affinities, covered by the literature on 'anthropology at home', is not what will be considered here. Rather, I shall focus on two factors of particular relevance to the study of organizations. The first is the likelihood that the ethnographer will share a common *intellectual* background with those she or he is observing in the organizational context: that the broad tradition of sociological understanding that informs the ethnographer is also a significant factor in the identity and purpose of the organization. The second is that ethnographers and organizations share a common *'instrumental'* nature.

The common intellectual background and the common instrumental nature make it likely that the ethnographer will find that she or he will be using an intellectual toolkit, a set of fundamental intellectual resources, that also plays a significant role in the life of the organization. Organizations, and ethnographers, make interventions in the 'natural' continuity of social life. Unlike social forms such as family or kin groups whose primary purpose, if they can be said to have a purpose, is to reproduce themselves, most organizations have an instrumental purpose which is the basis of their identity. They have to define the world that they work on before they can set to work, just as do professional practitioners of social description such as ethnographers. Their engagement with the world therefore involves a basic repertoire that begins with naming/identifying/defining, then proceeds to involving the phenomena defined in the 'work' that they exist to do, and finally makes syntheses or decisions. They are likely to share the predicament of professional social describers in having a limited repertoire of logical possibilities for describing the social world on which they work. The phenomena with which they engage will be apprehended either as discrete atoms linked by relationships, or as a continuous fabric of relationship awaiting separation. And amidst all of this, in common with ethnographers and other intellectual workers, they will measure what they do to some extent through the difficulty involved in getting it done.[1]

The common intellectual resources to be considered are therefore those related to the requirements of organizations and ethnographers in performing instrumental processes on the world, and to the repertoire of possibilities available for describing the social world in terms of continuities and ruptures, of relatedness and separateness. What follows is a case study illustrating the affinities between the ways that ethnographers and organizations make beginnings with their material, and the ways in which theoretical preoccupations familiar to anthropologists may also play significant roles within organizational contexts.

Case Study

The case study that follows is based on fieldwork carried out at the Child and Family Department Day Unit of a large mental health clinic in a large city in Britain between April 1992 and July 1994. In order to have access to the Unit I worked as one of a handful of unqualified volunteers. I have changed all names of people, places, and institutions in order to preserve the confidentiality of my informants. The Unit provides a therapeutic school-like environment for twelve children between the ages of five and thirteen with severe emotional and behavioural difficulties. Children are referred to the Unit after coming to the attention of a local government Education Authority and being 'statemented' by an educational psychologist as having special educational needs. As a placement of last resort the catchment area of the Unit is the whole of the northern part of the city. The broad aim of the Unit is then to provide education in a therapeutic environment, combined with specific treatments such as psychotherapy, in order to allow the expression and management of the child's perceived problems with a view to return to 'mainstream' educational provision. In practice few children return to the mainstream and most of the work at the Unit is focused on management: helping children and parents or guardians to stabilize rapidly deteriorating situations, even if this means no more than providing a secure and calming environment during the school day so that problems are not as bad as they might be at home during the evening and night.

---

1. In the course of this chapter I do not mean to suggest that the parallels I draw between ethnographers and organizations are definitive. Organizations can be seen, and see themselves, as both 'instrumental' and 'natural', working both on the world and to ensure their own reproduction. The question of the relative balance of these elements in an organization's identity is a useful one. I am emphasizing certain similarities as a strategy for enriching the ethnographic process rather than as a way of defining ethnography or organizations.

This setting provided a situation in which there were psychologists, psychotherapists, and psychiatrists who work within a broadly similar tradition of social description to that of anthropologists, with similar fundamental intellectual resources and from a similar professional position. They manage the social reproduction and occasional innovation of ideas about how to treat the prototypical category of person, the child. It provided me with an opportunity to look at the relationship between the production and the consumption of concepts of the person, while remaining close to the material processes of social exchange in the movement of children, and responsibility for children, back and forth between families and professional carers.

Children who are placed at the Day Unit of the Clinic's Child and Family Department stay there for a period of up to three years. There are no specific rules or procedures governing the length of stay of a child at the Unit, this being decided by the interplay of several factors. Ideally, from the point of view of the Unit itself, a child would stay until he or she had been able to take full benefit from the Unit, leaving when staff began to observe a maturity and composure significantly beyond that of the majority of the other children. This is felt to take approximately two to three years. In practice, however, the child's period of stay at the Unit is determined by many other factors, such as the effects of budgetary constraints on the referring Education Authorities, which have to meet the costs of keeping the children at the Unit, or the progress of arrangements with fostering or adoptive homes for the children. As a result, the period that a child stays at the Unit may vary from a few months to over three years.

Methodological Affinities between Ethnographer and Organization

The business of social description and prescription which is carried out by the Unit is directly comparable to the project of social description in anthropology. The first stage involves the defining of terms: classifying the child; setting out the objectives and points of reference of ethnographic research. The second stage involves establishing the relationships between the previously defined terms: the participation of the child in the life of the Unit; the participating ethnographer's observation of the subjects' lives in process. The final stage involves a synthesis which includes the terms and the relationships between the terms in a formulation which can be translated into and used in other contexts: the child's prognosis; the ethnographer's theoretical observations. This sequence is common to intellectual activity in general. The value of drawing attention to it in this context is that the ethnographer of organizations may be able to observe that just as she or he faces the practical problem of marshalling available resources of attention to best effect, so too the organization, in fulfilling its instrumental objectives, has to structure and direct its attention. In the context of my fieldwork at the Unit this similarity was particularly evident because of the specifically forensic nature of the work done at the Unit. Just as I was struggling to be a successful participant in the Unit while also trying to discover aspects of life at the Unit which I could relate to the body of anthropological theory that had brought me there in the first place, so too the staff of the Unit were struggling to manage the practicalities of dealing with severely disturbed children while at the same time saving some attention in order not to miss any signs of abuse or pathology which, if they constituted adequate evidence in the relevant statutory or medical context, might entail significant consequences. In this case the affinity between the ethnographer and the organization is easily seen, both sharing investigative, forensic aims. Most organizations, being instrumental, share this characteristic to some extent. In organizational settings where there is a task to be delivered or a problem to be solved it will be useful for the ethnographer to be aware both of her or his own problems of marshalling resources of attention and of similar problems faced by the organization and those who work in it.

Social Definitions

The arrival of a new child at the Unit is a process that begins with an educational psychologist working for a local Education Authority or a local government Social Services department making a referral to the Clinic's Child and Family Department. The referral is the point in the process at which the Clinic first becomes aware of the child, and is the beginning of a period during which, if the child is judged to be an appropriate case for treatment by the Unit, and the referring authority is able to fund the placement, the Unit will get acquainted with the child. The process of acquaintance takes several forms and operates at many different levels. At one extreme is the exchange of psychological assessment information between the referring educational psychologist and the educational psychologist at the Unit. Less formal is the process by which the history and diagnosis of the prospective new child is communicated through a chain of meetings to the staff of the Unit. This process involves some of the technical descriptive terms of the psychological reports, but also relies heavily on an anecdotal shorthand that identifies the new child by comparison with children already known to the Unit. At the other extreme is the process by which individual staff and children weigh up the new child as he or she gradually becomes part of the Unit. Between these extremes are many other contexts in which the child and the Unit have to get to know each other, reflecting the fact that the Unit is a highly complex organization, the purposes of which are worked out at all available registers of social life.

This process of acquaintance is a necessary consequence of the fact that the Unit is an instrumental organization functioning as a part of the interventions made by the state in the lives of its citizens. The Unit is directed towards social phenomena (the child and family), which it describes in order to accommodate them to its own terms of reference. What follows is a process of continual redescription until a final prescription (the parting diagnosis and prognosis) can be made.

The Acquaintance Phase

It might be said that it is inevitable that a newcomer will be given a different kind of attention to that given to someone who is well established within a particular environment. In the case of the newcomer, information is required which could not have been gathered until the arrival within the new environment. I would argue, however, that the mode of attention paid to new arrivals at the Unit does not entirely correspond with the need to put together a picture of the newcomer which suits the Unit's aims and terms of reference. The distinctive form of attention paid to a newcomer does not relax once enough is known for him or her to become a part of the Unit: it is not just a question of information. Rather, the intensity and duration of the period of acquaintance are dependent upon the relationship between the different modes of attention that the Unit operates through the career of a child in the Unit. At any one time, the Unit operates a variety of modes of attention in relation to the children, which can be divided into three basic phases. The first phase is that of defining, of labelling, and of static definitions, the most extreme form of which is the Statement of Special Educational Needs which places on an Education Authority the statutory obligation to provide appropriate education and care for a child. The second, central, phase is that of process and narrative, in which attention changes from the level of labelling and definitions to the relationships between those partaking in the life of the Unit. This is where the Unit feels its unique ethos to reside, where the organization is most strong and comprehensive. The third and final phase is that of the diagnosis in which the significance gathered from the second phase is translated through the layers of staff meetings and discussions to establish a point from which the child can move on.

Focus on Symptoms

Gemma was a seven-year-old girl, large and strong for her age, who had been placed at the Unit because her behaviour had become too difficult for the special school for children with moderate learning difficulties (MLD) at which she had previously been placed. Though she could appear calm and content, her speech and learning were severely below the norm for her age, and she was prone to sudden violent tantrums. She spoke in a bizarre and idiosyncratic way, beginning a sentence with a few intelligible words, but then trailing away into jumbled words and phrases, accompanied by knowing looks from coyly up-cast eyes, as if she were posing a riddle to be deciphered.

Gemma's mother was from the isle of Harris in Scotland. She had moved to Perth at the age of thirteen and her parents had divorced at about that time. She had moved to London with Gemma's father about five years before my fieldwork and had subsequently split up with him. She lived with Gemma and two younger children, and the father of the younger children, in a high-rise council flat which Social Services' staff had described as very untidy and dirty. They shared the flat with several pets which Gemma's mother said that she kept to compensate for the open spaces and 'nature' she missed in Harris. There had been long-standing fears by Social Services about Gemma's mother and step-father's violence, and about possible sexual abuse by Gemma's natural father, who made occasional visits to the flat.

At the beginning of her time at the Unit almost every aspect of Gemma's behaviour was a focus of concern; indeed when the Unit's senior child psycho-therapist gave a brief presentation of her work on ritual satanic abuse, mentioning that one of the factors associated with cases of satanic abuse was the keeping and misuse of exotic pets, the fact that Gemma had mentioned that her step-father kept pet tarantulas in the flat gave rise to a frisson of suspicion that satanic abuse might be involved in her case. By the end of Gemma's first month at the Unit it was well established that there were significant grounds for suspicion of sexual or physical abuse. Attention shifted away from anecdotal evidence about Gemma and her family, and away from the existing education and Social Services case files, to the discovery of fresh evidence of on-going abuse, particularly in the form of bruises and other marks on the body.

As a result, staff started to focus less on the analysis of the pictures Gemma was drawing during the day in the classroom and more on her physical appearance as she arrived each day at the Unit after the night at home. Each morning when the children and the staff assembled for 'news' (morning assembly) in the hall space at the start of the day, the staff would exchange glances as they looked at Gemma for any signs of fresh bruising. On many days there were new bruises to be seen on Gemma's arms, legs, neck, or face and Gemma, aware of the attention, would, coyly and without making eye contact with any of the staff, turn her body and lift her skirt or jumper so as to make her bruises visible. On the occasions when no bruises were visible, the staff's attention would often fall on the fact that her clothes were either very worn or very dirty, causing further concern that she was being neglected. On those occasions when other children were commanding the attention of the staff she could make herself the centre of attention by such oblique strategies as falling off her chair or running into the alcove around the fireplace, behind the ring of chairs the children and staff used for the meeting. Direct attempts by the staff to question Gemma about her bruises caused her only to turn coyly away, or to respond with incomprehensible mutterings. During this period the attention of everybody was closely fastened on the signs that could be detected on or from Gemma.

The End of the Acquaintance Phase

The particular form of attention that I have described as being operated by the Unit during its period of acquaintance with a new child is not entirely a function of the need to gather information. If that were the case then one would expect that form of attention to last for as long as the need to gather information about the child. What other factors might bring about a change in the form of attention paid to the child?

Gemma was the focus of serious concern about possible sexual abuse from the moment she started at the Unit, this concern manifesting itself principally in the daily monitoring of bruises and signs of neglect such as dirty clothing. There was a clear and pressing need to do everything possible to protect Gemma and to stop her being hurt. Enquiries made by the staff directly to Gemma's mother on the occasions when she came for meetings at the Unit, and through her 'Home/School Book', which Gemma (like all the children) took home every night for her parents to read the class-teacher's comments about the day, were answered with tales of Gemma's clumsiness at home, given as the cause of all the bruises. Indeed Gemma *was* clumsy, often falling over as a quite transparent way of attracting attention, but concerns persisted and the matter was referred to Social Services. In the meantime, though, I noticed that after a couple of months the attention paid to Gemma's bruises began to wane. I was very struck by the fact that though, as far as I could see, Gemma was as bruised as she had been at the height of concern about her, she was no longer the subject of the attention of the Core Team staff at the morning assembly, and that attention paid to her cryptic comments in the classroom had also fallen off. Attention was now paid to Gemma for a different reason, for she had begun to display some of the behaviour that her previous school had found difficult to cope with and which until this point she had not shown at the Unit. She started to have tantrums which developed without warning (or so it appeared) and which would begin as a sulky unresponsiveness. When asked what was the matter, or asked why she was not joining in with the rest of the class, she would jump up and run away, shouting angrily, 'Leave me alone, I hate you, I hate you.' When this occurred in the classroom she would run out into the hallway and then up the main staircase and into the winding corridor that passed through several fire doors and unlit sections through to the far side of the upper floor where the therapy rooms were. When somebody followed her to check that she was safe, and to bring her back if possible, she would scream and shout even louder, kicking and struggling violently if any attempt were made to take hold of her hand, and repeatedly demanding what, in the circumstances, was impossible: to be left alone.

Gemma had begun to explore the Unit's reaction to the behaviour which had seen her rejected by her previous school, and in so doing she demonstrated that she had left the period of acquaintance, of close and anxious attention, and moved on to the main, central phase of the Unit's career with a child, that in which the repertoire of relationships with staff and other children is explored within the context of the closely defined spatial world and timetable of the Unit. The signs and behaviour which had drawn such anxious and intense attention when Gemma first arrived remained and, it might be assumed, required just as urgent attention, but from now on they were more or less overlooked.

I observed the same thing happening with other children. A six-year-old boy, an elective mute, was the focus of excited attention during his early period, as staff vied to discern whether his mutism stemmed from a genuine inability or an arch refusal to talk. Yet when he too started to run off into the building, and put himself in danger by climbing onto precarious high places, interest in the minutiae of his expressions when trying to communicate waned. In many other cases I observed chronic anxiety about minute symptoms of behaviour or affect suddenly fade as the children became incorporated into the life of the Unit.

What explanations can be given for this observation? It would certainly be true to say that in the case of a child such as Gemma, for whom there is serious anxiety because of possible sexual abuse, it is to be expected that when the initial urgency of the suspicions of abuse has been succeeded by the frustrations of trying to establish evidence and proof of abuse in conjunction with the statutory authorities, discouragement at how little can be done, despite the very distressing strength of the conviction that the child has been abused, will make the maintaining of an urgent vigil for signs of abuse seem of little use. When the child has newly arrived at the Unit it is understandable that everything might seem to be at stake; both in terms of the future of the child and in terms of the reputation of the Unit in relation to the referring authorities and the previous place of education. When, after a few weeks, it is apparent that the world will not fall apart if the Unit does not immediately reveal the truth of the child's condition and history, it is also understandable that the anxious close focus should be relaxed.

But I think there is a different explanation for the change between the close attention of the early phase and the broader attention of the middle phase. Because of the way the Unit has to work, the initial phase of naming and defining is inherently unstable. The process that begins with the Statement of Special Educational Needs and ends with the anxious gaze of a member of the Unit staff looking for definite signs of abuse or psychological disturbance – a process which aims to fix a picture of the child, so that he or she can become an identifiable and appropriate item to be moved between parts of the education and mental health care system – is anathema to the central process and ethos of the Unit which – far from fixing positions and identities – is designed to provide a safe and tightly defined context within which to allow the elements of the child's psychological identity to shift and reform into more manageable arrangements. The paradox is that the Unit needs somewhere to start, but from that point onwards aims to undermine the tyranny of such starting points by working to multiply and shift perspectives. Such a range of perspectives may be seen in relation to a particular item of behaviour such as incontinence, which might be seen in the home environment as a rebuke to the authority of the parents; in the classroom at the Unit as a sign of a desire to withhold consent to participate in social groups and in the 'growing-up' of education; by the Unit's social worker as the occasion for a sharing of opinions from the whole of the family network; by a paediatrician as possible evidence of urinary tract trauma with slight possibility of sexual abuse; or by a psychotherapist as the articulation of a desire or intention largely unrelated to outside contingencies but of immense significance at that point in the narrative of that particular session. The basis of the ethos of the Unit is that as large as possible a range of different perspectives on the child will be found by the staff in the course of the Unit's daily life and that the child will be helped to manage life more easily if he or she is able to internalize a broader repertoire of perspectives.

I have already drawn on the fact that the Unit shares a common intellectual tradition with the social sciences, and operates, in a highly practical and contextually embedded form, a system of analysis that shares basic structural features with the social sciences. I have suggested that parallels can be drawn between the phase during which the Unit becomes acquainted with a child and the necessary starting point of sociological analysis in which social phenomena must be differentiated and defined. The necessity for a point of departure is in both cases a necessary evil: flawed and provisional. From the psychodynamic perspective, the early persistent and anxious focus on the newly arrived child is an invitation for something to *happen* with the child rather than for it to submit to definition. From this perspective it might be said that definition is perversely insisted on in the early phase, until the child, and the Unit's view of the child, are provoked into breaking free into the daily life of the Unit.

Affinities between the Ethnographer and the Organization

Having discussed some basic 'methodological' affinities between the ethnographer and the organization, I now turn to theoretical affinities. I have already noted that in my fieldwork at the Unit I shared an interest in the child as a prototype of personhood (from my anthropological perspective) with the people that I was studying (from their clinical perspectives). Awareness of theoretical debates was very much a part of the life of the Unit, even for those members of staff with no formal theoretical expertise.

By being equally an educational and a psychiatric/psychotherapeutic institution, the Unit takes on the contradictions between these two approaches. The main contrast in approaches is between one which sees the child as part of a network of family and wider social relationships in the context of a life career, and one which sees the child in isolation as the vehicle for the expression of symptoms of his or her psychological pathology. This contrast can be described as being between an extensive outlook and an intense internal focus and, while it is most often seen as the difference between the perspective of the teacher and that of the psychotherapist, it is equally present in the debates and struggles within the psychiatric team between behavioural and psychotherapeutic approaches, and in the competing claims of differing educational philosophies or requirements. Containing the contradictions between these different approaches (rather than being a Behaviourist *or* a Therapeutic Unit) is often talked about by the staff of the Unit as almost impossibly difficult, but ultimately it is felt that the difficulty is worth enduring because it allows the fullest possible treatment of the children. This difficulty presented itself in many different ways, but particularly where psychotherapeutic treatment, practical management of difficult behaviour, and disciplinary measures in response to seriously unacceptable behaviour came into conflict. During the period of my fieldwork, violence within the Unit was felt to be permanently at crisis level. Physical assaults, the throwing of sharp or heavy objects, and spitting (directed both at other children and at members of staff, predominantly the teachers and nursery nurses) happened several times daily, but periodically there would be an incident of such severity, or the sustained level of violence would become so intolerable, that the teachers and the nursery nurses would demand that a formal set of procedures be drawn up so that violent behaviour could be responded to by the temporary exclusion of children from the Unit. The psychiatric team vigorously opposed the exclusion of children, maintaining that the therapeutic environment must offer the children total containment. On several occasions the teacher in charge of the Unit took a unilateral decision to exclude a child, insisting that she *had* to protect her staff. On these occasions the psychiatric team made it clear that they felt that the teachers and nursery nurses were failing the children. On a day-to-day ad hoc basis there were 'behavioural' elements to the treatment that the children received. That is to say that the children were treated as if they were separate from the Unit and their behaviour could be modified if the Unit acted on them through such measures as the withholding of access to the garden at playtime or, *in extremis*, being excluded for a few days. But the open-ended therapeutic commitment to regard the children as belonging to the 'psychodynamic' whole of the Unit as a therapeutic environment was maintained in the ultimate refusal to draw up any guidelines setting out specific responses, such as exclusion, to unacceptable violent behaviour. Only through keeping faith with an unwritten treatment ethos was it felt that the Unit could continue its unique blend of treatments.

In the work of the Day Unit there is a link between the staff's ability to balance and reconcile the contradictory models of personhood – those reflected in the educational and the therapeutic elements of the treatment – and the child's ability to know himself or herself more correctly in order to be able to live more successfully.

Being couched between contrasting models of the person, the atom-self of boundary-drawing behaviourism and the inter-subjectivity of the psychodynamic, therapeutic tradition, the practical, working psychology of the Unit is a constant process of testing and reproducing the prevailing conditions of and for the nature of personhood, of the balance of boundaries and continuities in personal and social life. Strong, though only partly rationalized, links are made between the effort to understand and the effort to live successfully, so that a part of overcoming the gross difficulties of the lives of very unhappy children is the overcoming of meta-physical difficulties by the professionals charged with responsibility for the children's welfare. It was true for a majority of the children that their behavioural problems were so severe that they, their families or carers, and the staff of the Unit were faced with the constant imperative that if no improvement could be made the children would have to be, for example, taken into care, or moved to a secure psychiatric ward, or faced with drugs-based medical treatment. And thus practical problems of how to deal with the children during their day at the Unit were forced together with the problems of understanding both what was 'wrong' with the children and what could be done for them. Many of the children, including Gemma, were thought to present varying degrees of autism. But the theory that autism might exist in varying degrees is a controversial one. Some of the children presenting autism-like symptoms were thought by some members of the psychiatric team to be suffering from neurological problems that required urgent drugs-based medical treatment. Other members of the Unit's staff were convinced of the significance of a mild form of autism in these cases, while yet others just saw a desperately unhappy and withdrawn child. These diagnoses were thrown into constant competition through the system of daily and weekly meetings in which the staff, in groups varying in number from two to the whole staff, discussed how the Unit dealt with the children. The result of this was that people were aware both of the troubled history of the children outside and within the Unit and also of the various competing explanations for the problems, and the attendant different solutions. So in the daily, constant crises with the children, for example, in instances such as when it began to become clear during the course of an early morning that something was very much amiss with Gemma, the energies of the staff would be mobilized simultaneously to providing practical containment and comfort and to achieving some form of resolution to the intractable questions about diagnosis and treatment that the worrying behaviour gave rise to. Staff at the Unit live with the sense that if they could only, in that moment of crisis during the day, understand the truth about the nature of, say, autism and the relative merits of psychotherapeutic or behavioural approaches to treatment, then they could offer some hope of relief to their desperate charges. The urgency of the predicament thus makes it seem that the overcoming of difficulties of understanding is very closely related to the practical problems of managing a specific child in the Day Unit.

These theoretical concerns were very much a part of the staff's constant discussions about the children and about the nature and adequacy of the treatment that they were receiving. The sense of the importance of theory did not depend on consistent and coherent understandings across all members of staff; it consisted more in the awareness that there were always two basic and fundamentally opposed approaches. Terms such as 'behaviourist', 'therapeutic', 'psychodynamic', 'systemic therapy', or 'phenomenological' were used, not always strictly accurately in theoretical terms, to recognize the existence of antagonistic approaches which often entailed mutually exclusive rationales.

The importance of these 'theoretical' preoccupations was not limited to abstract discussion. They were reflected in the daily life of the Unit and in some of its most intractable problems.

The division of the staff of the Unit into two separate teams was both the most controversial issue and that which caused the problem that seemed most inescapable during the period of my fieldwork. The names themselves caused frequent grumbling. The Core Team (the teachers, the nursery nurses, and the administrative secretary) felt that 'core' as opposed to 'psychiatric' implied 'basic' as opposed to 'specialist'. At the same time the Psychiatric Team (two psychiatrists, a social worker, an educational psychologist, and a child psychotherapist) felt that 'core' implied 'indispensable' while 'psychiatric' implied 'external, optional extra'. On several occasions I heard discussions of the origins of the two labels, there being no consensus as to who had initiated them or how long they had been in use. There were two alternative labels, Educational Team and Clinical Team, which were occasionally used, pointedly, in meetings, but they were never used as the universal shorthand for 'the other lot'. There were indeed significant descriptive shortcomings to both labels. Only two of the five-strong Psychiatric Team were psychiatrists. Nevertheless, Psychiatric Team and Core Team remained the labels by which the two groups were known and in which rivalry and resentment continued to echo.

One basic fact divided and distinguished the two teams. The Core Team were with the children all the time and the Psychiatric Team were not. For the Core Team attendance at the Unit meant arriving before the children and leaving after they had left, united in containing the children throughout the day. For the Psychiatric Team attendance at the Unit meant leaving the main Clinic building down the road and arriving at the Unit in order to attend regular meetings, therapy sessions, or one-off meetings that occurred during the Unit's day. Whereas members of the Psychiatric Team tended to come and go individually, the Core Team arrived and left all at the same time. They gathered together for cups of tea or coffee before the children arrived and after they had left, their solidarity at the beginning and end of the day resolving its uncertainties.

The conflict between the continuous solidarity of the Core Team and the instrumental intervention of the Psychiatric Team was frequently evident in disagreements that occurred during the weekly Community Meeting, or during subsequent discussions about the meeting. The Community Meeting, in which all of the staff and all of the children met together in the dining room seated around the walls in a circle for exactly half an hour for the acting out of the community's 'psycho-dynamics', was often extremely disturbed and chaotic, giving rise to very worrying behaviour from the children. It was to be expected that the Psychiatric Team, for most of whom this half-hour session represented their only direct contact with children other than those with whom they were involved in therapy sessions, would be more alarmed than the Core Team by the extremes of behaviour often seen in the Community Meeting. The Core Team could more easily see such behaviour as the expressive climax of a period of anxiety or unhappiness that a particular child was undergoing, and have confidence in the fact that the child would return to a more manageable state, whereas the Psychiatric Team were inclined to see such behaviour as a sign that things were far more out-of-hand than they, in their absence from the Unit, had assumed. The result would be that the Psychiatric Team would insist that a particular child, or sometimes the Unit as a whole, had reached a state of crisis which required an urgent response and wholesale re-evaluation. By contrast, the Core Team would respond that no such crisis existed and that the behaviour that had so alarmed the Psychiatric Team was either the result of particular circumstances, such as the temporary absence from home of one of the child's parents or a build-up of anxiety before the half-term holiday, or part of a period of emotional acting out that had been observed over a longer period and which the Core Team were confident would be resolved positively by the under-standing and strategies that observation had given rise to.

The different responses to worrying behaviour in the Community Meeting illustrate the contrast between Core Team and Psychiatric Team attitudes: continuous solidarity, observation, and long-term strategy were opposed to the isolation of significant symptoms of behaviour and the need for urgent instrumental intervention. In practical terms this is an effective and complementary opposition, the deficiencies of each outlook being offset by the other, but in the conflict between the two staff teams it was rarely seen as such.

If the Core Team were the custodians of contingency, the Psychiatric Team, for their part, offered the benefits of being freed from contingency. They saw the children in highly formalized contexts which were sufficient in themselves, without any continuous supporting context. In contrast with the Core Team's internal life in the Unit, which was based on a shared knowledge and experience, with shared responsibility, of all that went on, the work of the Psychiatric Team was often unseen by the rest of the Unit. Members of the Psychiatric Team arrived at the Unit during the day for appointments and, having been let in through the front door by the administrative secretary, they passed unnoticed by the children and the Core Team staff to the rooms on the upper floor where they held meetings with each other or with children and members of their families, or where they had therapy sessions with the children. The practical basis for the Psychiatric Team's experience of time in the life of the Unit was the model of appointments in a daily diary, characterized by specific times for beginning and ending, with the absolute separation of one appointment and the next marked by the logistical requirement to travel between appointments in different buildings, or in different parts of the same building, and to keep on time. The theoretical model underlying this practical fact, and reinforcing it, was that of the 'therapeutic hour' of fifty-minute consultations, the beginning and end of which are observed rigidly and absolutely so as to mark the absolute distinction between quotidian time and therapeutic time.

The Psychiatric Team did not, therefore, share the Core Team's sense of continuity with the child. Seeing children on separate occasions, they saw them differently each time, noticing changes more readily than the Core Team (or, as the Core Team often insisted, seeing changes where none had really taken place). Whereas it was the role of the Core Team to manage continuity it was the role of the Psychiatric Team to enable change. Within the firmly policed boundaries of the therapy session new meanings are created for child and for therapist.

If the Core Team's continuity forms a part of the linear progress of the child's social career in life, and this is seen as a horizontal continuity, the therapy session, by-passing the threads of contingency, aims a vertical probe into the psychological history of the child. Whereas the Core Team staff member in the classroom is placed within the spatial disposition of other containing presences and the certainties of the unfolding timetable, the Psychiatric Team member in a therapy session is alone with the child in a bounded world in which space and time are collapsed into the therapist's focus on the psychodynamic significance of the child's behaviour.

The contrasting models of time and space that I have described above in relation to the roles of the Core Team and the Psychiatric Team, which each imply different models of personhood in their attitude to the children, are not entirely exclusive to each team. The antagonistic pairing of the two teams, together with the requirements of their respective roles, commit them towards one model rather than the other, but both, as mutually reinforcing opposites, are always co-existent.

'The Split'

So far I have described the way in which a basic repertoire of complementary ideas about personhood, rooted in the same traditions of social description as inform the ethnographer, structured the treatment the Unit offered the children. But this binary opposition between logically complementary poles was not restricted to the level of ideas about the work done, for it was underpinned by the structure of the organization itself.

During the period of my fieldwork at the Unit it was undergoing a change in its organizational structure which amplified its anxiety about its identity. When I began my fieldwork, in the spring of 1992, the Unit was run jointly by the local Area Health Authority, through the Clinic, and Council 'A' Education Authority. Council 'A' employed the teachers, then numbering three full-time and one part-time, covered the cost of educational materials, and provided the children's lunches. The Clinic was responsible for the health component, employing the nursery nurses, the psychiatrists, the educational psychologist, the psychotherapists, and the social worker, and providing and maintaining the building. The division within the Unit between health and educational components of its treatment was thus underpinned by an organizational split. Though the staff of the Unit worked closely together they were divided by relationships with quite different employers.

At the time of my arrival at the Unit two factors seemed to threaten its continued existence. A financial crisis, combined with a change of policy, led Council 'A' to withdraw its support for the Unit. At the same time a debate had begun within the Clinic as to whether it should opt out of the control of the Area Health Authority and become a Trust under the provisions of the government's Health Service reforms. A draft proposal for the structure of the Clinic as a Trust was being drawn up and it had become apparent that the large Edwardian house that was used by the Unit would represent one of the Trust's most significant realizable assets. This implied that the building should either be sold to raise money for capital investment in the Clinic, or be kept in use for a purpose commensurate with its high asset value. There was doubt as to whether the Child and Family Department Day Unit could generate enough prestige and fees to justify its use of the building.

The climate of uncertainty and anxiety over the institutional status of the Unit persisted until after the end of my fieldwork in July 1994. It provided a permanent thread of controversy through all of the many staff meetings, and though finally resolved by the Clinic gaining Trust status in the autumn of 1994, the new pressures of survival in the Health Service's 'Internal Market' mean that certainty about the Unit's current institutional status is mitigated by an unpredictable market in which Education Authorities placing children at the Unit now have to pay fees which are nearly ten times what they paid when the health component's cost was being absorbed by the Health Authority.

The changes that took place between 1992 and 1994 had profound implications for the treatment ethos of the Unit as well as its institutional structure and the job security of its staff. As Council 'A' Education Authority gradually withdrew from the Unit the balance of power shifted towards the health component of its treatment. The institutional split between the Clinic and Council 'A' had maintained a balance of power between the Core Team and the Psychiatric Team. This allowed their relationship and the definition of their respective roles to remain to a certain extent uncontested. The withdrawal of Council 'A' put the Core Team on the defensive and exacerbated conflicts over roles. The Psychiatric Team were concerned to defend their role as interpreters of the children's behaviour by defining the teachers' role as primarily educational as opposed to therapeutic. The Core Team, on the other hand, criticized the Psychiatric Team for their lack of practical involvement with the children, believing that the Psychiatric Team's reluctance to spend time with the children outside their own consultations reflected their attitude that the 'educational' component of the treatment should be merely that and that the teachers and nursery nurses should not attempt to interpret the behaviour of the children.

It was in recognition of the extraordinary strains that the Unit was undergoing that the head of the Child and Family Department at the Clinic agreed for some money to be provided for a therapeutic consultation for the staff of the Unit. An outside therapist would visit the Unit to take sessions aimed at working through the difficulties of the relationship between the two teams. This move was a logical extension of the fact that the relationship between the staff groups was regarded as being one of the most significant psychodynamic entities in the life of the Unit, with the weekly meeting of the whole staff, the 'Friday Meeting', being regarded as the arena in which the psychological dynamics arising from the two teams' work with each other, and with the children, could be explored in order that they be better exploited in the service both of the children and the staff. The children's day at the Unit ended after lunch on Fridays in order to make time for this staff meeting, and the consultation took place in this Friday afternoon slot, without the children.

The first session of the consultation was in November 1993. It took place in the large Edwardian house used by the Unit, though the experience of exposing the troubles of the two teams to outside attention was difficult, and different, enough for there to be much discussion about which room in the building would be most appropriate. In the end, for want of any more suitable space, the consultations took place in the hall space where the children had their morning assembly, or 'News', and in which the Friday Meetings, which had become so bitterly contested, took place. Though there was a wish to find an alternative venue to the place of the staff's weekly battles, finally it was acknowledged that the bitterness of the split could not be escaped merely by finding another room and might as well be faced in its usual setting. The session began by everybody introducing him- or herself to the consultant, Roberta – with the exception of Mark, the psychiatric senior registrar, who arrived fifteen minutes late. Roberta said that Mark's lateness might be able to stand for everybody's reluctance to face the problems of the two teams' relationship, a role which he accepted with good humour. Roberta then set the session in motion by asking everybody to go away and draw a picture to represent their view of the Unit. Spread out in rooms throughout the Unit, the staff spent the next twenty minutes drawing pictures on large pieces of paper, then bringing them back to one of the classrooms, where Roberta hung them on the wall so that they could all be seen together. The novelty of the experience brought the whole staff together, excited comments being made about how well everybody had done to produce such interesting pictures. Roberta looked at the pictures one by one, asking for people to speculate as to who was responsible. At this stage the atmosphere was still good-humoured, the unfamiliar experience of forensic attention normally directed at the children being directed at the staff themselves causing a solidarity of defensiveness of the whole staff group against Roberta. But more negative and searching comments began as the predominant theme of the drawings became clear. What was most striking was how many of the staff had represented themselves in isolation.

Once each of the pictures had been identified the euphoria caused by the novelty of the situation began to subside. There was a general sense of shock that so many of the pictures showed only the person who had drawn them, without any reference to the wider work of the Unit. 'What a difficult job you all have, feeling so alone in your work', said Roberta, and the discussion slowly polarized in response to this observation. Members of the Psychiatric Team said that it was typical that so many of the Core Team had drawn themselves with the children without any reference either to the Psychiatric Team or to the world outside. On the other hand, the Core Team resented the fact that members of the Psychiatric Team had represented the Unit as a whole as a problem. They felt that the Psychiatric Team's detachment allowed them to view the Unit as a problem rooted in the Core Team. The meeting ended with Roberta suggesting that it was a positive step that everybody had been able to acknowledge how much they all suffer from the bad relationship between the two teams, but despite this attempt at a positive gloss the atmosphere was depressed and angry.

The consultations with Roberta continued through into 1994, with sessions arranged approximately twice a term, at irregular intervals because of the need to secure continuing funding from the Clinic. Though the sessions were unanimously felt to be very valuable, it could not really be said that they had a positive effect. What they had in common was that they always served to emphasize and polarize the split between the two teams.

Eventually Roberta suggested that there must be a reason for the staff to cling so tightly to the split; after all, in session after session they had shown more determination to identify and define it than to heal it. She suggested some reasons for the necessity of the split in the Unit. Splitting, she said, was an important concept in psychodynamic theory and work. The child split the mother's breasts between the good and the bad; the one that provides and the one that denies. The children placed at the Unit were tormented by deep splits between the good elements of their parenting and the bad elements, the abuse. Maybe it was the burden of containing such deep splits which drove the children mad, and the reason for the split between the staff teams was that they were relieving the children of the burden of unendurable splits.

Or, from another perspective, it could be thought that the children were projecting into the staff a split between the good, desired parent and the bad parent. The staff would then be, maybe a little too unwittingly, playing out the children's fantasies of warring and destructive parents.

Roberta's suggestions were welcomed by the staff, who agreed that they seemed destined to take on and to live out a deep split. But the question remained, was this a good thing? Were they amplifying the torment of the children by perpetuating the split? Might it not be more important for the children to be presented with a model of unified containing care? Was the staff split, therefore, dangerously failing the children or providing them with the invaluable opportunity of being relieved of an unendurable burden? There seemed to be no answer to this question.

Difficulties were perpetuated rather than resolved.[2] The consultation ended with the recognition that if the split between the two teams serves to relieve the children of the difficulty of living with deep internalized splits, the difficulty has only been removed to another level. The split which relieves a difficulty becomes in turn the new difficulty. Of course it is a fact that many difficulties of the work of the Unit cannot be resolved, only better endured. Every day, situations with the children confronted the staff with conflicting imperatives, imperatives that counselled intervention and non-intervention, often with equal and simultaneous urgency. The difficulty which was so characteristic of life in the Unit was the measure of being torn, or balanced, between the conflicting imperatives, and the difficulty of antagonism between the two staff teams became the paradoxical measure of solidarity in the service of the children.

Conclusion

It was clear to me as I undertook my fieldwork that I was not the only social theorist at the Unit. Indeed, at the same time as I was applying my knowledge of social theory to what I was observing, the staff of the Unit were acting out social theory in the daily business of their work. We were, truly, close intellectual cousins, and the nature of our affinities and our differences was mutually illuminating.

This affinity between social scientists and organizations has deep roots in sociological ideas about social structure. When Mary Douglas describes van Gennep's metaphor of society, 'as a kind of house divided into rooms and corridors, the compartments carefully isolated and the passages between them protected by ceremonial' (Douglas 1975: 55; van Gennep 1960), she might be describing the labyrinthine Edwardian house of the Unit, or indeed the interior of many organizations. It is important that the ethnographer is not blind to this affinity.

---

2. Similar enduring staff conflicts are described by Melissa Parker in Chapter Seven below.

The case study that I have given in this chapter is of an ethnographic context in which it was very clear that the ethnographer and the subjects of the ethnography had much in common, but it will be equally true in other organizational contexts that awareness of certain basic similarities between the ways of working of the ethnographer and of the organization will enrich the ethnographic process. Seeing others as both expert and 'folk' social theorists allows the ethnographer to be better aware of her or his own position as both specific expert and participant in a much broader tradition of social description.

References

Douglas, M. (1975), *Implicit Meanings: Essays in Anthropology*, London: Routledge & Kegan Paul.

Van Gennep, A. (1960 [1909]), *The Rites of Passage*, London: Routledge & Kegan Paul.

7

Stuck in GUM: Life in a Clap Clinic
Melissa Parker

Introduction

Over the last ten years or so anthropologists have undertaken an increasing amount of research in health-care settings in the Western world (e.g. Donegan 1998; Kayser-Jones 1990; Krause 1998; Modell 1989; Rapp 1988; Sinclair 1997; and Pulman-Jones, Chapter Six in this volume). This chapter adds to that growing literature by focusing, for the first time, on a clinic specializing in the treatment of sexually transmitted infections. The clinic is part of a teaching hospital in a British city and the fieldwork took place over a two-year period between December 1993 and December 1995. In view of the dearth of anthropological writing, the chapter is deliberately descriptive and sets out to do the following: first, to describe the atmosphere and ethos of the clinic and, second, to demonstrate the different ways in which the emergence of the viral infection HIV in the 1980s has helped to create a culture of work that is unique to clinics which have a large number of patients registered with HIV and AIDS and specialize in the treatment of other sexually transmitted infections. With respect to the latter objective, the chapter analyses conflicts between staff as well as the fears and prejudices displayed by staff towards different types of patient in order to explore the extent to which wider social fears and concerns are both warded off and acted out within the clinic.

Before engaging with these issues, I present here a brief description of the clinic. This is followed by a discussion of the type of contact I had with staff and patients with a view to generating useful background information and highlighting both the strengths and the limitations of the research findings presented in this chapter.

A Description of the Clinic

The clinic is part of the Department of Genito-Urinary Medicine which, in turn, is part of a teaching hospital. The department is often referred to by its acronym 'GUM' and it is located in a modern, three-storey building. This building is solely used for clinical practice in genito-urinary medicine and HIV medicine as well as clinical research investigating a broad range of issues. These include clinical trials documenting the relative merits of different drug combinations for the treatment of people with HIV and AIDS; research seeking to develop an effective vaccine against HIV; and research investigating and developing non-invasive screening tests for the bacterial infection chlamydia.

With respect to clinical practice, there are three clinics. Each clinic is located in a different part of the building and has a different name. The first clinic is a walk-in GUM clinic (where anyone can walk in off the street and request to see a doctor, nurse, or health adviser without prior appointment). The second clinic monitors the success of drug treatments for infections such as chlamydia and gonorrhoea (which have been diagnosed and treated at the walk-in clinic) and it also provides follow-up treatments for chronic sexually transmitted infections such as genital warts and genital herpes. The third clinic is solely for patients who have been diagnosed with HIV and/or AIDS.

All three clinics are open five days a week and they are attended by a large number of people. In July 1995, for example, more than 5,000 people came to this particular clinic and the majority (70 per cent) attended the walk-in GUM clinic. A further 18 per cent attended the second clinic and 12 per cent attended the HIV clinic. A number of other services are also provided by the clinic. These include drop-in centres for male and female prostitutes respectively. The drop-in centres provide confidential, advisory services and the staff run special clinic sessions for those prostitutes who wish to be screened and/or treated for sexually transmitted infections.

Numbers of Staff

A large number of staff are employed at the clinic (approximately 80–100 people) and, in common with many other biomedical institutions, the employment structure is shaped much like a pyramid. At the top are the consultants in HIV medicine and genito-urinary medicine and then, in ever-increasing numbers, staff are employed at the level of senior registrars, registrars, and nurses. The nursing staff outnumber the doctors by a ratio of approximately 2:1 and there are a further four to six health advisers employed at the clinic as well as a large number of administrative and clerical staff.

It should also be emphasized that the clinic has a dual hierarchical structure. That is, there is a consultant who is also responsible for all clinical practice at the clinic and a consultant/professor who is responsible for all research undertaken in the department. In theory, these two heads work closely together. In practice, their relationship is full of tension and conflict and this is not always creative or to the public's advantage. It is also interesting to note that the majority of staff employed at the clinic are in their 20s or 30s. Even the consultants are young. When I first started working at the clinic, for example, the head of clinical practice was in her late 30s and the head of research in his early 40s.

Participant Observation in the Clinic

I first became interested in the medical speciality of genito-urinary medicine when I was asked to contribute to epidemiological, microbiological, and anthropological research investigating sexual networks and the transmission of gonorrhoea. The research project was funded by the Wellcome Trust and, since it was anticipated that the majority of participants were going to be recruited at a clinic for sexually transmitted infections, I was appointed as an honorary senior research associate at the above-mentioned clinic (where the study was going to be based) to enable me to have easy access to patients.

Throughout my time at the clinic, I had two distinct roles: first, I worked as an honorary health adviser with responsibilities to provide appropriate health advice to all patients who tested positive for gonorrhoea (as well as their sexual contacts who may or may not have tested positive for gonorrhoea) and second, in my capacity as a researcher, I undertook open-ended, unstructured interviews with some of these patients both in- and outside the clinic. Interviews with patients usually took place after I had dispensed appropriate health advice in my capacity as a health adviser.

In both cases I carried a bleep and whenever a patient tested positive for gonorrhoea (or returned to the clinic for additional treatment, tests, or a research interview) a member of staff would bleep me and I would go and find the person concerned. The rationale for working in this way was to acquire (in as friendly a way as possible) an understanding of the number and type of sexual contacts each person had had and to persuade that person to introduce me to each of his or her contacts as well as to the contacts' contacts. In so doing it was hoped that it would be possible to identify sexual networks and thereby further our understanding of the transmission of gonorrhoea.

However, the majority of people either refused outright to participate in the study (usually by saying something like 'I don't want no bloody social worker') or said that they would be willing to participate but did not have time to be interviewed that day. The latter group then arranged an alternative day to meet but made themselves scarce when it came to the time of the interview. The following example captures some of the frustrations and difficulties of finding people who had recently had gonorrhoea to participate in the research (and thus highlights the near impossibility of talking to contacts and identifying sexual networks): Andrew[1] was a 20-year-old, black Caribbean heterosexual male who was diagnosed with gonorrhoea in January 1995. He reported having had five female sexual contacts in the three months prior to his diagnosis of gonorrhoea at the clinic and he seemed

---

1. The names of men and women attending the clinic, staff employed at the clinic, and the clinic itself have been altered to preserve anonymity. Similarly, information that could lead to the identification of anyone mentioned in this chapter has been modified too.

happy about participating in the research 'so long as it was not on camera'. Indeed, he gave me one of his two mobile phone numbers and willingly agreed to a date for an interview. He did not turn up at the agreed time and when I rang him at 8.00 p.m. later that day the conversation went like this:

> *A:* 'ello.
> *MP:* Oh hi, is that Andrew?
> *A:* Yeah (*this response was against a background of loud disco music and lots of conversation*).
> *MP:* It's Melissa Parker here.
> *A:* Who?
> *MP:* Melissa . . . we met briefly at the Radcliffe Centre.
> *A:* Do I know you?
> *MP:* Yeah . . . you said you'd be willing to help me with some research that we're doing.
> *A:* Oh yeah (*acknowledgement in his voice*) . . . umm . . . ring back in 10 minutes.

I rang him ten minutes later and a smart, female-sounding voice said: 'The vodafone you have called is switched off. Please try later.' The next couple of times I rang I got the same response but a week later I got through. This time a man called Mark answered and said:

> *M:* Who is that . . . who is that?
> (*To which I responded by saying:*)
> *MP:* Is Andrew there?
> *M:* No . . . who is that?
> *MP:* It's Melissa, a friend.
> *M:* (laughing) How good a friend?
> *MP:* A reasonably good friend.
> *M:* Oh well, you'll get him on 4443-883355.
> (*Hesitating, he went on to say:*)
> You're not a police officer are you? . . . um, tell him Mark gave you the number.

I rang this number at least ten times over the next few weeks and each time the telephone was switched off. At this point I called it a day. Andrew was clearly unavailable and it seemed pointless to pursue him further.

Increasingly anxious about how I was going to undertake a substantial piece of research when I could not find anyone to talk to, I thus turned my attention to two more promising areas of research: the transmission of HIV, and writing an ethnography of the clinic. The former topic was not supported by senior staff at the clinic but I pursued it vigorously, and useful and interesting material was eventually generated (see, for example, Parker *et al.* 1998; Parker 1999). The latter topic also emerged by accident. I had not been employed to write an ethnography of a clap clinic and I probably would not have kept an on-going account of events, conversations, and conflicts at the clinic if the project I had planned to work on had not been such a failure. However, the clinic proved to be an extraordinary place to work and while the culture of work undoubtedly contributed to the difficulties of identifying sexual networks and understanding the transmission of gonorrhoea, it also proved to be a fruitful avenue of research in its own right.

The Atmosphere and Ethos of the Clinic

This section attempts to capture the unique atmosphere and ethos of the clinic by focusing on four themes which are central to the organization and running of the clinic: sex and sexuality; machismo and the intolerance of sensitivity; confidentiality and anonymity; and the clinic as a market place. The writing presented under each of these headings will ultimately be used to demonstrate the different ways in which the emergence of the viral infection, HIV, has created a culture of work that is unique to this particular clinic and, in all probability, other genito-urinary medicine clinics which have a large number of patients registered with HIV and AIDS in this city.

Sex and Sexuality at the Clinic

To an outsider, one of the most striking aspects of working in a clinic for sexually transmitted diseases is that it is characterized by a sexually charged atmosphere. Indeed, it would not be an exaggeration to say that the atmosphere is more charged than any other work environment that I have ever been in and that I have ever heard anyone else describe. It is unique and it was, in fact, the first thing that struck me when I was shown around the clinic in December 1993. Indeed, one diary entry dated 20 December 1993 simply stated:

> John (a white, English, gay male nurse in his early 30s) was in the laboratory of the walk-in GUM clinic looking down a microscope at a urine sample. Stella (a white, English, research nurse in her late 20s) came up behind him and greeted him by putting her arms around his waist. She hugged herself tight against his buttocks and, playfully, pulled out the front of his trousers – heavily suggestive of the fact that she was going to put her hands down the front of them. My first thought was: 'Oh my God! Is this how people greet each other here?' And: 'I don't have to do that as well, do I?'

A month later, and still perplexed by the extent of sexually charged interactions between staff, I noted in my diary that I had overheard and/or participated in four different conversations within the space of 30 minutes. All of these conversations were full of innuendo and they either explicitly referred to a desire for sex or explicitly acknowledged sexual feelings between different members of staff. Each conversation was fairly insignificant in itself but together they drew attention to the fact that sex permeates even the most mundane thoughts and requests. The following vignettes describe some of these exchanges.

Example one A white, male, heterosexual doctor (aged about 30 years) walked into the laboratory of the GUM clinic in January 1994. He had been working at the clinic for about a week and asked one of the nurses about the whereabouts of another nurse. The nurse replied: 'Oh, he's tied up with another patient.' At this point a group of four nurses (who were also standing around in the laboratory) started to laugh and chorused 'Tied up? . . . that sounds interesting doesn't it?!' The rather innocent, fresh-faced doctor looked a bit bemused but he clearly needed to talk to the nurse in question so he persisted by saying: 'What shall I do next?' The nurses responded in a teasing manner by saying: 'Well, you could go and join in . . . you could always lie on top of them.' At this point everyone in the laboratory groaned. It was, undeniably, a weak joke.

Example two This interchange was quickly followed by a chat between Carole (a black Caribbean nurse in her early 30s) and Paul (a white English 24-year-old gay male nurse). On this particular occasion Paul was telling Carole about a conversation he had just had with a doctor called Charles. Charles was about to leave the clinic to take up a new post elsewhere and Paul found him 'very pretty'. He thus told Carole in a matter of fact way that he had said to him: 'You know, you should let me have you [consent to sex] at least once before you go.' Carole responded with exasperation and fondness in her voice: 'Oh . . . you need one of those closet things . . . so that we can lock it [penis] up and throw the key away.'

They laughed and Paul went on to ask Carole whether or not he should contact a 17-year-old male whom he had met at a club a few days previously (with a view to having sex with him). He drew attention to the fact that although the man was young he had taken the initiative by giving his telephone number to Paul and it was not as if Paul was that old himself. As he wrestled with the issue of the age of consent and power relations it struck me that he felt totally uninhibited about discussing recent sexual developments in his life with an array of staff listening in and adding their twopenny piece.

Example three At the same time as this conversation was going on, a male senior registrar hugged and kissed a male nurse in the corner of the laboratory. Several staff acknowledged the sexual exchange occurring by giving each other a nudge and a wink but they did not think it was particularly unusual. It was just their way of saying 'hello' and wishing each other a Happy New Year.

Example four I was sitting in the receptionists' work area of the downstairs walk-in GUM clinic reading a patient's notes when the following exchange took place between a Spanish male heterosexual doctor and a black Caribbean female receptionist: the doctor had asked the receptionist 'to pull' a patient's notes and she had not got round to doing it. He had thus come into the receptionist's work area to complain about not having them and in a jokey, overtly sexual manner said: 'If you're not careful I'll take you outside and show you what I've got.' The rather busty receptionist replied by saying: 'And if you're not careful, I'll take you up on your offer!' At this point all the receptionists convulsed into a fit of giggles and the doctor beat a hasty retreat.

Needless to say, I was no more exempt from the joviality and sexual comments than anyone else. Thus a psychiatrist who ran a clinic for patients with psycho-sexual problems thought nothing of saying in the corridor, at the top of his voice and surrounded by patients and staff: 'I'm more in love with you than ever, Melissa' and 'I'll submit myself to anything you require . . . just say the word.' Such comments are part of the 'anything goes' ethos and no one batted an eyelid.

Sexual banter often features in the relationships of heterosexual and gay-identified staff working in different kinds of organization in the UK. Unlike the majority of workplaces, however, it was striking that at this particular clinic a large number of sexual partnerships and friendships were established across hierarchies and that sexuality was often perceived to be a more important link with colleagues than professional status. Not surprisingly, therefore, one of the first questions that anyone asked about new members of staff was: 'Are they gay or are they heterosexual?' And, in the words of one female gay health adviser: 'The fact that sexuality is a bond across hierarchies is a big attraction of the post.'

Moreover, some of the most fiercely contested issues within the clinic reflected divisions between the 'hets' (heterosexuals) and the 'gays'. For instance, there were often discussions about whether clinics should be set up exclusively for gay men and, if they were, whether these patients should be able to choose the sexuality of their doctor and, similarly, whether staff should be able to choose the patients they worked with according to the patient's reported sexuality. So far, clinics have not been set up along these lines. This, perhaps, reflects the fact that the majority of consultants are white and heterosexual and it would never be in their interests to witness these developments (as they would have access to fewer HIV patients and this would affect their research output).

Nevertheless, it was striking that the gay male nurses frequently socialized and developed sexual relationships with the gay senior registrars, consultants, and administrative staff. Similarly, the gay female nurses socialized far more with the gay female health advisers and doctors than with other staff of similar rank within the organization. Divisions along these lines undoubtedly made the day-to-day working life of those heterosexual men who were employed at more junior levels within the clinic rather difficult. Indeed, they tended to retreat into the arms of the female receptionists at the walk-in GUM clinic as they were a group of predominantly young women in their 20s and 30s who were vigorously heterosexual.[2]

Machismo and the Intolerance of Sensitivity at the Clinic

A second issue to emerge during my time at the clinic was the fact that the staff employed at the walk-in GUM clinic and/or the HIV clinic and drop-in centres had to respond to an enormous number of difficult cases each day. In November 1995, for example, a senior registrar at the walk-in GUM clinic told me about the work he had done the previous day. Among other things, this had involved seeing three patients in the morning. The first patient had had to be told that he was HIV positive and the second patient that he had cancer of the testicles. The third patient presented with pneumonia and the doctor had to advise him to have an HIV test as he showed every sign of being HIV positive (which he was subsequently shown to be). The afternoon also proved to be difficult as he had to spend the best part of an hour with a patient who was distraught by the fact that she had genital herpes. When he was exhausted and about to go home, a patient turned up late for an appointment and intensely distressed. She had genital warts and showed signs of having been physically abused. This was, undoubtedly, a 'bad' day but it was striking that the doctor, in common with all other doctors and biomedically trained staff at the clinic, viewed the volume of difficult cases as 'all in a day's work'; and he did not convey any emotions about the volume of tragedy that he had been asked to deal with that day. In short, it would not be an exaggeration to say that a sort of machismo informed the way in which many staff talked about patients to other staff and, on occasions, the way in which they dealt with the patients themselves. The following case study illustrates this point further.

Case Study Theresa is a graduate in her mid-twenties and works at the clinic's drop-in centre for female prostitutes. She has an engaging, warm, open manner and spoke lucidly about the fact that (as with so many other units within the National Health Service) she and other staff at the centre felt under increasing stress as they were so understaffed and unsupported. Indeed, she described one particular occasion when she spent the best part of five hours trying to sort out accommodation and benefits for one of the prostitutes visiting the centre.

---

2. The fact that staff members' sexuality influenced the type of relationships they established with other staff members and the type of relationships they established with patients (see the following section for a detailed discussion of this point) reflects the growing influence of the gay lobby in influencing the provision of sexual health services, and particularly for men who are HIV positive and have been diagnosed with AIDS.

The woman had turned up in a dreadful state as she had been physically threatened by her pimp over the weekend. She described how he had threatened her with a large knife and, reliving the trauma, pulled out the knife he had used and started waving it around in the air. Theresa felt untrained and ill-equipped to deal with the situation. In fact she had been terrified by the woman's actions as no one else had been in the building at the time and she felt that the woman could easily have attacked her with it or attacked herself.

Distressed and concerned (both for herself and for other staff at the drop-in centre) Theresa made an appointment to see the business manager for GUM and HIV medicine as she wanted to use the opportunity to convey the importance of increasing the numbers of staff at the drop-in centre as well as improving security arrangements. But the manager's response was dismissive and she simply replied: 'Well, that's nothing! Jane Crowther was bitten by a patient last week!'

This, incidentally, was not a view shared by a psychiatrist who worked at the same hospital and saw Theresa for supervisory sessions once a week. He felt that an enormous load was being placed upon her (and on other staff at the centre) and commented on the fact that he saw about five such cases in a year whereas she was being asked to see about five in a week. Theresa was clearly heartened by his response as staff within the clinic rarely, if ever, responded in this way.

The intolerance of sensitivity My own experiences within the clinic also highlight this latter point. I arrived at the clinic having undertaken a large amount of research in Africa. I did not, however, have any previous experience of working within the National Health Service. I thus spent the first few weeks tracking health advisers in their day-to-day work with a view to acquiring sufficient experience to be able to see patients who had been diagnosed with gonorrhoea in my capacity as an honorary health adviser and researcher. Within six weeks of my taking on the role of a health adviser, however, a meeting was called by the health advisers with the senior management at the clinic. They were not happy about my presence within the clinic and wanted to remove my status as a health adviser. Their grounds for removal (and, therefore, the possibility of recruiting large numbers of patients to the study of sexual networks) were twofold: first, they did not think it was possible to combine the role of health adviser and researcher. They argued that patients found the dual role confusing as they were never sure where the health advice ended and the research began and this was unacceptable. The provision of quality health advice had to take precedence over everything else (though it has to be said that not a single patient had complained). Second, I was simply not the right person for the job. I was, as far as they were concerned, far too 'sensitive' and 'fragile'.

At the time, all the health advisers were female and gay and to help argue their case they drew upon the support of the business manager (a woman who was gay herself and professed to support other gay female staff at the clinic) and the consultant responsible for clinical practice within the clinic (a heterosexual woman who loathed the consultant/professor responsible for research within the clinic and had never wanted to have this particular project in the clinic in the first place).

A fierce battle took place but, in the end, they won the argument and my status as an honorary health adviser was removed . . . at least for a while. These events were, of course, most unpleasant and confusing and it was only much later that I came to understand what had happened. Briefly, the health advisers felt resentful and threatened by my presence in the clinic. They were resentful because at least one of them would have liked to be appointed to my post (but they had not applied for it as they felt they did not have the appropriate academic qualifications); and they felt threatened as my presence played to their own insecurities: I was not a nurse, I did not have a background in sexual health, and yet within a few weeks of coming to the clinic I was perceived by many staff to be doing many aspects of their work as well as they themselves. To their minds, this only confirmed their precarious and lowly status within the clinic. None of the senior management appreciated just how experienced and good they were at their work (for if they did they would have wanted to have appointed a health adviser to the post) and since the funding of clinic posts was constantly under review, they were worried that as soon as there was a financial crisis their posts would be the first to be abolished.

They could not, of course, go to senior figures within the clinic with these concerns and thus they came up with something that everyone could identify with: I was too sensitive. After all, anyone who had worked in a clinic for sexually transmitted diseases for any length of time could recognize the dangers of being too open and sensitive to other people's difficult life situations.

With respect to these problems, it is interesting to note that they were eventually resolved in a classic way: one of the most articulate, thoughtful, and influential health advisers was paid, out of grant money, to work on a closely related research project on a part-time basis. In so doing, she became fully involved in the research investigating sexual networks and the transmission of gonorrhoea. It thus became possible to rely on the strength of her ties within the clinic to ensure that contact could be made with patients who received a positive diagnosis for gonorrhoea. In other words, the problems resolved themselves and I was gradually integrated back into the life of the clinic. Within a few months my status as an honorary health adviser was reinstated and I was allowed to see patients who had been diagnosed with gonorrhoea. In fact, by the end of the study, the very people who proved so hostile to me turned out to be some of my best informants and greatest allies at the clinic.

It is also important to mention that the health advisers' concerns about their lowly status and job security were fully justified. In the summer of 1996, for instance, there was a funding crisis and, disillusioned with their position in the clinic and the increasing likelihood that some of their posts would be abolished, four of the five health advisers resigned together. The fifth health adviser resigned a few months later. These posts have not been reinstated as the view taken by the senior staff at the clinic is that health advice can be delivered just as well by doctors and nurses and that it is not necessary to fund posts solely for the purpose of handing out appropriate health advice.

Confidentiality and Anonymity at the Clinic

The third theme addressed in this section concerns the issue of confidentiality and anonymity at the clinic. The image projected to the public is that of a clinic which provides a confidential, non-judgmental service, and the staff are thus obliged to ensure that they do not discriminate by sexual orientation, ethnicity or gender. There is a substantial body of legislation as well as codes of professional conduct to support this outlook but the reality, not surprisingly, proved to be altogether different. One particularly vivid illustration of this was entered in my diary under the heading: 'Pets at the clinic' and it said:

Today I had lunch with some of the nurses and health advisers in the common room. A young, male nurse came into the room towards the end of our lunch hour and started to describe the morning's events at the downstairs walk-in GUM clinic: a man had presented himself at the clinic with an unidentified animal stuck up his anus. The tail was hanging out and he came to the clinic to ask someone to pull it out. The young nurse went on to say that he and another colleague had been in a room adjacent to the male patient when he was having it pulled out. They had managed not to laugh out loud (as they knew the walls were paper thin) but their shoulders had heaved with silent laughter.

There were at least 12 people in the common room when the nurse described this event. It was striking that amidst embarrassed, shocked, and horrified laughter, others joked. One of the health advisers, for instance, had said that the clinic should replace its current sign 'welcome to the Radcliffe Centre' with one reading 'pets are us'!

The nurse, encouraged by the laughter, went on to describe the man's clinic notes. Against the acronym LSI [last sexual intercourse] the doctor had written '?'; and against the acronym PSI [previous sexual intercourse] the doctor had written: 'chicken (dead)'. Reflecting on these notes, he then said: 'Does this mean he had sex with the chicken once it had died or that it had died after he had had sex with it?!'[3] The laughter continued but as soon as it subsided, the nurse said: 'I tried really hard to like him . . . honestly I did . . . [but] he stank of urine.' He then went on to describe how other aspects of the

---

3. A female nurse said that he should write to Sainsbury's to let them know that people are using chickens for sexual purposes as it would give a whole new angle to marketing and Christmas. She went on to say, 'You can imagine him picking up chickens' and she gestured with her hands about how it might be done, including looking at the size of the chicken's anus. Another staff member, continuing on the theme of having sex with chickens, commented on the fact that 'baste at hourly intervals' now took on whole new meanings.

patient's behaviour had really annoyed him such as the fact that it had taken him ages and ages to move from one end of the room to another. By the end of the lunchtime break, the general consensus among the staff present was that the clinic's ethos had gone out of the window as not a single person in the room had managed to be non-judgmental.

The next example also illustrates the difficulties of maintaining a non-judgmental outlook. In fact, it suggests that the nature and extent of discrimination at the clinic varied according to the gender and sexual orientation of the patients. The example concerns people who repeatedly test positive for gonorrhoea. That is, people who receive a positive diagnosis for gonorrhoea as many as three or four times over a period of several years. These people are often referred to as 'repeaters' in the epidemiological and clinical literature; and the health advice they receive is sometimes delivered in a hostile and antagonistic way. This is on the grounds that they did not appear at all concerned about the consequences of repeat infections either for themselves or for their partner(s). Unfortunately, the majority of people suffering from repeat infections at this particular clinic were black, Caribbean, heterosexual, and male. The health advisers at the clinic (who, at the beginning of the study, were all white, female, and gay) were openly hostile and aggressive about these types of people when they talked among themselves, and any patient falling into this category was quickly labelled 'Mr GC'.[4] One health adviser, elaborating on the 'Mr GC' stereotype said: 'You know the type . . . he's tall, black, carries a mobile phone, and sits with his legs splayed out so that he can trip you up whenever you walk past him in the corridor.' At this point she gestured to the crutch indicating that the shape of his balls are always revealed by the tight clothes that he wears. After a brief silence she went on to say: 'Oh yeah, and when you see him, he says, "Give us the drugs . . . I don't want no lecture".'

The health advisers' hostility, antagonism, and distress were sometimes palpable in a 'GC interview'. In January 1994, for example, I observed the following inter-action between a white English, female health adviser and a black Caribbean, heterosexual, male patient: the patient had just been diagnosed with gonorrhoea for the fourth time in two years. He appeared to be fairly nonchalant about the diagnosis. That is, he shrugged his shoulders and did not articulate any concerns about whether he had transmitted this new infection to or acquired it from any of his female contacts. He also refused to be drawn about whether he would contact any of his female sexual contacts with a view to encouraging them to come to the clinic to be tested for gonorrhoea. The health adviser became increasingly angry and frustrated with his public persona and rounded on him at the end of the interview by saying: 'If you go on like this your dick will fall off.' He left the

---

4. 'GC' is the acronym used by staff at the clinic for the bacterial infection Neisseria gonorrhoea.

consulting room a few minutes later and, despairing, she turned to me and said: 'I hate patients like that.'

It would be quite misleading to suggest that health advisers were the only group of staff to struggle with codes of professional conduct requiring a non-judgmental attitude. It would also be misleading to suggest that black Caribbean, male, hetero-sexual patients were the only group of patients to be on the receiving end of staff hostility. Moreover, there were several occasions during my time at the clinic when the confidentiality of patients was breached on an individual and collective basis. For example, the following occurrence was reported by a female doctor at one of the clinic's monthly staff meetings in 1995: a patient with an HIV diagnosis was waiting in one of the consulting rooms of the HIV clinic for a nurse to come and carry out some routine tests and noticed a piece of paper on the ground. He picked it up and realized that it was a computer print-out listing all the patients who had died while registered at the clinic with HIV. Among other things the list specified their dates of birth and TCell counts at the time of their death. The patient, not surprisingly, was upset that such sensitive and confidential information was being left on the floor for staff to kick around and he was concerned by the disrespect implied by such carelessness. The doctor reassured the staff at the meeting that a formal complaint had not been made but urged everyone 'to take great care' and not to get 'too complacent'.

In sum, there were several indications to suggest that staff struggled to provide a confidential and non-judgmental service. The marginal and least articulate patients (including the deceased) were particularly vulnerable to breaches in professional conduct. This was largely due to the fact that staff were required to see a large number of patients facing difficult and often intractable health problems each day. The culture of work promoted a robust and emotionally detached attitude to work and the difficulty of sustaining this outlook meant that some of the most vulnerable were susceptible to professional misconduct. It is also likely that the desire to create a 'safe haven' for HIV patients to retreat to, and the difficulties – if not impossibilities – of talking about the difficulties of working with some of these patients (such as men who openly talk about infecting other men) meant that anger and hostility was often displaced onto others.

Money Speaks: the Clinic as a Market Place

The final theme addressed in this section concerns the increasing tendency by staff to view the clinic as a market place. This outlook primarily reflects the impact of political and economic changes imposed upon the National Health Service in the 1980s and early 1990s but, whatever the explanation, it would not be an exaggeration to say that considerable attention is now paid to monitoring the number and type of patients attending the clinic as this influences the amount of funding received and the type of services that can be provided.

That the clinic was best viewed as competing in a 'market place' with other clinics for patients (who, incidentally, were increasingly referred to as clients) could be seen at the monthly meetings held for all staff: the first item on the agenda was an overview of the number of patients who had attended the three clinics during the previous month. On those occasions where there was an increase in the number of new patients registering at the clinic, the clinic business manager and the head of clinical practice always made a point of congratulating everyone for successfully finding and recruiting these patients. This was particularly the case with patients who had been diagnosed with HIV, as each new HIV patient brings in at least £12,000 a year. In short, more patients mean more money and this, in turn, influences the quality of services provided. Moreover, clinical staff cannot contribute to research investigating the relative merits of different drug combinations unless patients with HIV are recruited to the clinic and a reduction in numbers means a reduction in research funding (which is another important source of income to the clinic).

Another indication of the importance of maintaining, if not increasing, the number of patients registered at the clinic is the fact that information about the number of patients (and particularly HIV patients) registered at a clinic is perceived to be extremely sensitive and confidential. For example, a senior registrar in HIV medicine at the clinic told me in November 1995 that he had recently been shown around a smaller hospital with a view to applying for a consultant's post. He had not asked anyone about the number of HIV positive patients registered at the hospital – even though the post entailed caring for HIV positive patients – as to ask would somehow cast aspersions on the unit. To his mind, the very question would send out the wrong message to the appointments panel as it would suggest that he was concerned that the consultant's post might be a low-status one.

The Hunt for Patients: Outreach Work The desire to increase the number of patients registered at the clinic (and particularly patients who are HIV positive) means that staff are increasingly asked to undertake outreach work in a variety of settings. This includes attending gay clubs to hand out free condoms and leaflets about the clinic; visiting schools to provide information about sexual health; attending family-planning centres to advertise the services provided by the Department of GUM; and attending freshers' fairs at universities and further education colleges to advertise the services provided by the clinic. Similarly, considerable time and effort is put into thinking about how to attract patients to the clinic who are HIV positive but do not, as yet, know their status. For instance, the business manager asked one of the gay male senior registrars whether or not he would be willing to set up a special clinic session for men into S&M sex. This suggestion was based on the idea that men into S&M sex would probably be having high-risk sex and if they could be attracted to a clinic catering for their specialist needs then this would be a promising way of identifying new cases of HIV infection. The doctor, incidentally, was uncertain as to whether or not he should run the clinic. He felt that he was too well known on the S&M scene and that it was potentially awkward for him to see patients whom he might have met in very different contexts elsewhere. Other doctors were also concerned about the precedent that such a specialist clinic might set if this particular doctor ran the clinic, namely, that male, gay-identified doctors would feel that they could have greater claim over the gay patients and the 'het' doctors would be left with the 'het' patients. The 'het' doctors were particularly concerned by this – not because they particularly wanted to run a clinic for men into S&M sex (on the contrary, some of them could think of nothing worse) but because they wanted to have access to the gay, HIV-positive patients as their research output depended on them having access to sufficient numbers of HIV patients. To date, the clinic has not been established but it is an illustration of the thought that is given to attract new patients with undiagnosed HIV infection.

HIV at a Clinic for Sexually Transmitted Diseases

So far this paper has described the atmosphere and ethos of a clinic specializing in the treatment of sexually transmitted diseases. Wherever appropriate, attention has been drawn to the various ways in which the emergence of HIV in the 1980s has helped to create a culture of work that is unique to departments of genito-urinary medicine which have large numbers of patients registered with HIV and AIDS in Britain. This section adds to this contextual information with a view to suggesting the following: first, HIV has transformed the medical speciality of genito-urinary medicine in an extremely short period of time. Second, many of these changes have benefited the medical speciality of genito-urinary medicine but the benefits are not equally distributed. Indeed, there are several indications to suggest that the quality of care varies according to HIV status.

With respect to the first point, Allen and Hogg (1993) suggest that genito-urinary medicine was perceived to be a low-status, 'Cinderella' speciality by medics until the mid- to late 1980s. Many of my informants reiterated this point. In fact, one senior registrar expressed this view in the following way: 'The only branch of medicine that had a lower status was that which specialized in the psycho-social problems of geriatrics.'

This is no longer the case. The discovery of HIV in the 1980s and the concern that was subsequently expressed by governments and international agencies that HIV presented a major public health problem meant that substantial resources were channelled into the research, treatment, and diagnosis of this infection. With respect to the medical speciality of genito-urinary medicine this precipitated major and profound changes. Many clinics specializing in the treatment of sexually transmitted diseases were moved from old and dreary sites to modern ones and/or they were refurbished. Resources were also provided to create a large number of new clinical and/or research posts including consultant positions in HIV medicine and research professorships in HIV medicine. Moreover, the roles and responsibilities of nursing staff and health advisers also changed and this has been usefully documented in the Monks Report (1988) as well as by Allen and Hogg (1993).

However, there is a growing body of evidence to suggest that patients who are HIV positive and/or suffer from AIDS receive a quality of care that is superior to that given to patients diagnosed with non-fatal, sexually transmitted infections. The differential care (and by implication the differential status) is reflected in the use of space within the clinic as well as the types of relationship staff establish with patients. The following descriptions of the walk-in GUM clinic and the HIV clinic at The Radcliffe Centre illustrates this point further.

The Walk-in GUM Clinic

The walk-in GUM clinic is on the ground floor. It is a rather depressing place and resembles a social security benefit office. There are very few consulting rooms with natural light or windows; the air-conditioning does not work properly and space is in short supply. The health advisers' room, for instance, is about twelve feet square. It has three desks crammed into it and several large filing cabinets. There are no windows and the room is used by up to six health advisers at any one time.

Patients attending this clinic walk into a large waiting area lined with hard black plastic chairs. They take a ticket from a large paper roll attached to one of the walls and when the number on their ticket flashes up on a red digital screen they walk to the far end of the room to see one of the receptionists. Here they take a seat and the receptionist records basic social and economic information about them (such as their name, age, nationality, and current address). It is possible for three people to be registered simultaneously by three different receptionists as hessian-covered partitions ensure that patients cannot be fully seen or heard by other patients registering at the same time.

The waiting area promotes a formal and anonymous atmosphere. The receptionists wear a uniform and a distance of about three feet separates patients from the receptionists at the registration desk. They also ensure that all patients are provided with a clinic number and, in common with other staff at the walk-in clinic, never refer to a patient by name in public space.

Consultation times with doctors are scheduled to run for ten to fifteen minutes and many staff described the service provided at this walk-in clinic as a 'conveyor-belt system'. A polite and distant atmosphere characterizes the majority of interactions between staff and patients. The following account of a patient's consultation with a doctor helps to capture the routine and, at times, de-personalized nature of consultations at the walk-in GUM clinic.[5] The consultation took place in a windowless, box-like room in March 1994. The patient was about 24 years old, white, English, and male. He was called into the consulting room by a white Irish female doctor in her 30s who opened the conversation in the following way:

Dr: I'm Dr Horton and this is Dr Parker who is one of our research staff. She would like to sit in so that she can get the hang of things around here. Now, what can I do for you?

Pt: I'd like to have a blood test . . . well, actually I'd like to know if I have AIDS.
(*He then went on to say that he knew he was a bit of a hypochondriac but he had recently lost weight and was sweating a bit.*)

Dr: I have to take a full sexual history so that I can see if you are at a high or low risk for HIV . . . Do you have a regular partner?

Pt: Yes.

Dr: Girlfriend or boyfriend?

Pt: Girlfriend.

(*The doctor wrote this down and without looking up asked:*)

Dr: Roughly how many partners have you had in your lifetime?

(*The patient hesitated, so the doctor continued:*)

Dr: Tens? Hundreds? Thousands?

Pt: Hundreds.

Dr: Low or high hundreds?

Pt: . . . um, low.

Dr: You mean one hundred? Two hundred? Three hundred?

Pt: About a hundred . . . um, more maybe.

(*The doctor made a note of this while asking in a routine manner:*)

Dr: Have you ever had sex with a prostitute?

Pt: I've never had intercourse with a prostitute but I've had oral sex with one.

Dr: Have you ever had sex with anyone from South America, North America, Sub-Saharan Africa, or South-East Asia?

Pt: No . . . Oh, actually, I was in America last year and some of my partners were American.

Dr: Have you ever taken drugs intravenously?

Pt: Yes, I've had my wisdom tooth out.

(*The doctor tried to muffle her laughter and then explained that she meant injecting drugs. The patient responded that he took drugs such as grass, ecstasy, and cocaine and then anxiously told her:*)

Pt: You'll see it in my blood.

Dr: (laughing) We won't see it as we won't be looking for it. Now, I'd like you to drop your trousers and your pants to your knees.

(*Inspecting a mark on his penis, she said:*)

Dr: You have a wart.

5. It is based on notes that were taken about five minutes after the consultation ended.

> *Pt*: Does that mean I'm more likely to have HIV?
> *Dr*: It's much easier to get warts than to get HIV.
> *(The doctor then explained that he would be referred for treatment to the upstairs clinic where he would have it frozen off.)*
> *Pt*: Frozen off! (with panic in his voice) Isn't there any other way of getting rid of it?
> *Dr*: You could have it cut out!

At this point the patient agreed that it was preferable to have it frozen off and he departed in the knowledge that he would now be referred to the upstairs clinic as well as to a health adviser to discuss the full implications of having an HIV test.

The rapid fire of questions and the speed with which patients such as the one mentioned above pass through the walk-in GUM clinic is viewed by some staff as a desirable state of affairs. Others felt that a 'crap service' was provided. Either way, it could not be more different from the HIV clinic.

The HIV Clinic

The HIV clinic has a very different atmosphere to that of the walk-in GUM clinic. It is on the first floor and the reception area is bright, airy, and spacious. It is carpeted and a large number of comfortable chairs (with arm rests) are provided for patients registered at this clinic. In contrast to the walk-in GUM clinic, a warm, friendly, and informal atmosphere is promoted. The receptionists do not wear a uniform and they are on first-name terms with the majority of patients. In fact, many patients kiss the receptionists hello on arrival and it is not uncommon for nurses to hug and comfort patients if they are distressed. The clinic sessions with doctors are also run in a friendly and informal manner. Patients are able to have longer consultations of approximately thirty minutes and, if problems arise that are beyond the remit of the senior registrar or consultant, they can be referred to a number of other professionals providing in-house services such as acupuncture and nutritional advice. Advice is also available from a welfare benefits officer and, where necessary, patients can be referred for free psychiatric and psycho-therapeutic care.

Other indications of the friendly and informal atmosphere promoted by staff working at the HIV clinic include the fact that patients often refer to the waiting area as a 'good cruising joint' and 'a nice place to hang out'. In addition, the clinic organizes Christmas parties for patients attending the HIV clinic. These parties are usually held at gay venues and patients are encouraged to bring their friends and lovers. These aspects of care and attention, in combination with the regularity and duration of consultation times, often means that a rapport develops between staff and patients. Indeed, it is not unusual for patients to leave staff gifts in their wills in gratitude for the care they have received and the staff, in turn, sometimes attend their patients' funerals.

In sum, the physical environments of the walk-in GUM clinic and the HIV clinic are very different from each other. The resources available for patient care and the type of relationship that tends to develop between staff and patients also differs and there is compelling evidence to suggest that the quality of care varies according to HIV status.

Conclusion

This chapter has focused on a clinic specializing in the treatment of sexually transmitted infections. It has tried to convey the atmosphere and ethos of the clinic by focusing on four themes central to the organization and running of the clinic: sex and sexuality; machismo and the intolerance of sensitivity; the myths and realities of providing a non-judgemental and confidential service; and the increasing tendency to view the clinic as a market place. I have suggested that the identification of HIV in the 1980s and the geographical concentration of HIV infections and AIDS cases in this part of Britain have influenced every aspect of life in the clinic. A very specific culture of work has been created which, in all probability, is also found in other GUM clinics with a large number of patients registered with HIV and AIDS. I have also suggested that, within the clinic, the quality of care varies according to HIV status; and that patients with non-fatal sexually transmitted infections are sometimes treated in a hostile and dismissive manner which contrasts markedly with the high-quality care offered to patients suffering from HIV and AIDS.

References

Allen, I. and Hogg, D. (1993), *Work Roles and Responsibilities in Genitourinary Medicine Clinics*, London: Policy Studies Institute.

Donegan, E. van (1998), '"I wish a happy end": Hope in the Lives of Chronic Schizophrenic Patients', *Anthropology and Medicine*, **5**: 169–92.

Kayser-Jones, J.S. (1990), *Old, Alone, and Neglected: Care of the Aged in the United States and Scotland*, Berkeley: University of California Press.

Krause, I.-B. (1998), *Therapy across Culture*, London: Sage.

Modell, J. (1989), 'Last Chance Babies: Interpretation of Parenthood in an In Vitro Fertilization Programme', *Medical Anthropology Quarterly*, **3**: 124–38.

Monks Report (1988), *Report of the Working Group to Examine Workloads in Genito Urinary Medicine Clinics*, London: Department of Health.

Parker, M. (1999), 'HIV Transmission in Urban Environments: London and Beyond', in L. Schell and S. Ulijaszek (eds), *Human Biology in Industrialized Countries*, Cambridge: Cambridge University Press.

——, Ward, H., and Day, S. (1998), 'Sexual Networks and the Transmission of HIV in London', *Journal of Biosocial Science*, **30**: 63–83.

Rapp, R. (1988), 'Chromosomes and Communication: The Discourse of Genetic Counselling', *Medical Anthropology Quarterly*, **2**: 143–57.

Sinclair, S. (1997), *Making Doctors: An Institutional Apprenticeship*, Oxford: Berg.

Part IV
Development and Politics

8

Social Research in Rural Development Projects
David Mosse

Introduction

In this chapter I will explore some issues and dilemmas involved in undertaking ethnographic research within rural development organizations. These reflections derive from experience working as an anthropologist within rural development in different organizations in India. My particular interest, however, is not in the conventional anthropological problem of how to produce an ethnographic description of another people or place, nor even in doing an organizational ethnography, but rather in the way in which social research is undertaken by actors in and for development organizations – both 'aid workers' and those the aid organizations are attempting to help – and in the way that research is used by the actors themselves in support of their own ends. The research methods discussed are therefore, to different degrees, intended to be participatory.

After explaining something of the context of my own interest in social research in development projects, I will introduce some recently popularized participatory research methods. The use of these methods presents some interesting problems which I will explore before looking at alternative approaches to information production in rural development. A number of these are closer to the way in which anthropologists normally work. Finally, I will return to some of the problems and dilemmas of attempting social research *within* organizations, and in particular the difficulty of balancing the demands of engagement in development agencies with critical analysis of their institutional processes.

Anthropology in Development Organizations

A development project, whether concerned with agricultural improvement, rural water supply, participatory irrigation, or any other activity is a particularly complex form of organization. A project is not a bounded entity formed around consensual goals and ideas (even though it may represent itself as such), but a 'political' system in which different perspectives contend for influence and authority. It involves multiple actors and stakeholders; not only project staff and participating villagers, but also donors, consultants, bureaucrats, senior agency managers, and local government representatives, among others. Within each of these there are distinct interests, concerns, and priorities. These may be defined by gender, age, and position (field workers, project management, senior agency executives), or competing development agendas (e.g. gender equity *vs.* increasing production; poverty reduction *vs.* environmental protection).

Given these different views and the tensions between them, a project can be seen as a negotiated, but frequently unstable, operating consensus among the different players and perspectives, including those of 'villagers', farmers, or consumers – or in planning jargon, the 'primary stakeholders'. Unitary and official representations of projects often mask this complexity. A development project also involves a whole series of interfaces: farmers/project staff, fieldworkers/supervisors, staff/management, consultants/team, government/agency, among others. Each of these is a site for competing meanings. There is, then, no single perspective from which to undertake an ethnography of a development programme, or even to describe what is happening.

My own perspective comes from engagement as a development actor (manager, trainer, and consultant as well as researcher) within different types of organization and of project in India, including an international NGO, a bilateral aid agency, and various local NGOs. I have had various tasks, including the development of project design, implementation strategies, the assessment of impact, the development of policy, or the management of an office. In all of these I have been among those seeking to advance certain interpretations and meanings, specific readings of events and priorities for action, over others. Indeed, development practice involves constant negotiation, advocacy, and the strategic deployment of information as much as its production through research.

More particularly, the comments offered here derive from my experience as an anthropologist working in two different settings. The first is as part of a multi-disciplinary team supporting an agriculture project in the Bhil tribal region of western India, i.e. in the adjacent districts of Rajasthan, Gujarat, and Madhya Pradesh. The second setting is research on NGO- and state-managed irrigation development in Tamil Nadu.

My ethnographic perspective has depended considerably on my relationship to the organizations concerned. In the western India agriculture project, I have been a project 'insider'. This is an ODA/DFID-funded project with the stated objective of involving male and female members of Bhil tribal farming households in the improvement of livelihoods though work on crops, agro-forestry, small-scale irrigation, soil and water conservation, and savings and credit, and addressing the constraints of deforestation, deficit agriculture, rural indebtedness, and seasonal migration (see Jones *et al.* 1993; Mosse 1994, 1996; Mosse *et al.* 1997). I was directly involved in the design and negotiation of this project in 1990–1991. I also supported the recruitment and training of staff and the design of approaches to participatory farming-systems development from 1993, and the early formulation of village plans. Subsequently my role has been in review, monitoring, impact assessment, and ancillary social research (e.g. on livelihood strategies, tribal debt, and seasonal labour migration).

In Tamil Nadu, my relationship to irrigation development organizations has been that of a more conventional researcher, in this instance pursuing ethnographic and historical work on indigenous tank-irrigation systems. Here I have been an 'outsider' researcher, with restricted access to the internal practices of the agencies involved, whether of government, universities, or NGOs.

It is probably true to say that most of my insights into organizational processes have come from the former 'insider' role rather than the latter 'outsider' role. In other words, as an anthropologist I have learned about organizations by working within them (as adviser, consultant, or manager). This means being a reflective participant – or perhaps engaging in 'observant participation' rather than 'participant observation'.

Even within a single organization I have found my role and perspective changing significantly. This has certainly been the case with my work over seven years with the tribal farming project. Initially I was deeply involved in the mechanics of *doing*: designing, recruiting, training, supervising, etc.; once the project was established, my role began to change. I became a critical observer of actions and effects, encouraging review and reflection, acting as an advocate for field-level perspectives, providing feedback to management and donor, and influencing changes in approach as the project learned from experience. This was a task shot through with tensions and the need to negotiate or bargain for desired changes, often through forming tactical alliances with my technical colleagues.

More recently, and in part through reflective writing, these two modes – participation in, and critical reflection on, project processes – have become more separate. Indeed I have become more conscious of the two discourses and practices of development and anthropology respectively as distinct. But I do not cease to move between them, and find this journeying fruitful. Like ethnography in other cultures and places, insights come from translation, from the juxtaposition of different perspectives on the same phenomena – in this case that of development actor and critical ethnographer – and a heightened consciousness of the processes that structure our own thought. In other words, through developing a critical separateness from the project, it is possible to view my own accounts and actions as a product of the project discourse.

Let me illustrate some contrasting perspectives. In forging a new participatory and poverty-focused *agriculture* project in the early 1990s it was necessary to link activities which promised to guarantee benefits for the poorest and for women to widely endorsed views of the nature of the problem – namely low production, land fragmentation, deforestation and soil erosion, and the isolation of tribal villages from services of the state (e.g. education, health, agricultural extension, etc.). The focus of my work was on countering top-down, subsidy-driven programmes with community-based planning and action. There was a constant need to identify opportunities for farmer involvement (especially by women), to emphasize low-cost, low-subsidy interventions, and to focus on the needs and interests of the poorest, in order to ensure equity in access to benefits. In order to influence project design and strategy, it was necessary to be acquainted with local people's assumptions about the role of natural resources in livelihoods (e.g. the importance of farming, forestry, or horticulture as against artisanal activity or migrant labour), as well as knowing about the capacity of local communities to manage resources sustainably, and the need for participatory action.

But this operational perspective is one of several; it is also one which, from a different point of view, can be challenged. The poverty of tribal villagers need not be seen in terms of low production arising from pressure on land and tree resources or isolation from government services, but rather as the result of historical and political processes. Included here would be the effects of the registration of land for revenue purposes under British rule which established land as private property, and – together with stricter administration of forest land – ended an earlier tribal practice of allocating usufruct rights for unoccupied land by mutual agreement. A more sedentary form of agriculture, and the need to pay cash land tax, brought a range of intermediaries and middlemen, shopkeepers, and moneylenders into these remote areas. Today, tribal farmers are often involved in seasonal migration to urban construction sites which ties them into on-going relations of debt to moneylender/labour contractors. Rather than seeing migration as a consequence of pressure on resources, it is possible to view environmental degradation as the result of a historically specific set of political relationships which have ensured that tribal communities subsist in marginal regions. Today, labour migration is not a problem in itself. It is a central part of tribal livelihoods. What is problematic is the relationships through which farmers access informal urban labour markets, the linking of migration to debt, and the small proportion of the value of their labour which poorer migrants are able to retain. Such an analysis implies a different set of problems, a different type of strategic action, and work with different agencies (e.g. government labour offices, NGOs working in urban sites, trade unions, employers' organizations, legal aid organizations).

There is no one true perspective. Subsidies, for example, do indeed undermine local initiative, and do damage the long-term maintenance of soil and water conservation or forestry plantings, and so need to be minimized. But, from the other perspective, subsidies are to be maximized for their part in protecting a livelihood system which depends upon short-term seasonal wage labour. Viewpoints are institutionally grounded and adopted tactically in the pursuit of given goals. In fact, the role of an anthropologist in development organizations is often to combine different perspectives, and so to challenge the tendency of closure within a given analysis or narrative. The result of such efforts in this western Indian project have been, for example, to refocus attention towards debt and migration, and to break up monolithic ideas of 'community'.

Ultimately, then, the ethnography of a development institution is an ethnography of the structuring of the thought and practice of its actors (including myself); it involves direct acknowledgement of the socially mediated nature of my own knowledge and practices. But this reflexive practice has to take place within the flow of events and commitments. An active engagement in meetings, discussions, debates, arguments, or conflicts potentially involves a parallel process of self-observation, note-taking, and writing. But this is unmediated by an explicit research agenda. Indeed, it is in practice very difficult to do two things at the same time: actively to push forward an agenda, and simultaneously to reflect critically on this.

Towards the end of this chapter, I will return to the question of the tensions involved in taking (or articulating) an anthropological perspective within an organization. But these comments are really by way of personal background. What I want to focus on next are some more specific approaches or methods of social research and information production employed by organizations involved in rural development.

Social Research *by* Actors and *for* Organizations

Ethnographic research methods have been adapted for and used within, or more particularly *by*, development organizations to serve their own agendas. In these situations the role of the anthropologist changes. Rather than producing data and delivering an analysis, the researchers facilitate actors in documenting and reflecting on their own practices, whether these are the institutional practices of development workers or the agricultural practices of villagers. The aim of research is to encourage innovation and improve learning. This involves significant departures from academic modes of research.

In this section, then, I will refer to methods which have evolved largely within development rather than in academic settings. There are two clusters of methods here, which are captured under two labels: 'Participatory Learning' (also known as Participatory Rural Appraisal or PRA); and 'Process Documentation Research', or 'Process Monitoring'. These are two rather different approaches to social research in development which, for convenience, I will refer to as 'participatory' and 'process' research respectively. The first is rather better known than the second, but both potentially shift ethnographic practice in new directions. Six related points need to be made about them.

1. These research methods in different ways stress the *direct involvement of actors* (project staff, participants, or 'beneficiaries') in the production and analysis of data.

2. To different degrees, they involve *continuous information production* over a period of programme work rather than a 'snap-shot'. The focus is not on the development 'output', but on the dynamics of development processes, different perceptions of relationships, transactions, decision-making, or conflicts and their resolution in a context of change.

3. There is often an *orientation to the present*, 'an intimate relationship with what is happening right now' (Gilbert, personal communication, cited in Mosse 1998a: 10). In project-cycle terms, process research methods focus on programme *implementation* and depart from the dominance of planning or evaluation discourses in development.

Relatedly, PRA and 'process research' are explicitly *inductive* rather than deductive in orientation; that is to say, they have an open-ended concern with project contexts and happenings rather than the modelling of expected change from known inputs. While close to ethnographic common sense, this is a significant departure from those many project information systems which are structured around the monitoring of predetermined indicators. In other words the concern is with the complexity of the social life of a project rather than focusing attention on the question, 'Has input x brought about change y?'

4. 'Participatory' and 'process' research methods both have a strong *action-orientation*, which means that their outputs are, in the first instance, directed towards participants who are in a position to react to them whether 'beneficiaries' or programme managers. The feedback is often rapid, rather as the strategic adjustments during a football match. But the significance of learning by doing is not only in the immediate utility of information. There is also a methodological premise that intervention and change make visible certain structures underlying social systems which are otherwise invisible. The axiom is: '. . . if you want to know reality you must try to change it' (Volken *et al.* 1982, quoted in Uphoff 1992: 275). In other words, action-orientation makes for a better interpretative social science of practice. However, it should also be pointed out that strongly action-oriented research can also narrow the frame of reference, as indeed can planning-oriented PRA. This is one point at which (as I will explain below) 'participatory' and 'process' research diverge. The intention of the latter is not appraisal for planning, but rather to focus on events, relationships, and diverse impacts on the particular or improbable individual person, idea, or event, as well as more regular influences of contexts, roles, interests, and constraints.

5. While engaging institutional actors, research (especially process research) is situated outside of normal structures and the routine flow of programme activities and monitoring information. Indeed it is intended to by-pass the usual filtering and packaging involved in hierarchical organizations. (I will comment later on the degree to which this is possible.)

6. Finally, both participatory and 'process research' methodologies give recognition to the *inter-subjective* nature of the research process and (at least potentially) treat the perspectives and judgements of researchers, monitors, or participants as data in their own right.

Several of these developments in 'applied' social research correspond to contemporary 'post-positivist' trends in anthropology, addressing issues of both representation and relevance. There is no place for invisible, omnipresent, and unquestioningly authoritative anthropologist-narrators.

There are also several reasons why development organizations themselves are interested in more detailed knowledge of their own processes, and are increasingly willing to make use of participatory and semi-ethnographic methods. Briefly, various turns in development policy and practice make for new demands for information and qualitative analysis (cf. Mosse 1998a). In a complex series of changes in development discourse, five trends stand out. First, there has been a shift away from narrow technology-led projects towards the more complex objectives of social and institutional change. Secondly, these involve more complex management situations. Instead of the expatriate-managed technology-transfer project, international development today more commonly involves inter-organization collaboration and local networks. Thirdly, there has been a shift away from simple input-output project models and greater acknowledgement of the unpredictable and complex nature of 'development'-induced social change. Fourthly, awareness of the limits of 'blue-print' planning has led to a shift towards more flexible and iterative (repeatedly reassessed) planning approaches. Fifthly, there is now widespread support for participatory 'bottom-up' approaches to development.

These complex interrelated shifts cannot be discussed further here. It is enough to know, first, that there is growing interest in the use of qualitative and ethnographic methods within development contexts, and second, that at least some of these are employed reflexively to understand better the workings of development organizations themselves.

Let me now turn to the research methods themselves. First, I will provide a very brief introduction to currently popular participatory research methods. Then I will consider the application of these to social research in development organizations. This will raise certain critical issues which serve to introduce, 'process documentation research' as an alternative approach to reflexive organizational practice.

Participatory Learning and Action as used in Development

Participatory Rural Appraisal (PRA) has been described by one of its leading proponents, Robert Chambers, as a 'growing family of approaches and methods to enable local people to share, enhance and analyse their knowledge of life and conditions . . .'(Chambers 1997: 102). PRA methods have principally been developed for generating information for planning with rural communities. However, they can (with adaptations) be used as a means by which any group of people analyse their situation, including members of an organization.

PRA is based on certain key assumptions or principles. The first principle is that social actors are themselves the 'experts' in understanding complex inter-linkages involved in their life-situations and therefore should be involved not only in generating information (for outsider analysis and presentation) but in actually doing the analysis (using local categories). A second principle is that research techniques can be adapted for different situations and especially for the recording and representation of information by non-literate men and women. Outsider researchers need only have a limited, facilitating role. A third principle is the visual sharing of information often in the form of maps, models, or diagrams and the generation of information which is public, correctable, manipulable, and owned/verified by participants themselves. Information is retained by participants or circulated close to its point of generation through participatory record-keeping, monitoring, etc. Fourthly, information is regularly cross-checked by using more than one method to verify accounts (the principle of triangulation). A key assumption (fifthly) is that participatory research is an empowering process involving, as it does, role-reversals between the researchers and the researched. In short, PRA, as Chambers puts it involves 'rapid, progressive learning, is iterative, flexible and exploratory'.[1]

PRA Methods Themselves

So, what sort of methods are involved? As Chambers and others are quick to point out, there is no fixed set of PRA methods. Methods are rapidly evolving and innovations are constantly being made. Core methods commonly used include semi-structured and group interviewing; the recording of local histories or 'timelines'; participatory mapping and modelling (e.g. of settlements, agricultural landscapes); seasonality diagramming; and various techniques for estimating, ranking, and comparing (including 'wealth ranking', a technique to establish local criteria of social differentiation). PRA methods emphasize the use of local materials (e.g. stones or fruits as counters). The context of PRA varies enormously depending on the purpose of the exercise but often involves researchers working together with local residents through a structured set of activities, the results of which are used as a basis for planning development activities. The outputs of PRA exercises

---

1. Taken from loose sheets handed out during a PRA workshop, Seeganhalli village, Karnataka, 1989.

are important, but often the discussion and debate that surround the exercise are particularly informative.[2]

None of the research techniques used in PRA are, in themselves, fundamentally new. Most have been developed and used in other contexts first. Visual representation and informal mapping and diagramming, for example, were developed as methods for agro-systems analysis at the University of Khon Kaen in Thailand (Khon Kaen University 1987; cf. Chambers 1997: 112). The involvement of local people as researchers and experimenters and the exploration of the complexity and diversity of local farming systems was a part of farming-systems research in the 1970s and 1980s. More radical 'participation' streams within PRA derive from traditions of action-reflection research among activist NGOs in Latin America and South Asia (notably the influence of Paulo Freire's ideas of 'conscientization'). More directly influential were the approaches of the more extractive precursor to PRA, namely RRA or 'rapid rural appraisal' (which made use of group interviews, key indicators, group walks, aerial photography, chronologies of local events, portraits, and case studies) and the idea of 'indigenous technical knowledge' which was popular among development agencies in the mid-1980s. Finally, the qualitative elements of PRA – work in indigenous categories and the ideal of local residence – derive from the older tradition of anthropological participant observation (Chambers 1997).

PRA and Research in Organizational Settings: Practice and Problems

Let me illustrate with an example from Western India the kind of development context within which PRA is used. The Kribhco Indo-British Rainfed Farming Project (KRIBP) (begun in 1992 and still ongoing) is a participatory farming-systems development project situated in the Bhil tribal region of Gujarat, Madhya Pradesh, and Rajasthan. The project aims to improve the livelihoods of poor farming families by actively involving them in generating location-specific natural-resources development plans (focusing, *inter alia,* on crop improvement, soil and water conservation, agro-forestry, minor irrigation). In the early stages of this 'participatory planning', villagers and project staff jointly used PRA techniques to identify

2. There is now a large literature on different PRA methods and readers interested in details of technique or records of the experience of use of PRA are referred to the *Participatory Learning and Action Notes (PLA Notes)*, published by the International Institute of Environment and Development (London), and to the PRA/PLA information packs produced at the Institute of Development Studies, Sussex University (Brighton). There is also a critical literature which has provided a challenge to some of the claims made for PRA, or examined its practice in a little more detail. (For critical accounts see Mosse 1994, 1996; Pottier 1997; PLA Notes 1995.)

livelihood problems and workable solutions, and to negotiate project interventions. Typically, initial PRAs are rapid-research events. Small teams of project staff stay in villages for four or five days guiding villagers through a structured set of group exercises and interviews. For example, villagers develop maps or models of their neighbourhood and landscape on the ground, identifying attributes of their social and physical environment. These may be accompanied by 'transects', discussions on the constraints and opportunities in relation to natural resources while walking in different directions from a high point in the landscape. Maps and 'transect' diagrams are used, in a preliminary way, to identify problems (such as areas of soil erosion or tree loss) or opportunities for resource protection. Techniques of seasonal diagramming are used to indicate periods of shortage, cycles of debt and seasonal migration, variable availability of food or work, or the seasonal patterns of ill-health. Visual representations of trends enable discussion of changes over time in diet, yields, prices, or types of wage labour. Such discussion of trends links to the representation of local histories as 'timelines'. Techniques of matrix ranking are used to explain (to outsiders) the different types and qualities of tree or grass species, and to express preferences, and a rather specialized form of ranking based on card-sorting is used to identify local criteria of wealth and well-being. This 'wealth ranking' provides a basis for provisionally grouping households into broad socio-economic categories (e.g. 'deficit', 'self-sufficient', and 'surplus' households).

Since, as I have argued elsewhere (Mosse 1994), women face constraints in participating in PRA 'research', it proves important to work with them separately in smaller groups, often in domestic settings. Bhil women faced practical constraints to participation in PRAs in terms of the demands on their time which restricted their ability to be available collectively, at central locations, for continuous periods of time. Women (depending upon age and status) were also constrained socially in their ability to participate in activities in public spaces in the presence of outsiders. It was also rare that women were able to articulate needs or concerns which deviated from socially accepted gender roles. Finally, some of the PRA techniques themselves may have excluded women's perspectives. In early KRIBP PRAs 'the representation of knowledge and experience in maps, tables, charts and so forth involved a formality which appeared to mark it out as the province of men' (Mosse 1994: 513).

In the KRIBP project, therefore, initial general PRAs were followed by work with smaller groups of women. There were also focused PRAs dealing with specific issues (e.g. the availability of livestock, health, or fodder) which contributed to the formulation and budgeting of a programme of action.

While PRA has commonly been used by development workers in order to facilitate community-level problem analysis and planning, it has also been used for participatory research within organizations. Indeed, some techniques such as the diagramming of institutional linkages are intended to enable members of organizations (as much as 'villagers') to represent and analyse the social and work relationships in which they are engaged, spheres of influence, social proximity, distance, hierarchy, competition, and so forth. In training exercises it is common for students of these techniques to model their own institutions and their place within them.

In the teaching session on which this chapter is based, for example, a hetero-geneous student group including BA, MSc, and MPhil students from the Human Sciences Department at Brunel University used linkage and Venn diagram methods to explore different perspectives on student-department relationships. The simplest form of this exercise involves representing individuals/institutions by different-sized or -coloured circles and placing them (on the ground or on a sheet of paper) at different distances to determine importance (size) and social distance (relative position). Since the intention is often to establish significant differences of per-spective, the group divided themselves up by type of degree. (Other distinctions such as age or gender could also have been used.) The different small groups did, as expected, produce very different representations of the structure and relationships of the Department and their place within it. These different representations then provided the basis for discussion both of the research process and of the organ-izational dynamics of the Department.

Whether carried out in Indian tribal villages or among UK students, participatory research takes place in a particular social context and produces a distinctive type of information. By virtue of being participatory, these research exercises are also unusually visible: individuals work with a large group of their peers, in the presence of persons in authority (teachers, heads of department, or village leaders) and in front of outsiders (who in development settings are often resource-bearing outsiders to whom the right image has to be conveyed). In this sense participatory research is often a very *public* type of activity. The public nature of the research has a strong bearing on who participates, what is said (or drawn), and what is not said (or not drawn). (At Brunel the output of one student group was influenced by the presence of staff among them.) There may be unspoken ground rules for safe discussion, or official models of organizational behaviour from which it is difficult to depart (cf. Pottier and Orone 1995).

More generally, the way in which a group (villagers or students) represent their situation (its charted output) is a product of its own social dynamics. These dynamics are themselves produced by existing social relationships. In the case of KRIBP, the exclusion of women was only one of several ways in which PRAs came to be orchestrated locally in such a way as to exclude divergent opinions and the interests of non-dominant groups, whether these were factions, minor lineages or clans, or distant hamlets. Public expressions of community interest were capable of concealing private interests. A striking example was where – as it became apparent in retrospect – a community desire for education (expressed though the PRA event) disguised the individual interest of the village headman who wanted a hand-pump near his house. The need for education meant a school, schools came with hand-pumps, and the placing of both could be influenced locally (Mosse 1994).

With the advantage of hindsight, it is clear that, in almost all cases, initial project PRAs took place under the control of key villagers and their supporters. PRAs took place on their land or by their houses, or in public spaces or social contexts over which they held sway. These were often the same 'brokers' through whom the project had gained entry into villages, and whose interests (and those of their client groups) featured prominently in the early record of community needs and priorities. I remember being impressed in 1992 by the way in which, in one village, KRIBP fieldworkers had incorporated *bhajans* (informal devotional singing sessions) into the PRA event in order to place it within a locally understood informal context. Later it became clear that the *bhajans* had a more important social effect. It served to mark the proceedings of the PRA (and subsequent project activity) as the province of members of a *bhajan mandal* (devotional group) in the village, a group which was dominated by older men and which represented a clan-based social group (headed by the leader of one village faction) who, identifying themselves as *bhagat Bhils*, claimed a measure of separation and status superiority over other villagers. The link between PRA and *bhajans* only served to underline and exclusion of other interests in the village.

If representation of livelihood needs are shaped by local power relations they are, in an even more profound way, shaped by the assumptions, preconceptions, and interests of the development agencies and projects involved which promote them. The way in which KRIBP objectives came to be articulated through PRA has been discussed elsewhere (Mosse 1996). An important question is, how effective are PRA techniques at elucidating the very social/power relationships which structure their own outputs?

In general, participatory research has been more successful in some areas than others. In the KRIBP project in Western India, PRAs often proved very effective at generating agro-ecological information related to farming systems and watershed development. However, they were far less useful in generating an analysis of social relations: village-level patterns of dominance or dependence, credit relations, factions, conflicts, or spheres of influence. Such social knowledge was indispensable to fieldworkers who had to integrate activities aimed at enhancing production (irrigation, soil and water conservation, agro-forestry, etc.) with principles of gender equity and long-term sustainability. Indeed, a basic grasp of the social dynamics of a community – as many anthropological fieldworkers quickly realize – is necessary in order to reside and work effectively. Project fieldworkers, in their notes and diaries, often recorded their shifting perceptions of the villages in which they worked, sometimes synthesizing into diagrams their analysis of sub-groups, alliances, leadership, and influence. While these had a superficial resemblance to the linkage diagrams of PRA, they could never, in fact, have been generated *in the course of* a participatory research-event.

The strong desire of communities or organizations to represent themselves as harmonious, well integrated, or functional, means that public PRAs involve a 'micro-politics' of consensus which obscures rather than reveals local social relations. This presents a major constraint to analysis of the social relations of villages, projects, or institutions more generally through PRA-type research methods. Indeed, in work on the West India tribal project, it was through the *participant observation* of PRA events and their contexts (and *not* the direct application of PRA techniques) that elements of local power relations, and the relationship between villagers and project staff, came to be understood (as in the case of the *bhajan* group mentioned above). The best material for analysis of relationships of the 'project setting' were not found in the consensual output of chart, map, or diagram but in the absences, the gaps, the corrections, the staff interpretations, the different receptions given to male and female workers, the rewards, disagreements, conflicts, and inconsistencies (Mosse 1998a). PRAs provide critical events in which to observe social relations. This sort of joint reflection on events is where 'process' approaches to research in development agencies come in.

Process Monitoring and Documentation Methods: Examples

Conscious of the biases contained with early PRAs, in the KRIBP project, together with a colleague, Mona Mehta, I began to facilitate structured and critical reviews of PRAs to improve their usefulness for planning. At the same time we began to encourage the field teams to recall, discuss, and review other project events, working through various significant happenings, creating a history of actions, and describing these from as many dimensions and points of view as possible. Patterns of participation, the identities of prominent actors, the rationale of decisions were all considered. The events selected for discussion could be anything from the visit to an agricultural research centre, to the planning and implementation of a programme, to the theft of saplings from a project tree nursery. In what loosely resembled 'situational analysis' (van Velsen 1967), the structured review of key events/interventions helped reveal local social networks, highlighting for the project staff the significance to outcomes of factors such as clan difference, religious difference, patronage, factional conflict, and leadership struggles. As far as the staff were concerned, reflection on action generated a kind of knowledge about social relationships which was concealed in PRA events. It also focused attention on the *processes* of intervention and the role of staff themselves.

Although every case was different, there were some common patterns in the effects of early project work which helped field staff in developing entry strategies in new villages. For example, a key component of success in villages had been the development of strategies to avoid or neutralize disruption from village leadership, by identifying individuals or groups within a village having the right balance of *authority* and yet *independence from patronage*, as the starting point for programme development. In some cases, the KRIBP staff shifted away from the village leadership to more independent hamlets or clans; they found support from returned migrants; or they shifted from the older to the younger generation, finding alternative more supportive persons among sons or more often nephews of village leaders (Box 1).

Box 1: Influence and Opposition

In one Rajasthani village the headman or *tadvi*, through whom KRIBP had entered the village, began to oppose project activities, such as a crop loan scheme and the new *anganwadi* (child-care centre). He inhibited villager participation in the otherwise popular credit scheme and forbade his son from becoming a signatory of its new bank account. The crop loan scheme, unlike earlier community initiatives led by the *tadvi* (getting an electricity connection or bridge for the village), did not support his style of patronage and leadership. Indeed potentially it threatened his own money-lending (and land-mortgaging) activities. But, while the *tadvi* was able to control his son (and his daughter-in-law who had run the child-care centre before it collapsed) and indirectly to influence other villagers dependent upon him to withdraw from the programme, he was opposed by his brother's son, Lalji. This young man had the tacit support of his father, who was a man of stature in the community but was not prepared openly to come into conflict with his brother. Lalji led a group of younger men supportive of the project's interventions. Work at the hamlet level resulted in the formation of three kin-based neighbourhood groups for the purposes of crop loan repayment. These were headed by Lalji and other younger men (his cousins) normally excluded from prominence in village-level meetings. With the tacit support of older leaders, including their fathers, these young men successfully pressed ahead with the credit programme without the *tadvi* (Mosse *et al.* 1995).

As Appadurai (1989: 271–2) has pointed out, conventional interview-based research techniques (including PRA) usually attempt to capture the outcomes of events, the identifiable net outcomes of social processes: organization and leadership, structures, new linkages, input supply lines, community decisions, etc. However, many important data are manifest not in the outcome but in the quality of the transaction, in the relationships implied, and in the aspirations and expectations, as well as in the post facto outcomes (ibid.). The reviews of project activities and processes undertaken by the project focused on transactions, but unlike PRAs did not involve the villagers concerned. In that sense they arose more from participant observation than from participatory research. Despite their fruitfulness in understanding the dynamics of project-community interfaces, the monitoring of development events in the project never continued beyond the initial few facilitated sessions largely because they generated a type of information not easily assimilated to institutional interests of the project as a whole (see p. 175–6).

Elsewhere, however, the observation and recording of events by project staff or outsiders has been more systematically undertaken, in a method which has come to be known as Process Documentation Research.

Process Documentation Research

This term was first coined at a workshop in the Philippines in 1978 as a label for research into field-level implementation of a programme to improve communal irrigation by developing farmer institutions for irrigation management, which was part of the broader objective to transform the National Irrigation Authority from a government bureaucracy to an autonomous agency self-financed through water charges (Veneración 1989). Full-time social scientists took up residence in selected villages along with project staff. They attended all project activities and meetings, interviewed staff, analysed records and began detailed observation and documentation of the workings of the programme and the processes of 'water user group' formation and functioning. Detailed and daily diaries of events record the interactions of villagers and project staff and other agencies, the significance of wider processes – party political contests, leadership struggles, resistance from contractors, caste conflicts, etc. – to institutional development, the opinions, and attitudes and judgements of key project and non-project actors (notably absent from PRAs). Process documenters synthesized their observations into regular narrative reports, as well as contributing to manuals on field intervention methods (how to organize meetings, manage association funds, promote effective leadership, etc.).[3]

In the later 1980s and 1990s similar research has been initiated within programmes of 'participatory irrigation development' in Tamil Nadu and Gujarat in India and in Thailand, as well as in forestry programmes in the Philippines and Gujarat (e.g. Parthasarathy and Iyengar 1998). The precise combination of methods varies. Sometimes the 'process documentors' are members of the project team (Tamil Nadu), while at others they report separately to a research institute. In each case the primary objective is to enable the programmes as a whole to learn from implementation experience and in this light to modify strategy and policy (Mosse 1998b; Bagadion and Korten 1991). This involved programme decision-makers at project,

---

3. Documentation methods are not limited to monthly reports, but also include subject papers, working papers, newsletters. Networks and fora are important parts of some process-monitoring programmes.

national, and international (donor) levels coming together to form working groups to review information on processes. This represents a significant departure from the normal upward flow of information in development organizations.

But beyond immediate programme-implementation uses, process documentation (PD) reports allow for analysis which can challenge aid agencies' own narrow instrumental perspectives on development. The PD reports from the Tamil village of 'Nallaneri' between 1989 and 1994, for example, provided a rich record of events in the establishment of a local water-users' association (WUA) and the repair and improvement of a local tank-irrigation system under a European Commission and Ford Foundation funded programme. Among other things this record could be used to trace the shifting pattern of alliances and disputes around the new irrigation association, showing the importance of new institutions in the articulation and contestation of leadership and upper-caste honour.

The long-term process documentation showed that the significance of the water-users' association extended way beyond irrigation management and wetland agri-culture attracting the attention of urban-based kin who had no interest in cultivation at all. In fact, for a long period the WUA proved far more capable of mobilizing funds for extensive litigation (over rights to leadership) than for tank repairs, demon-strating that this, like many such associations, was an institution of village politics as well as of water management. The process documentation also traced a parallel process in which the NGO- and state-backed Association provided a major focus for low-caste social mobility. Upper-caste Mudaliar and low-caste Harijan members of the village could be seen to evoke and manipulate development ideals of 'community' in pursuit of quite separate strategies of social change. Mudaliar leaders sought to retain some measure of status and dominance by building the new WUA on an old system of privileged 'shares' (*pankus*) in tank resources clearly indicative of their caste power. Harijans, on the other hand, perceiving that this intent behind the new 'public service' roles and institutions challenged their own restricted partici-pation, withdrew their support and labour, or bargained for new privileges (including office-holding in the WUA and rights of access to tank resources) (Mosse 1997).

The Process Documentation Research employed in this case is, in fact, one of several efforts to use ethnographic methods *within* development organizations, including Laurence Salmen's approach of 'participant-observer evaluation' devel-oped in 1982–4 for work in urban Latin America (Salmen 1987). Salmen used ethnographic methods (residence and participant observation in project areas for five months plus small, focused surveys) to identify different and contrasting perceptions of achievement between beneficiaries and project professionals in World Bank urban upgrading projects. 'Process research' also bears on the concerns of a body of actor-oriented sociological work which focuses on the 'interface' between communities and development agencies (e.g. Long and Long 1992) and which further develops the 'situational analysis' of the 1960s. Equally relevant for the development of 'process research' is the renewed interest in the anthropology of organizations (Wright 1994). But what distinguishes Process Documentation Research is, first, the close and continuous recording of local programme activity and, second, its integration into development organizations and policy processes.

Process Documentation Research does, however, present a number of difficulties both as a device for influencing policy/project management and as a tool for social research. I will just comment on the latter (on the former, see Mosse 1998b). On the positive side, PDR has made policy-makers aware that development effects are socially complex and locally diverse. It has contributed understanding of matters such as leadership in villager organizations, the complexity of local-agency inter-faces, the shifting bargaining power of different groups and genders, and the functioning of resource user groups as dynamic and evolving political institutions.

But there have also been problems. Principal among them is the ambivalent status of the 'process documentor'. As external agents, process researchers meet resistance from agency staff, while as insiders they present too close an identification with the purposes of the project and lack a critical independence from the project studied. A research strategy based on long-term (six to seven years) recording of events as they happen is anyway expensive, and, even more importantly, depends upon field researchers possessing exceptional skills. They are required to have intimate knowledge of the project, good rapport, documentation skills, critical independence, and sufficient local and subject knowledge to enable interpretation of events and the attribution of significance. These are rare skills. More often there is an overemphasis on note-taking and report production as against selective observation, discussion, and analysis. (Oral reporting might in many situations provide a more useful feedback.) In Geertz's terms (1973: 7), the lack of inter-pretation means a predominance of 'thin' over 'thick' description. The notion of 'documentation' itself gives a spurious sense of objective reporting. In fact 'process documentation' is anything but a 'clear window into the rich detail of uncensored experience' (Korten 1989: 14). Selection and interpretation is the more difficult to handle because it is not explicit. Certainly there is often a narrow focus on project activities which can miss relevant local events.

Institutional Ethnography

Recently, 'process research' (of a slightly different kind) has extended beyond individual projects and programmes and been used in more complex inter-agency settings to analyse how partnerships (an increasingly important part of development practice) actually work. Lewis (1998), for example, describes attempts to undertake an 'institutional ethnography' of donor-government-NGO collaborative links involved in Bangladesh fisheries development. This involved examining inter-agency relationships through, *inter alia,* tightly structured problem-solving workshops followed by semi-structured interviews with participants, the use of tape and video to record discussions, and content analysis to mark shifting attitudes and experiences.

This institutional ethnography had two sorts of output. First, there were a number of practical effects: better adapted fisheries technology 'packages', improved inter-agency (NGO-GO) communication, and revitalized NGO networks. But second, and more critically, research began to question the whole 'partnership idea' by analysing the different motivations involved. As Lewis concludes, research indicated that the principal collaborating technical agencies 'need each other far more for the individual institutional survival of each agency than the average low-income farm household in Bangladesh needs new technology for aquaculture' (Lewis 1998: 104–5). As elsewhere, the ethnography was able to suggest how institutional needs perpetuated misperceptions of development problems (in this case portraying technology constraints rather than socio-economic issues of resources access and tenure as the principal bottlenecks of fisheries development).

In drawing attention to problems, distortions, and institutional interests underlying the discourse on 'partnership', the ethnography hit sensitivities which rapidly undermined its legitimacy. The research project was resisted and eventually closed prematurely.

Power and Information

The experience of tension in undertaking independent ethnographic analysis of development organizations is commonly reported, especially where research draws attention to the weakness of prevailing models, and points to contradictions or the gap between intention and action. But these tensions are unsurprising. The difference between ordinary ethnographic work and the sort of client-oriented ethnography I have been describing is that the latter is research which takes place *within* and *for* organizations. As such it has to contend with the fact that organizations – and especially development organizations which exist in a nexus of information, evaluation, and external funding – are, among other things, systems for the production and control of information. Development organizations have highly evolved mechanisms for filtering and regulating flows of information. Indeed it is particularly evident here that information generation and its use is inseparable from specific interests. These interests conspire to decide which versions of reality are legitimate in that, for example, they give legitimacy to chosen courses of action or existing structures. In short, contrary to the tenets of academic research, in organizational settings information is rarely viewed as a 'public good'.

There are several issues here. At the most general level very few, if any, organizations are conducive to the free flow of information. Where it falls within the domain of management control, research is likely to serve to reinforce existing perceptions, assumptions, and prevailing consensus models, or meet the organizational imperative to report success. As such it is tolerated and supported. More commonly, however, ethnographic or process documentation research modifies existing flows of information or creates new ones beyond management control. In this case, it quickly loses legitimacy, is treated as suspect, resisted, undermined, or, as in the Bangladesh fisheries case, terminated.

Moreover, there is the general problem that ethnographic work – typically exploring and revealing complexity of social relationships and the untidy business of practice – runs up against organizational needs for simplicity and to reduce complexity. Much resistance stems from the perception that research is unnecessarily wasteful of staff time and serves only to reduce the desired manageability of the social world.

It is not only those in management positions who seek to control information flows. Middle-level and field-workers often systematically withhold or distort information from senior executives and conceal poor performance. This is not only to place their own work in a good light, but also to support the claims and demands of the communities or leaders for whom they work. In short, information gets lodged in different parts of an organization, its flow is controlled, guarded, and restricted by individuals holding conflicting priorities (cf. Edwards 1994). More generally, within agencies (as in social life), information is often very clearly a private good, part of an actor's private endowment and a source and instrument of power in negotiating one's position in organizations (Baland and Platteau 1993). This means that there can be powerful individual and collective resistance to any exploration of the sorts of everyday practice in which ethnographers might be interested.

Ethnographers or 'process researchers' are not themselves independent from the relations of power within which information flows are nested. As researchers we operate within frameworks which align us to certain perspectives rather than others, we have points of entry to negotiate and confidences to maintain; and in organizational settings as 'observant participants' we may find ourselves using information strategically to pursue particular ends. The overall point is that ethnographic work in organizations makes the link between power and knowledge unusually clear, endorsing the post-positivist point that knowledge is not made valid by its relation to its object (its objectivity), nor by the consensus underlying its assertions 'but by its relation to our pragmatic interests, our communal perspectives, our needs and our rhetoric' (Baumann 1996: 4, citing Cahoon 1996; cf. Mosse 1998a: 25–6).

The loss of legitimacy that comes from separating information flows from the domain of management control is a common experience in organizational ethnography. In several cases this has ultimately led to the closure of process-monitoring programmes. This loss of legitimacy is expressed in various ways: process work is undermined, for example, when researchers face non-cooperation; it may be neutralized by lowering the status of process monitors, by denying them access to meetings or documentation, or by carefully circumscribing the areas in which they can work. Indeed, the mere fear of information leaks can make access to organizations by social science researchers extremely difficult. Arguably, this is particularly so in development organizations in which success depends so much upon interpretation and representation.

Does this make an ethnography of organizational practices in development impossible, unless pursued by a reflective 'insider', or are there alternatives? In the context of development programmes, recognition of the problems of the power-knowledge nexus has led some to abandon externally oriented analytical objectives altogether. Instead, social 'research' is used as a means for *engagement* in consensus-building *within* programmes rather than to analyse institutional performance and relationships. As the idea of independent synthetic accounts is abandoned, 'process research' takes on the role of improving performance, enhancing inter-agency understanding, advocacy, facilitation, or nurturing. Process researchers – whether they focus on the processes (meetings, etc.) of village-level user groups (e.g. forest-protection groups), of project-level teams, or of high-level steering committees – produce information in order to facilitate agreements, to hold officials to verbal agreements, to validate policy changes, or to resolve differences (cf. Mosse, Farrington, and Rew 1998). These recent experiences significantly expand the scope of social research in development.

This type of research involves work *within* existing organizational domains and attempts to shape and mould existing flows of information rather than to cut across them. In practice this means being willing to allow agencies to set the agenda, abandoning certain analytical research objectives, and being able to respond to local needs for problem-solving or the production of promotional material. Such an approach undoubtedly has some power in advancing development initiatives, in creating the necessary consensus, resolving differences, and validating progressive change in organizations. But these achievements have their price in terms of the loss of critical reflection. As such they may equally allow the perpetuation of misconceived models, may foster self-serving institutional collaboration, or may contribute to the production of usable fictions and sellable products covering over the gaps between intention and action.

Conclusion

Research in organizations tends to face in one of two directions. On the one hand, it is oriented towards critical analysis, producing an 'institutional ethnography', or an understanding of the 'architecture' of a project, including the structure of interests and motives. Research concerns here tend to be defined outside of the programme where the ultimate consumers of the information lie. On the other hand, some forms of action-research are firmly embedded in the institutions and processes they reflect upon. Their orientation is towards resolving problems, the working out of consensus, collaboration, or change within the programme setting.

While not entirely incompatible, these two orientations pull in different directions. We end therefore by revisiting the tension between analysis and engagement. This brings a dilemma. The more that the study of project processes are independent, critical, and unrestricted by organization concerns (the more ethnographic it manages to be?), the greater will be its loss of legitimacy and practicality, while the more the analysis is instrumentally focused and tied to project concerns, the less interpretative power it will have (cf. Alvesson 1993: 30, 33). Finally, this tension finds a parallel in the distinction between participatory and critical research perspectives. The more 'participatory' the analysis of communities and institutions is, the less it is likely to reveal about the social dynamics of the participants themselves.

References

Alvesson, M. (1993), *Cultural Perspectives on Organizations*, Cambridge: Cambridge University Press.

Appadurai, A. (1989), 'Small-Scale Techniques and Large-Scale Objectives', in P. Bardhan (ed.), *Conversations Between Economists and Anthropologists: Methodological Issues in Measuring Economic Change in Rural India*, Delhi: Oxford University Press.

Bagadion, B.U. and Korten, F.F. (1991), 'Developing Irrigators' Organizations: A Learning Process Approach', in M.M. Cernea (ed.), *Putting People First: Sociological Variables in Rural Development* (2nd edn), Washington: Oxford University Press for the World Bank.

Baland, J.M. and Platteau, J.-P. (1993), 'Are Economists Concerned with Power?', *IDS Bulletin*, **24**(3): 12–20.

Baumann, P. (1996), 'A Review of the Literature on Information Generation and Exchange: Implications for Process Documentation and Process Monitoring', unpublished ms., Overseas Development Institute.

Cahoon, L. (ed.) (1996), *From Modernism to Post-Modernism: An Anthology*, Oxford: Blackwell.

Chambers, R. (1997), *Whose Reality Counts? Putting the First Last*, London: Intermediate Technology Publications.

Edwards, M. (1994), 'NGOs in the Age of Information', *IDS Bulletin*, **25**(2): 117–24.

Farrington, J., Gilbert, E., and Khandelwal, R. (1998), 'Process Monitoring And Inter-Organizational Collaboration in Indian Agriculture: Udaipur District and Beyond', in D. Mosse *et al.* (eds).

Geertz, C. (1973), *The Interpretation of Cultures: Selected Essays*, New York: Basic Books.

Jones, S., Khare, J.N., Mosse, D., Smith, P., Sodhi, P.S., and Whitcombe, J. (1993), 'The Kribhco Indo-British Rainfed Farming Project: Issues in the Planning and Implementation of Participatory Natural Resource Development', *KRIBP Working Paper No. 1*, Centre for Development Studies, University of Wales, Swansea.

Khon Kaen University (1987), *Proceedings of the 1985 International Conference on Rapid Rural Appraisal*, Rural, Rural Systems Research and Farming Systems Research Projects, University of Khon Kaen, Thailand.

Korten, D. (1989), 'Social Science in the Service of Social Transformation', in C.C. Veneración (ed.).

Lewis, D. (1998), 'Partnership as Process: Building an Institutional Ethnography of an Inter-Agency Aquaculture Project in Bangladesh', in D. Mosse *et al.* (eds).

Long N. and Long, A. (eds) (1992), *Battlefields of Knowledge: The Interlocking of Theory and Practice in Social Research and Development*, London and New York: Routledge.

Mosse, D. (1994), 'Authority, Gender and Knowledge: Theoretical Reflections on The Practice of Participatory Rural Appraisal', *Development and Change*, **25**(3): 497–526.

—— (with the KRIBP Project team) (1995), 'Social Analysis in Participatory Rural Development', *PLA Notes*, **24**: 27–33.

—— (1996), 'The Social Construction of "People's Knowledge" in Participatory Rural Development', in S. Bastian and N. Bastian (eds), *Assessing Participation: A Debate from South Asia*, Delhi: Konark.

—— (1997), 'The Ideology and Politics of Community Participation: Tank Irrigation Development in Colonial and Contemporary Tamil Nadu', in R.L. Stirrat and R.D. Grillo (eds), *Discourse of Development: Anthropological Perspectives*, Oxford: Berg.

—— (1998a), 'Process-Oriented Approaches to Development Practice and Social Research', in D. Mosse *et al.* (eds).

—— (1998b), 'Process Documentation and Process Monitoring: Cases and Issues', in D. Mosse *et al.* (eds).

——, Ekande,T., Sodhi, P., Jones, S., Mehta, M., and Moitra,U. (1995), 'Approaches to Participatory Planning: A Review of the KRIBP Experience', *KRIBP Working Paper No 5*, Centre for Development Studies, University of Wales, Swansea.

——, Farrington, J. and Rew, A. (eds) (1998), *Development as Process: Concepts and Methods for Working with Complexity*, London and New York: Routledge.

——, Gupta, S., Mehta, M., Shah, V., and Rees, J. (with the KRIBP team) (1997), 'Seasonal Labour Migration in Tribal (Bhil) Western India', *KRIBP Working Paper* (mimeo), Centre for Development Studies, University of Wales, Swansea.

Parthasarathy, R. and Iyengar, S. (1998), 'Participatory Water Resources Development in Western India: Influencing Policy and Practice Through Process Documentation Research', in D. Mosse *et al.* (eds).

PLA Notes: Notes on Participatory Learning and Action. No. 24, '*Critical Reflections from Practice*', October 1995, London: International Institute for Environment and Development.

Pottier, J. (1997), 'Towards an Ethnography of Participatory Appraisal and Research', in R.L. Stirrat and R.D. Grillo (eds), *Discourses of Development: Anthropological Perspectives*, Oxford: Berg.

—— and Orone, P. (1995), 'Consensus or Cover-Up? The Limitations of Group Meetings', *PLA Notes*, **24**: 38–42.

Salmen, L. (1987), *Listen to the People: Participant-Observer Evaluation of Development Projects*, New York: Oxford University Press.

Uphoff, N. (1992), *Learning from Gal Oya: Possibilities for Participatory Development and Post-Newtonian Social Science*, Ithaca and London: Cornell University Press.

van Velsen, J. (1967), 'The Extended-Case Method and Situational Analysis', in A.L. Epstein (ed.), *The Craft of Social Anthropology*, London: Tavistock.

Veneración, C. (ed.) (1989), *A Decade of Process Documentation Research: Reflections and Synthesis*, Quezon City: Institute of Philippine Culture, Anteneo de Manila University.

Volken, H., Kumar, A., and Kaithathara, S. (1982), *Learning from the Rural Poor: Shared Experiences of the Mobile Orientation and Training Team*, New Delhi: Indian Social Institute.

Wright, S. (ed.) (1994), *Anthropology of Organizations*, London and New York: Routledge.

9

'Among Professionals': Working with Pressure Groups and Local Authorities

Simone Abram

Introduction[1]

This chapter concerns the ethnography of policy. Policy is formed within an organization – in this case local government – and it ought, therefore, to relate to anthropological discussions of organizations. The 'anthropology of organizations' has tended to imply a parallel with organizational studies – that is, the study of businesses, public bodies, governmental offices, and so on – in response to the use of the notion of 'culture' in organizational studies literature (see Wright 1994: 1). Work on local government 'organization' has tended to focus on service provision, and rarely on policy processes, despite ethnographic work from other disciplines on policy activities such as planning. However, rarely is the 'public' role in planning policy preparation brought into these ethnographic analyses, and this is the key area where anthropological experience can inform debates on 'public participation' in policy formulation. The lack of proper public voice in policy processes, particularly regarding international development, has long been of concern to anthropologists (and remains so: see Sillitoe and Bicker 1998, and Mosse, Chapter Eight of this volume). However, as I have pointed out elsewhere (1998), in cases where the lives of social groups are overwhelmed by the forces of international capital coming from outside, particularly from other countries, it is easy to feel justified in defending 'indigenous knowledge'. In the case of the local government of housing policies, the differences in local knowledges and forms of knowledge become more difficult to analyse, especially because the anthropology of development has not made a major contribution to the debate on forms of democratic government per se (with the notable exception of Robertson 1984; cf. Gardner and Lewis 1996: 68–75).

This chapter introduces an ethnography of a policy that appears in a Local Land-Use Plan for a district in the south-east of England. The focus on a specific

1. The fieldwork research referred to in this chapter was funded by the ESRC (Research Award No. 000222057). I would like to thank Jonathan Murdoch, David Gellner, and Eric Hirsch for their comments on earlier drafts.

policy allows a multi-perspective ethnography that encompasses not only the planners preparing policy, but the politicians responsible for making decisions, and multiple, competing, local residents' groups and landowners or developers attempting to influence decisions. The chapter begins with a very brief introduction to planning in England. (A similar system applies in Wales; the legislation regarding Scotland and Northern Ireland is separate.) It then moves on to introduce the setting of the ethnography, indicating the complexity of relations between competing groups, and the transformation in the expression of resistance throughout the period of policy debate. The chapter demonstrates the tension between the politics of policy-making and the technical competencies of 'experts', such as professional planners. We will explore the efforts of local pressure groups to negotiate the relationship between the politics and the techniques of planning, in the context of local competition over the future of a particular settlement under pressure for growth.

Why an Ethnography of Planning?

The planning system for housing in Britain is the arena for decisions on what gets built where. The legislation and procedures change constantly, but currently the system is hierarchical and can be described as 'plan-led'. In very simple terms, this means that the government, through the Department of the Environment, Transport, and the Regions (DETR), uses the census to forecast housing requirements over twenty-year periods, as the basis for a decision on how many new dwellings will be required in that period. These figures are passed down to county-level authorities, who generally negotiate with each other on how regional projections will be distributed. Counties then distribute their own household figures between districts.[2] Local decisions on individual applications for development permissions must then be made in accordance with prepared plans. In other words, if a plan indicates that a certain amount of development will be permitted at a certain site, permission will normally be given to whoever applies to carry out that development. Particularly in south-east England, where the pressure for development has been increasingly intense for several decades, local pressure groups are beginning to realize that if they want to retain some control over local development, or if they wish to prevent building on particular environmental sites, they must ensure that the plan does not indicate this site for development, otherwise any local enquiry will be obliged to follow the plan, often despite strong local objections. Hence, more and more local groups are getting involved in local and strategic plan-making in the name of local environmental protection.

---

2. Since local government reorganization in the late 1990s, a new and less systematic system puts districts and unitary (mostly urban) authorities together into strategic planning groups very similar to the prior counties, to produce joint strategic plans (see http://www.planning.detr.gov.uk/ppg12/7.htm).

Ethnographic research on planning is beginning to appear from within planning theory, where there is recognition of the importance of planning policy for environmental management and of the social implications of settlement policies (e.g. Yiftachel 1997), although this work owes more to the geographical than the anthropological tradition of ethnography. Foucauldian analyses of ethnographic experience are currently popular in Planning Theory debates, and some excellent ethnography focuses on the roles of key powerful actors within planning 'networks' (e.g. Flyvbjerg 1998). A few anthropologists have begun to consider the local politics of planning (e.g. Vike 1996), and this chapter suggests that it constitutes an important area for ethnographic study, since the issues under debate concern the future of not only the physical but also the social environment that many of us inhabit. We need only glance at the British local or national newspapers to find concern over new housing development, or travel around the country to see new housing estates appearing at a rapid rate on fields around all the towns and cities, and many villages as well, while in other areas houses are lying empty. Sites of Special Scientific Interest are often destroyed to build new roads, or for open-cast minerals mining, and alternative 'environmentally friendly' settlements are threatened by landlords who want to build executive housing estates for commuters. (For a particularly vivid example of this, see Holtsfield Residents' Association 1998.) All these developments are governed by planning laws, but much of the application of the law is organized through local government planning officers who subscribe to particular rationalities which make them deaf to appeals from certain quarters. This renders some citizens voiceless, not necessarily through lack of knowledge or even education and wealth, but it ensures that planning is distanced from general concerns raised by objectors through the use of limiting discourses.

Earlier research on the use of public consultation in the preparation of strategic policy raised some questions on the activity of planning (see Abram *et al.* 1996, 1997; Murdoch and Abram 1998). It was very clear that a great deal of effort was required from local residents to have even the smallest influence over local government decisions on the future of settlements through the statutory procedures for public consultation in planning-policy formulation. This raised a number of questions about participative and representative democracy. For instance, why was so much stress placed on public participation in planning when so little attention was paid to the views of people who did participate? Why did people feel the need to participate when they had elected local politicians to represent their interests? Why did planning policies appear to go against the interests of many residents? Answers to these questions might also reveal why so many more people did not participate in the preparation of planning policy, a problem that concerned many planners and politicians alike.

In any case of local authority practice, the pragmatic management of public participation, or consultation, has its roots in some much deeper questions about local democracy and political activity. Local authority officers, in this case planners, are the intermediaries between local politicians, the public and the central state authority (government), and therefore the relations between these individuals and groups are crucial to the effectiveness of any policy process. What became clear during this research project was that each of these sets of people had different understandings of development and of the environment, as well as of democracy, and that this deeply coloured both relations between them and their approaches to planning. In order to look at this more closely, I embarked on a detailed ethnography of local planning, where I examined the different perceptions of development among the various participants in planning negotiations.

Studying the Policy Process

This later project focused on the production of a new district-wide plan for a district in the county of Buckinghamshire, north-west of London. However, the research project was based neither solely in the planning office nor in a single 'community', if such a thing can be said to have substance. The focal point around which the ethnography revolved was related to a set of policies which identified a field in a village as a suitable location for the development of a housing estate whose size altered through the policy process from 300–400 houses down to around 100. The conceptual 'target' of the ethnography was binary, being both the preparation of the plan itself and notions of villageness held by residents in the village. In other words, while part of the research was recognizably 'village-based', the most important aim of the research was to record and analyse the processes by which policy was formulated by the many different, often competing, actors involved (see Wright 1995).

One of the difficulties of this ethnography, therefore, was the need to try to make contact with many different, often conflicting groups. Initially, I expected most resistance from the local authority officers, because I anticipated that their official positions would make it awkward, first, for me to persuade them to give up sufficient time to talk me and, second, for them to present anything other than the 'official line' to me about their work. In the event, however, these fears were not fully realized, possibly influenced by the fact that my employer at the time was a well-known school of Planning. Several, but not all, of the planners in the District Council offices were glad of the opportunity for reflection on their roles and activities, one not often presented to them amidst the routine everyday round of their work.

However, time spent with planners was organized formally in terms of meetings, and I was not offered access to council offices.[3] It was possible to hold informal discussions with planners on other occasions, though. A public exhibition of the

---

3. This contrasts dramatically with more recent fieldwork in Norway (2000), where full and open access was offered by a district council, which also made an office available for me as guest researcher.

draft local plan held on a bitter January day attracted only a handful of visitors, leaving plenty of opportunities for me to chat with planners and participate in their discussions about their lives and roles, as they described how they had decided to become planners, and compared careers. It was clear that contrary to what many villagers believed about planning the planners held to a belief in a 'greater good': they made clear their belief in the need for more housing for 'concealed households' and for provision to be made for changing living patterns. A striking commonality of purpose was evident among these professionals, who expressed a belief in their role as providers of housing, a basic human right, for those who needed it. Striking, also, was a level of recognition of the limits to their ability to achieve this, expressed as resignation, perhaps cynicism and a degree of ill-ease with their roles as servants to political groups they sometimes personally disagreed with.

A certain form of rationalization of this problem was also discussed. The planners explained the limitations on them as to what they could achieve. Much of this was steeped in planning discourse that could be distilled from governmental Planning Guidance Notes. For instance, I asked one planner why they should want to develop a large amount of new housing in the district's main town, and he explained that it was necessary because the government wanted four million houses built and all the other places round London are already built-up and under severe constraints, whereas the town can expand. The town has long been identified in regional guidance as a sort of 'sacrificial site' for expansion which keeps the pressure for development off the exclusive southern areas of the county (see Allen, Massey, and Cochrane 1998: 87), and the district planners began their planning approaches from this starting point.

The planners discussed the difficulty of separating professional roles from personal politics, and characterized the problems they faced in working with politicians of different parties. They joked about pompous local 'squires', recounted horror stories of right-wing bigots demanding preferential treatment over the unworthy poor, and referred to influential episodes in their personal development, including an enlightening encounter with Greenpeace, an eye-opening training course with the RSPB, and the responses from local residents to one planner's ANC and 'support the miners' car stickers. This fortuitous meeting formed the basis for continuing discussions with some of the planners who felt able to discuss planning policies with me openly and frankly. It also offered me an initial insight into the lives of the planners as whole people who often remain hidden behind their professional personae as disinterested local government servants. This contrasted strongly with the characterization of planners by many local residents as alternately misguided, incompetent, anti-environmental, or as being pawns trapped in a bureaucratic system. Here was a demonstration of the tension between the politics and techniques of planning made visible through the difficult relationships between professional planners and politicians.

Local Responses

The District Local Plan (DLP) emerged from a changing statutory planning process. Until 1995 districts were obliged to produce separate plans for urban areas and rural areas, so when new requirements appeared for district-wide local plans, the planners began to merge their existing documents with the requirements of the strategic County Structure Plan for Buckinghamshire. Plans are repeatedly updated, and new plans are often based on revisions of former plans, which makes it difficult to identify a discrete policy process. However, the preparations of the new plan for the district began when district council planners prepared a set of issues papers introducing the idea that planning for the district required an overall strategy. Much of the strategy was prescribed by central government, suggesting that new development should be concentrated in existing settlements that were well served by public transport and public facilities (shops, health and education centres, and leisure facilities). The first draft version of the plan, which went out to public consultation in 1996, contained an interpretation of that strategy which proposed to concentrate development in the main town and in the larger settlements in the rural areas. Political input to this early plan was quite understated. The council had recently ceded from Conservative to Liberal Democrat control, and many of the councillors on the planning committee were quite inexperienced, with little knowledge of planning. The full council had agreed a strategy that appeared to be environmentally orientated, promoting 'sustainable development'. Once the plan was published and awareness was raised in the district of the proposals contained within it, the politics of planning began to appear increasingly significant to the physical and social future of the District and the communities within it.

As the District Plan of the settlements proposed for further development became known to residents, a number of groups began to coalesce around certain responses to the plan. Most reaction came from one large village in the rural area of the District, which had experienced approximately a ten-fold growth in population since the 1950s. Villagers reacted in various ways to the proposals for a new housing estate on one edge of the village, and their responses could be summarized into three main positions, which we can label 'pragmatic planning', 'old villagers', and 'no growth'.

'Pragmatic Planning'

In this view, villagers with many years of experience of responding to planning proposals and enquiries recognize that the district has a large allocation of housing to find sites for. Given the district's proclaimed desire to follow a 'sustainable' planning strategy, interpreted as the preference for development in places with good public services and public transport links, it appeared inevitable that the village would be identified for further housing over the next twenty years. It was therefore in the villagers' interests to make sure that the figure allocated should be limited to a 'reasonable' amount and that it should be well situated and well designed. This view was promoted by the Village Society, some of whose members were professional planners working in other districts.

'Old Villagers'

This term was often used to describe members of families long-established in the village. As well as kinship, the implication was that 'old villagers' had personal or collective memories of life in the village prior to the massive expansions during and after the Second World War. Rather like Zonabend's description of the war forming a juncture between the endless past and the modern present (1984), villagers reflected on an earlier period when it was imagined that village families were identifiable, all villagers knew each other personally, and villagers built new houses for their growing families within the village, from local materials, particularly 'witchert' (mud and straw), a building technique used well into the twentieth century. For many of these 'old villagers' the latest round of growth was simply another step in a long process, and often they accused those protesting against it of being hypocrites: had the old villagers objected to growth in previous plans, the new protesters would not be living in the village to protest against further development.

'No Growth'

A large body of village residents responded to the prospect of further expansion with horror. The idea that a new set of green fields (currently used for crops) should start to be built on threatened their notion of living in a rural area. They imagined the countryside being 'concreted over', and the picturesque English village transformed into a suburban landscape. The site was bounded by houses on two sides and roads on the other two sides and, once part of the site was released for housing, there would be little 'rational' argument against releasing the rest of the site for housing. At stake, therefore, was not a question of a hundred houses on a few acres, but the potential for up to a thousand houses on the whole site. It would only require the council to release land for business purposes elsewhere in the village, thus creating more employment, to justify large-scale housing development, until the village became just the kind of large, impersonal town that those who had moved in over the previous ten or twenty years had consciously wanted to avoid. This argument held a powerful sway over many residents who also recognized that some of the village's services were already stretched. The health centre was in financial difficulties and was in need of another partner, although there was no room to expand its present accommodation. Waiting lists for GP appointments were increasing, with no prospect of improvement. The village primary schools were also having difficulties in accommodating certain classes with large age-cohorts (particularly at the more fashionable 'church' school) so that some class sizes were larger than normal. The idea that one hundred new families could be added to the GPs' lists and their children be included in the bulging classes seemed nonsensical. Villagers subscribing to this view began to organize into a pressure group, which adopted the title of 'Protection Society'.

Official, state-sponsored representation for the village consisted of a Parish Council and two District Councillors. The village also had a (Conservative) County Councillor, whose seat also covered some small neighbouring settlements. The Parish Council, while normally an elected body, had not had sufficient candidates to hold an election, so its members were unelected. However, far from being a list of village noteworthies, as it had been in the 'old village' days, its members represented each of the above views, including 'old villagers', incomers of long standing, and people who had moved to the village more recently. They also represented a range of party political standpoints, although all members insisted that party politics should not inform local Parish politics. Two members of the Parish Council were also local landowners, who were therefore unable to participate in any debates over the local plan, since they potentially stood to gain financially from the release of land for housing. The two district councillors, though, were both Liberal Democrats, although only one of these councillors was active during most of the preparation of the plan, the other having moved away. The latter resigned only some months later, leaving the village with only half its representation on the District Council in the interim. This appeared to be a party strategy to minimize the chances of losing the seat.

In response to previous plans, only the Parish Council and Village Society made collective objections. When the County Structure Plan was being prepared, a few years previously, the Village Society sent a delegation to the Examination in Public (a sort of informal public enquiry) to press for the removal of the mention of the village as a 'Key Rural Settlement', which they felt would lead to massive development pressures in the local plan and which had, in fact, been specifically recommended against during an earlier planning dispute by the Secretary of State (the government minister who has the final say on contested planning decisions). They were successful, although most of the other villagers were unaware of this since general awareness of structure planning was low. Broad interest in the plans only arose with the specific suggestion that a new housing estate might be built on a green field in the village, when a small 'ginger' group (i.e. a group of villagers trying to provoke interest in the issues) distributed leaflets suggesting 'thousands of houses' would come to the village, prompting a large turnout to a village meeting, at which the Protection Society was formed.

However, before it appears too neat to suggest that three groups held three different views, we must note that many of the Village Society members also joined the Protection Society. Furthermore, members of each society were on the Parish Council. As Howe has suggested (1998), resistance to powerful institutions is rarely singular, and in this case, among the 'powerful' as well as the 'weak', there was commonality and conflict. While many of those making objections could hardly be described as 'weak' in terms of education, wealth, or access to public institutions, they were still rendered relatively powerless in the planning process by the exclusivity of the planning discourse. In fact, what distinguished the groups was partly their familiarity with this discourse and associated practices, and what became evident through the plan-preparation process was the transition of pressure groups' arguments from 'common sense' to 'planning discourse' in their quest for effectiveness.

The Protection Society, beginning from a position of outrage and emotive resistance, prepared statements for villagers to send to the District Council planning office, and distributed them throughout the village. These letters suggested that the village was already bulging, and that an additional round of housing estates would urbanize the village beyond acceptability. The efficiency of this method of public-consciousness-raising was such that of some 3,000 responses to the publication of the Draft District-wide Plan, around 1,800 were from villagers, protesting at the policy to build on a green field. This action effectively put a great deal of pressure on the local politician to act in the interests of his constituents, and in doing so highlights one of the major confusions among local people over how planning policies are arrived at.

Channelling Emotions

The objections sent by village residents, along with comments on the plan from all respondents (including business groups, developers, Parish Councils, etc.) were received and collated by District Planners, whose duty was to present them to councillors with a set of recommendations as to how the Council should respond to them. It is particularly clear at this point in the consultation process how planners attempt to transform political pressures into technical arguments, a process they articulate through a specific discourse on the limitations of planning powers.

Many village residents first assumed that if 'the whole village' were to object to the policies, on the grounds of not wanting further development, then this would persuade planners that they had made a mistake in identifying the sites. However, planners were keen to point out that public consultation was not supposed to act as any kind of 'opinion poll'. One planner explained, attempting to redefine the boundaries between politics and technical limitations, as follows:

Say a thousand people wrote in and said, 'This will destroy our property values' (and that's what a lot of people have said). That will have next to no value in planning terms. And one person can even write in and say, 'You can't get access on this site because I've measured it and you can't get access because you'll have to knock down half the street' or something; that one comment will have far more weight than a thousand about property values.

This forms almost a truism in British planning: that is, first, that planning is a technical activity rather than a vehicle for public representation, and, second, that few 'members of the public' are aware of this. With this discourse, planners attempt to duck political pressures, and exclude broad social problems from their technical 'solutions' by invoking governmental limits to planning's powers and domains. Technical 'knowledge' holds inherent superiority in planning over emotional, social, psychological, or political knowledge, and the planner's explanation rationalizes and reproduces this continued preference.

This preference for 'technical' 'planning' knowledge also upholds a common planning perception of a generalized, planning-ignorant, and selfish 'public'. The notion of 'educating the public' plays an important role in the conceptual vocabulary of planning, legitimating planners' 'expert' knowledge in contrast to widespread ignorance, and justifying a common refusal, or perhaps inability, to listen to people's responses to plans by categorizing them as planning-unaware. However, many planners do recognize this as a categorization that is not universally applicable, since, as Forester (1989) argues, technical planning is only one of a range of tech- niques that planners employ; and, as one of the planners said:

> In fact, in those thousand comments, you will get a lot of planning-related comments – people aren't that stupid, they have a lot of planning-related concerns.

Despite this acknowledgement, the planner reiterated the notion that individual residents as 'members of the public' are self-interested, with reference to one of the guiding principles of planning:

> Planning is for the public interest. It's the public interest in the widest possible sphere. It's not about the residents today, with their back garden, it's about everybody's living in the future and private amenity has some part to play in that, but it can't be an over- riding concern against everything else.

The planner then backed up this assertion with a reference to Governmental papers:

> The new PPG1 [Planning Policy Guidance notes issued by the Government] – there's stuff in there about how you evaluate substantial numbers of objections and the duty of the politicians and the duty really of evaluation of proper terms so it's worth reading, that's a good document to understand where we're coming from.

This suggestion encapsulates a very powerful ideology within planning, that of the 'public interest' being served by 'strategic' decisions. This is the notion, stressed in recent planning legislation (Planning and Compensation Act 1991) that at each level of planning – national, regional, county, or local – individual planning policies and decisions are guided by 'strategic' general principles, from which good planning results will flow in logical progression. However, planners rarely stress that strategic decisions are made by politicians, quite possibly not in the interests of the 'greater public'. For instance, a strategy to concentrate development in existing urban areas could be said to be simply protecting exclusive, wealthy areas occupied mainly by people who vote for a particular party, at the expense of 'town-cramming' for those who cannot afford to move into, or to remain in, more desirable areas. However, all political decisions must be examined by government-appointed planning inspectors, and can be challenged by the Secretary of State, who can, in turn, be challenged in the High Court if decisions appear not to comply with planning legislation. The politics of planning, therefore, operate within the technical limitations of planning legislation, but within those limits (themselves set by political choices since, effectively, government makes legislation) political courses can be followed. What is clear about the relationship between planning and politics is that there is a complex interaction between the two whereby each reins in the other and, in turn, follows the other's leads.

Learning Planning Speak

Given the complexity of the relationship between politics and technical expertise in planning, and their constitution of an ignorant and self-centred 'public', any form of local resistance requires a high degree of both technical knowledge and political influence, and a great deal of perseverance. Different groups within the village demonstrated different degrees of effectiveness in this process, not merely reflecting their experience of planning. Indeed, those most experienced in planning had often become incorporated into planning discourse, thereby limiting their ability to contradict strategies and tacit assumptions implied in the technical jargon of planning.

The Village Society's approach had been to put forward sound planning principles to the planning committee, to be considered also at a public enquiry on the plan, accepting the need for the District to find housing sites, and regretting their decision to site it in the village. However, having admitted that they accepted the strategy, they had then to argue that some housing must be accepted in the village, leaving them only to argue that it must be minimized and strictly controlled. Their detailed experience of planning procedures (their advisers including a retired government planning inspector) drew them in to planning discourses concerning the demands on government to accommodate development pressure, and the factors that suggested that the village was an appropriate site for growth. It could be said that they were, to some extent, doing the planners' work for them, and translating their own feelings about the future of the village into technical planning terms themselves. This contrasted sharply with the initial broad and emotive reactions of the Protection Society.

However, since the preliminary consultation on the draft plan, the Protection Society committee had spent a great deal of time and effort (and money) investigating the rules of the planning system. They had read government guidance notes and legislation, taken advice from a planning solicitor, and joined the national Association of Small Historic Towns and Villages. They had talked to other pressure groups and canvassed support from the other villages that had raised resistance to the plans. They had also spoken with District Council planners to discuss the alternatives for the allocation of housing. While the planners had attempted to convince the villagers of their reasons for putting forward certain proposals, the Protection Society members had used the opportunity to calculate how they could reformulate their arguments to make them carry more weight. The Protection Society group began to focus on the necessity for the plan to go to a public enquiry before it could be formally 'adopted' by the District Council, and in the year between responding to the first Draft plan and the publication of the 'deposit draft' (the version of the plan that would go to public enquiry), they had developed a great deal of planning knowledge, and a new strategy. They had seized on the government's preference for the re-use of previously occupied land (so-called Brown Field Sites) over land that had not been previously built on ('Green Field Sites'). They began to argue that the District had a duty to use Brown Field sites before any Green Fields were breached, and that this applied equally to the rural parts of the district as to the urban areas. They also argued that developing the site in the village would increase traffic, since it was nearly a mile to the railway station from the site, which was at the opposite extremity of the village. They began to acknowledge that they were not completely 'anti-growth', as they accepted that 'infill' would allow an increase in village housing whether or not the new site was allowed, and that they were happy to see continued, small-scale growth. They also acknowledged, as they had from the beginning, the need for low-cost housing in the village. This latter factor was almost universally recognized in the village, as housing costs had spiralled since the 1960s, and the children from low-income homes were all obliged to move to cheaper areas to find their own accommodation.

This gradual transformation from an emotive, 'felt' argument into a calculated, 'planning' argument was noted by the local planners. For them it represented a reining in of 'emotional' response into a technically informed discourse. One commented:

If you look at the Protection Society, early on, a lot of it was irrelevant but gradually it evolved into planning-speak. They've taken on the jargon and to a degree they've taken on the thinking and they're using that, so they've matured that as an argument.

As the villagers began to translate and rationalize their arguments into a planning discourse, planners found themselves more able to 'work with' them and negotiate potential alternative policy proposals. However, in adopting this discourse, the Protection Society had to drop references to their concerns over health provision, urbanization, or the potential increase in vandalism from a growth in the number of young, unemployed residents with no meeting places or leisure facilities.

Paradoxically, planners also recognized that part of their own duty was to 'educate and inform' the public and to consult them over their future plans, and this duty must be carried out with some minimum effectiveness. Planners also have to respond to all sorts of public reactions, and they need to channel emotional responses through technical filters in order to redirect often aggressive or angry respondents. Their occasional experiences of blatant racism and snobbery lead them often to a level of cynicism over the responses they receive at public meetings. Another planner explained these two points:

If we are inconsistent in the way we consult people, then the validity of the process can be challenged in law, and maybe the plan eventually made null. So we've had that sort of fairly intelligent tactic played upon us. Individuals get very, very angry when they approach us. They find it very difficult to speak; one has to be patient in dealing with them. There are others who make threatening gestures, physically poke you. Their behaviour is basically threatening. But there are others who acknowledge that you've got a job to do, your job is to inform them and they will exploit that to the full – they will cross-examine you, but in a good-natured way, in order to get as much information. Indeed, one man said to me last week, 'Do you think I now have sufficient information to enable me to make the case against this proposal? What more can you supply that might enable me to?' There's a very telling question!

Planners' recognition that residents' views must be tutored does not prevent them from using pacifying tactics. In one instance, an angry resident came to a village planning exhibition, saying 'I know it won't make a blind bit of difference what I think about this. You're going to do it anyway aren't you? What can I do about it?' The planner quoted above let the woman rage, then stepped back towards her, saying, 'Here's what you can do: you can take one of these forms that we have brought with us today, and you can write there exactly what you think about the plans, and you can return the form to my office before the end of the consultation period. That is what you can do to have your say, and the council have a statutory duty to consider whatever you say.' This graphically demonstrates the planner's tactics in trying to channel emotional anger into technical discourse.

He was well aware that such emotional responses would not be useful in justifying the council's plan to a public enquiry, or to a planning appeal made by frustrated developers, and would therefore do little to change the policy to build in the village. While her response might possibly influence local politicians, planners are often uncomfortable with such outbursts, and try to redirect them into the technical arguments which form their professional expertise.

Planners occupy an ambiguous role in the preparation of forward plans. While they are responsible for preparing technical details and offering alternatives for politicians to choose between, they are also cast in the role of presenting the politicians' decisions to the public through these 'public consultations'. Occasionally, politicians turn up to public planning displays, known as 'surgeries', which are held in the main sites identified in the plans. As the planner explained, again:

> We have had local members [councillors] attend what we call surgeries, these local exhibitions-cum-meetings. They're not formal meetings where we make a presentation, we just make ourselves available to be questioned, to provide information and to equip people to respond to the consultation as best we can. So local members tend to turn up because they are the people, the councillors representing that particular ward. I think they're there not to promote the plan or to defend the plan, I believe they're there to gauge public opinion. Indeed, to do their job as representing those local people. But – and they play it different ways – some people say, 'Yes, I will defend you. You tell me what you want to say and I will say that at council, I will be your local representative, I will speak up for you at council.' There will be others who will say, 'I've got to hear what you've got to say, that is my job, but I'm also a member of council and a member of a corporate decision-making body, and I have to try to incorporate what you say with the interests of the greater majority.' My responsibility is not to any one community, whereas members do have responsibility to individual communities, the communities they represent. I am employed and appointed by the council to represent the council as a whole, and my interest is what I believe to be the interests of the whole of the council, trying to weigh everything, the interests of all the communities at the same time.

In this short speech, the planner reiterates his belief in 'public interest', while also disowning the plan and showing that politicians often do not assume responsibility for the 'corporate' decisions of the whole council. It is the planners' duty to justify the council's decisions through planning arguments, and they do this at surgeries and at public enquiries, even, sometimes, when they know the arguments to be, at best, 'weak'.

Politics Bite Back

In this discussion of the power of technical discourse at the expense of wider social or political interests, it is easy to imagine a technocracy dominating policy-making, against which politicians are rendered powerless. However, this is not a fair representation of the policy process. Although politicians' decisions can and are judged by judicial enquiries based on planning law, they do hold a great deal of control over detailed site allocations and individual policy. Politicians also have to play a number of roles in policy-making, attempting to take control of technical decisions, but also having to negotiate the interests of their constituents with those of other politicians from their own party groups, and those of other parties. Furthermore, District Councillors are under pressure to adopt a 'corporate' or 'strategic' Council perspective to consider the interests of the 'whole district' over their narrow sectoral interests, and adopt a role described by Councillors and officers as 'responsible' (as opposed to an 'irresponsible', localistic approach). In other words, councillors are under pressure to agree a general strategy and stick to it, whatever the consequences for their own wards. This, in particular, can lead to cynicism and mistrust from constituents who may feel that their councillor is failing to represent their interests sufficiently well, and therefore not carrying out the duties he or she was elected for. The strategic view is very problematic in local politics, precisely because it is often seen as contrary to the interests of particular sectors of constituents, and because it makes local decisions difficult for pressure groups to alter.

The adhesion to strategy effectively means that once a political approach is agreed, it is very difficult for local objectors to alter decisions, making it more important that objectors respond to strategic policies before they can know what the implications of these policies will be. The difficulties of getting people to respond to 'abstract' strategic policies is often cited by planners as an example of the public ignorance of the importance of planning, and of residents' narrow-mindedness in only caring about their locality once it is threatened, and showing no interest in broader issues. At stake here is the construction of a notional 'public' with poor planning qualities. As shorthand for this approach to planning, the acronym 'NIMBY' (Not In My Back Yard'), and variations on it, have become common currency in planning debates. The tendency of strategists and developers to dismiss any local or site-specific objections to their proposals as 'NIMBY' has reached such a level that at the beginning of debates on the plan at the local council, the chair of the planning committee requested that the term not be used, since it undermines proper consideration of all views.

In fact, the real import of a large body of objection is the pressure felt by politicians whose position as local representatives is threatened by unpopularity. Only when a large body of objections to development in the village was received by the council did the local councillor, who was at that time also standing for parliament, begin to try to dissuade his colleagues from continuing with their proposals. In an act of political bravura, he put forward a vote during a planning committee meeting to redistribute the allocation of housing for the village among several other, smaller villages, also minimizing the allocation for a small town under Conservative control, and thereby ensuring support for his proposal. Members of his own political group felt obliged to support the proposal since he was at that point the leading member of what was the leading political group. The planners were despondent: the consequences, they knew, would mean an extra year added to the timetable for preparation of the plan since the new proposals would have to be drafted with appropriate background papers and sent out for public consultation, any responses collated and debated by council, and a new draft plan prepared to reach the same position in the plan-preparation process that they thought they had already reached. While the politician may have considered the move would increase his popularity, in fact it proved to have been a highly risky manoeuvre. Many of his party colleagues were angry that he had turned away from the strategy they had spent two years preparing, that of concentrating development in the existing largest settlements, and were disappointed in the new policy which, to them, was 'unsustainable', since it proposed building houses in villages where residents would have no alternative to private car transport.

The planners were disappointed, not merely because of the extra work (which they were prepared to accept as part of their job) but because they would find difficulty in justifying this turn of events to a planning inspector at public enquiry, as it was such a transparently political move which would be almost impossible to dress up as sound planning policy, and this would make their plan vulnerable to pressure from developers to build on what they considered to be 'less sustainable' sites. They also knew the policy would be extremely unpopular in the smaller villages, and as they would be the public face of the policy, they would 'take the brickbats'. Many villagers, also, were far from satisfied with the change in allocation, since 150 houses remained in the village allocation, and were now to be considered on more than one site, which represented more sites for conflict and the dissipation of resistance. However, the amended policy was passed, written into the draft plan and taken to public consultation despite the technical objections of the planners and other politicians.

In conclusion, we can see that preparing a plan is an obstacle course through legislation, politics, and public representation. Roles are cast which are difficult to influence, and 'public consultation' is an extremely partial activity. This effectively allows the central state to effect change at the local level, by directing citizens either to adopt or struggle with the roles they have been allowed. If they argue from outside the planning discourse, they must have resort to a great deal of political influence; otherwise they must become expert in planning procedures in order to 'catch out' the planners on technical issues. While this is possible, and does happen, it requires a massive dedication of effort from citizens to become highly informed about planning techniques, for them to face professional planners whose full-time occupation is the preparation of planning policy. For developers, both tactics are adopted, but most importantly (contrary to popular opinion), the latter tactic of catching out local planning committees on technical procedural details is a common ploy. Planners know that many competing actors, including extremely articulate and experienced planning barristers acting for particular interests (especially developers or landowners), will be attempting to pick holes in their technical arguments, and they must therefore try to ensure that the politics of planning are constantly drawn back into the realm of technical detail.

Conclusions: Positioning the Ethnographer

In contrast with classic ethnographic studies, the sort of study described above requires the ethnographer not only to understand one particular group, and then represent them to the rest of the world (on a model of 'advocacy'; see Huizer 1996), but to understand the encounters between different groups. Anthropology has paid increasing attention to the encounters between groups, such as that between bureaucrat and citizen (Lipsky 1980), or between medical officer and patient. These are well-recognized examples of the encounter between forms of knowledge, but recent work has considered the relations between sub-sets of these groups, such as between groups of welfare officers (Cullen 1994) or the individuals whose work is to mediate between such groups, such as Housing Aid workers (Edwards 1994), or the relations between welfare officers and politicians (Vike 1996). In the context of ethnography of policy, there may be many different forms of social organization operating in reference to a single policy, some of which may be better defined than others. The idea of a policy network – attempting to 'map' all those who take a part in preparing a policy – indicates how complex merely identifying such actors can be (see Marsh and Rhodes 1992).

The ethnographer must become familiar with each of the different groups separately, in order to understand encounters between the groups. This presents particular problems of trust and loyalty. It has traditionally been the case that ethnographers have worked hard to gain the trust of informants from one social group, and have retained some loyalty to that group. In development encounters, this has often proved to be problematic, since anthropologists who act as advocates for a group to a development agency may find themselves without significant influence, but those who gain influence with development agencies may find their loyalty to 'their' group comes under strain. This may also be the case in studies of organizations, where ethnographers working at the lower echelons of an organization may often have to address the perception that they are 'management spies'. Indeed, when a study is commissioned by senior management, this perception may have some truth, and efforts to gain the confidence of workers may require a laying down of boundaries about what may or may not be divulged in the final report.

For anthropologists who wish to study encounters between groups, there may also be a requirement to suspend loyalty, or to retain a more neutral position.

It may or may not be possible to gain the trust of all parties to a dispute or conflict, or an anthropologist may need to split their loyalties, but the individual must decide how to respond to the tendency to be pushed into the role of mediator between groups. The role of anthropologist of policy in between groups echoes that described in the ethnography of science and technology, as the quest to conduct a 'symmetrical' analysis. It is important to distinguish between the notion that an individual can represent all sides of an argument, and the idea that they might be 'apolitical' or, more unrealistically, 'objective'. Even the most disinterested observer cannot be described as apolitical. Recent French ethnography of science has chosen to adopt a stance described as 'symmetry', which has two meanings. In relation to the ethnography of laboratories or other forms of scientific research, ethnographers like Latour (1993) have argued that scientific arguments must be incorporated into the ethnography as problematic statements, rather as beliefs or myths are in classic anthropological texts. As Latour indicates, the early sociology of knowledge only attempted to explain deviations from reason, whereas truth needed no explanation (ibid.: 92). Latour follows Serres' argument that if you want to explain flying saucers, you must be able to use the same explanation for black holes: in other words, we can only understand why some forms of explanation fail if we understand how others succeed; that is, truth and falsehood should be treated equally. Latour pushes this further, and adds another dimension to the idea of symmetry, whereby society and nature should also be incorporated equally into our analyses of the world, and the anthropologist should consider both human and nonhuman actors within the ethnography. He notes that the tendency of the West to define everyone else as having authentic cultures, whereas the West supposedly does not, is a reflection of the distinction between nature and culture central to Western self-understanding. In response to this, he argues for a symmetrical ethnography which attributes equal weight to all the different arguments of the participants to any debate. In order to represent fairly any situation, the anthropologist must not apportion weight to one argument over another, but must only trace the networks of power that lead to one argument winning out over another. There is some similarity here with the methods of Foucault, whose historical, genealogical method attempted to achieve a similar goal (see Davidson 1986). Latour therefore stresses the equality of voices between the analyst and the field, which creates a hybrid text, 'a mixture of "them" and "us", of "our" ways of talking and "theirs"' (Murdoch 1997: 751). The anthropologist is thus not apolitical but can adopt a disinterested stance, and try to follow through the process by which one particular view becomes dominant over others.

At the beginning of my study of local planning, the planners, politicians, and three residents' groups were in all conflict with each other. However, I explained the aims of my study and my desire to understand all the points of view to people in each group; all my informants took it upon themselves to offer a righteous version of the situation. In other words, most of my key informants took upon themselves the role of tutor, and by posing as an interested student, I put my informants in a position of authority within my encounters with them. However, before I conducted any interviews, I familiarized myself with each of the groups, and thereby allowed them to become familiar with me. Through participation in various local social activities, and through my presence at council meetings, my interest could be seen to be genuine, and my willingness to participate became apparent. In fact, by doing voluntary work and joining village groups, I acted as a 'good villager', and by attending council meetings, I acted as a 'good citizen', rather than simply a nosy outsider, and gained some respect from the people I wished to learn from. Moreover, through some level of shared experience, as Judith Okely has noted (1994), I was able to understand some non-verbal communication, and to appreciate those sentiments and arguments voiced by my correspondents.

As with all fieldwork, ethnographers necessarily present themselves as wishing to learn from informants. In the case of fieldwork among professionals, it is important to differentiate professional knowledge acquired during training from professional practice. Ethnographers who are qualified professionals in the field that they study have the advantages and disadvantages of the ethnographer 'at home' in that they have a depth of insight into the cultural resources of the professionals, but may be so familiar with the profession that it could be difficult to problematize some of those deep assumptions. In fact, it is often some time after fieldwork that these become apparent, since explaining your experience to other people often prompts you to rethink this experience and reformulate it according to different questions.

In most fieldwork situations, we are looking for symbols and signs of communication, which act as shorthand for more complex concepts or systems. Often these symbols are so familiar to those who use them that they do not even notice them, although they articulate a fundamental belief or practice to those people. One of the jobs of the anthropologist is to recognize these symbols or metaphors, and to problematize them, and to ask people to reflect upon them in order to make them explicit. This is in itself a political activity, since it causes people to be reflective about their own lives and language, and it may be welcome or quite offensive to the people we ask. If knowledge is power, then different kinds of knowledge offer different forms of power, including our own anthropological forms, and it is crucial that we both address this issue and acknowledge it in our ethnographic practices.

References

Abram, S. (1998), 'Introduction', in S. Abram and J. Waldren (eds), *Anthropological Perspectives on Local Development*, London: Routledge.

Abram S., Murdoch, J., and Marsden, T. (1996), 'The Social Construction of Middle England: The Politics of Participation in Forward Planning', *Journal of Rural Studies*, **12**(4): 353–64.

Abram, S., Murdoch, J., and Marsden, T. (1997), 'Planning by Numbers: Migration and Statistical Governance', in P. Boyle and K. Halfacree (eds), *Migration into Rural Areas: Theories and Issues*, Wiley: Chichester.

Allen, J., Massey, D., and Cochrane, A. (1998), *Rethinking the Region*, London: Routledge.

Cullen, S. (1994), 'Culture, Gender and Organizational Change in British Welfare Benefits Services', in S. Wright (ed.), *Anthropology of Organizations*, London: Routledge.

Davidson, A.I. (1986), 'Archaeology, Genealogy, Ethics' in D.C. Hoy (ed.), *Foucault: A Critical Reader*, Oxford: Blackwell.

Edwards, J. (1994), 'Idioms of Bureaucracy and Informality in a Local Housing Aid Office' in S. Wright (ed.), *Anthropology of Organizations*, London: Routledge.

Flyvbjerg, B. (1998), *Rationality and Power: Democracy in Practice*, tr. Steven Sampson; Chicago: University of Chicago Press.

Forester, J. (1989), *Planning in the Face of Power*, Berkeley: University of California Press.

Gardner, K. and Lewis, D. (1996), *Anthropology, Development and the Post-Modern Challenge*, London: Pluto Press.

Holtsfield Residents' Association (1998), *Holtsfield: It's Where We Belong – And Where We Plan To Stay!* http://iip.co.uk/www/holtsfield/

Howe, L. (1998), 'Scrounger, Worker, Beggarman, Cheat: The Dynamics of Unemployment and the Politics of Resistance', *JRAI* (N.S.), **4**: 531–50.

Huizer, G. (1996), 'Anthropology as Advocacy', *Etnofoor* **9**(2): 31–50.

Latour, B. (1993), *We Have Never Been Modern*, tr. C. Porter, Cambridge, Mass: Harvard University Press.

Lipsky, M. (1980), *Street-level Bureaucracy: Dilemmas of the Individual in Public Services*, New York: Russell Sage Foundation.

Marsh, D. and Rhodes, R.A.W. (eds) (1992), *Policy Networks in British Government*, Oxford: Oxford University Press.

Murdoch, J. (1997), 'Inhuman/Nonhuman/Human: Actor-Network Theory and the Prospects for a Nondualistic and Symmetrical Perspective on Nature and Society', *Environment and Planning D: Society and Space*, **15**: 731–56.

—— and S. Abram (1998), 'Defining the Limits of Community Governance', *Journal of Rural Studies*, **14** (1): 41–50.

Okely, J. (1994), 'Vicarious and Sensory Knowledge of Chronology and Change', in K. Hastrup and P. Hervik (eds), *Social Experience and Anthropological Knowledge*, London: Routledge.

Robertson, A.F. (1984), *The People and the State: An Anthropology of Planned Development*, Cambridge: Cambridge University Press.

Sillitoe, P. and Bicker, A. (1998), 'Development's Demand for Indigenous Knowledge': workshop for the 5th Biennial EASA conference, Book of Abstracts, Frankfurt.

Vike, H. (1996), 'Conquering the Unreal: Politics and Bureaucracy in a Norwegian Town', University of Oslo, Unpublished PhD thesis.

Wright, S. (1994), 'Culture in Anthropology and Organizational Studies', in S. Wright (ed.), *Anthropology of Organizations*, London: Routledge.

—— (ed.) (1994), *Anthropology of Organizations*, London: Routledge.

—— (1995), 'Anthropology, Still the Uncomfortable Discipline?', in A. Ahmed and C. Shore (eds), *The Future of Anthropology*, London: Athlone Press.

Yiftachel, O. (1997), 'Nation-Building or Ethnic Fragmentation? Frontier Settlement and Collective Identities in Israel', *Space and Polity*, **1**(2): 149–69.

Zonabend, F. (1984), *The Enduring Memory: Time and History in a French Village*, Manchester: Manchester University Press.

–10–

Understanding the Working Environment: Notes Towards a Rapid Organizational Analysis
Stella Mascarenhas-Keyes

Introduction

In recent years, anthropologists have increasingly elected or have had little choice but to obtain research or research-related work in a variety of organizational settings. Furthermore, as the sites of knowledge production and consumption have changed (Loder 1992), anthropologists will increasingly be located within organizations or funded by non-academic institutions which have their own agenda that constrains the autonomy of the researcher. Such research is invariably policy- and practice-oriented and, therefore, has to lead to recommendations for action. In order to carry out research successfully in such working environments, it is essential to understand the organizational context. I arrived at this view after a large research project called Computer Access, which I was co-ordinating, failed to achieve most of its aims because of wider problems within and between the multiple organizations involved in the project. I had not foreseen these problems partly due to lack of experience and appropriate academic training.

Prior to taking up this post, I had undertaken two research projects. The first one involved a sociological study using self-completion questionnaires of an urban population living in London. This was an independent study funded by a large, well-known, elite philanthropic organization whose role was restricted to financial oversight of the project. I undertook the study under the auspices of a small, ethnic community organization and, although I worked to a steering committee, I had a considerable degree of autonomy. My second piece of research was for my doctorate and involved fourteen months' overseas fieldwork as an autonomous researcher. I was funded by the then Social Sciences Research Council. While in the final stages of writing up the doctorate, I obtained the job of research co-ordinator of the Computer Access project in a large non-governmental organization (NGO). I was told that I was successful in the national competition because of my research background. However, as I came to realize, training and experience as an autonomous, academic researcher does not sufficiently prepare one for working within a non-academic organization. The more one understands the organizational context in which one works, the more effective the outcomes, whether this is writing a proposal for funding, implementing a research project, or negotiating the take-up of recommendations arising from social research. A detailed ethnography of an organization is only necessary if that is the major aim of the research. However, if the research is focused on a particular topic or issue which is of interest to the organization in fulfilling its overall mission, then a rapid organizational analysis of the working environment is both necessary and sufficient.

In this chapter, I briefly describe the Computer Access project and then provide an organizational checklist which researchers may find useful in order to understand the context in which they are working. I illustrate how the checklist would have helped me by reference to the Computer Access project.

Case Study: The Computer Access Project

The project was the brainchild of a non-governmental organization which I shall call Voluntary Services Council (VSC) who successfully managed to obtain a grant of half a million pounds from a borough council. The three-year Computer Access project was focused on 'disadvantaged' people who were defined as black and ethnic minorities, women, and the disabled. It aimed to look at their existing access to training and employment in the computing field, to provide, on an experimental basis, different types of computer training and to make recommendations for increased and equitable access. VSC set up its own co-ordinating team at its headquarters which I was to manage. It was agreed that five voluntary organizations who worked with particular constituencies of 'disadvantaged' people should be selected to participate in the project. In order to choose these organizations, VSC held an open competition. It asked voluntary organizations to submit a research and development proposal which would give them substantial computer hardware and software and three staff. There was tremendous competition and eventually five organizations were chosen, each focusing on a specific 'disadvantaged' community as follows:

- Roots Trust (RT) whose constituency was Afro-Caribbean
- Women and Work (WAW) whose constituency was women
- Indian Organization UK (IOUK) whose constituency was South Asians
- Star Information Technology (SIT) whose constituency lived in a specific geographical area and which comprised people from a cross-section of ethnic backgrounds
- Disability Focus (DF) whose constituency was the disabled.

In addition, two computer companies were selected to provide equipment. The organizational chart for the project is given in Figure 10.1.

Each of the five organizations had a contract with VSC which disbursed funds at regular intervals to them. As the chief executive officer, I was responsible for the design and management of the project and worked to a steering committee. This committee comprised various members of VSC staff and council, as well as representatives from each of the five organizations. The central co-ordinating unit at VSC had three staff: myself, an assistant with expertise in computing, and an administrative worker. All the five projects also had the same complement of two professional and one administrative staff and a more or less equivalent skills constellation and background. I was the first person appointed and, subsequently, was involved in the recruitment and selection of all the remaining seventeen staff. The local staff were housed at the local NGO, and were jointly managed by myself and the director or a designate of the local NGO. The framework I had planned was that the research would have a general component that was common to all local projects, and a specific component which took account of local project specificities. The computer-training component I envisaged would be undertaken within an action research model and therefore would be research-based. The selection of computer hardware and the type of training courses set up would be based on research to identify constituency 'needs'. The training programme would run in phases and be evaluated after each phase, with the results being incorporated in the next phase.

My mistake was to focus solely on the research and development side of the project: what methods to use, how to identify sample populations, how to analyse the quantitative and qualitative data, what to do with the findings, etc. I had envisaged that the project would operate on the model of autonomous research, each researcher working separately but to a common timescale and plan within a larger framework. The model was naively premised on an autonomous researcher working

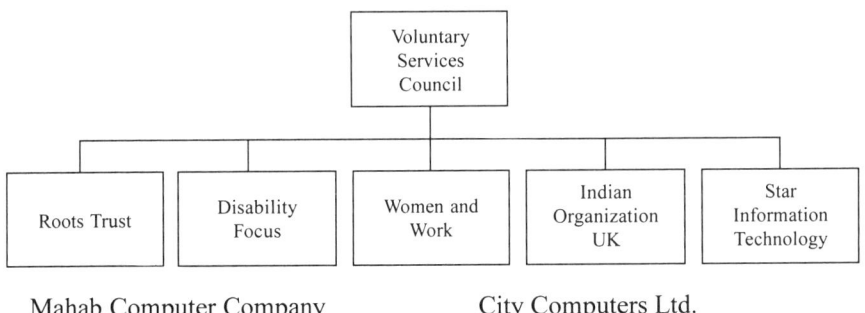

Figure 10.1 Computer Access Project

in a politically neutral context. I came to be increasingly frustrated by the personal, and inter-community and intra-community micro-politics, and the often irreconcilable, competing demands of the multiple organizations. I wrongly, and in hindsight arrogantly, thought that such behaviour was deviant and the fault of ignorant people who did not understand what constituted 'proper research'. In order to understand the institutional and political complexity and work effectively within such a dynamic context, I should have raised certain questions and undertaken a rapid organizational analysis using a checklist of the type I am now going to discuss.

Type of Organization: What Types of Organization are Involved in the Project?

There is considerable confusion generally as to what is meant by the label NGO. In its widest sense it includes: relief and welfare agencies, technical innovation organizations, public service contractors, popular development organizations, grassroots development organizations, advocacy groups and networks. Part of the problem is that the classification does not fully differentiate between the function, ownership, and scale of operation as part of a subcategorization of these organizations. As a result, everything from a neighbourhood organization concerned with better lighting through to an organization operating globally, such as Oxfam, is equally labelled NGO.

It may be helpful, therefore, to distinguish between two types of NGO:

- membership organizations staffed and elected by the people they are meant to serve and represent (such as farmer organizations or parent-teacher associations in schools).
- non-membership organizations staffed by people who are socially, professionally, and at times ethnically different from their clients.

In the VSC project, all the NGOs were non-membership organizations staffed by middle-class professionals. Some of them worked with membership organizations: for instance, WAW worked with a women's group – a membership organization – from a deprived housing estate.

Organizational Structure: What are the Structures of the Organizations I am working with and what is my Location within them?

Information about the structure of an organization may exist in publicity brochures. It will give some idea of the scope and complexity of the organization, and, for instance, whether there are specialist departments dealing with different activities (see Figures 10.2a-d). Role, task differentiation, chain of commands, and reporting arrangements vary considerably between organizations.

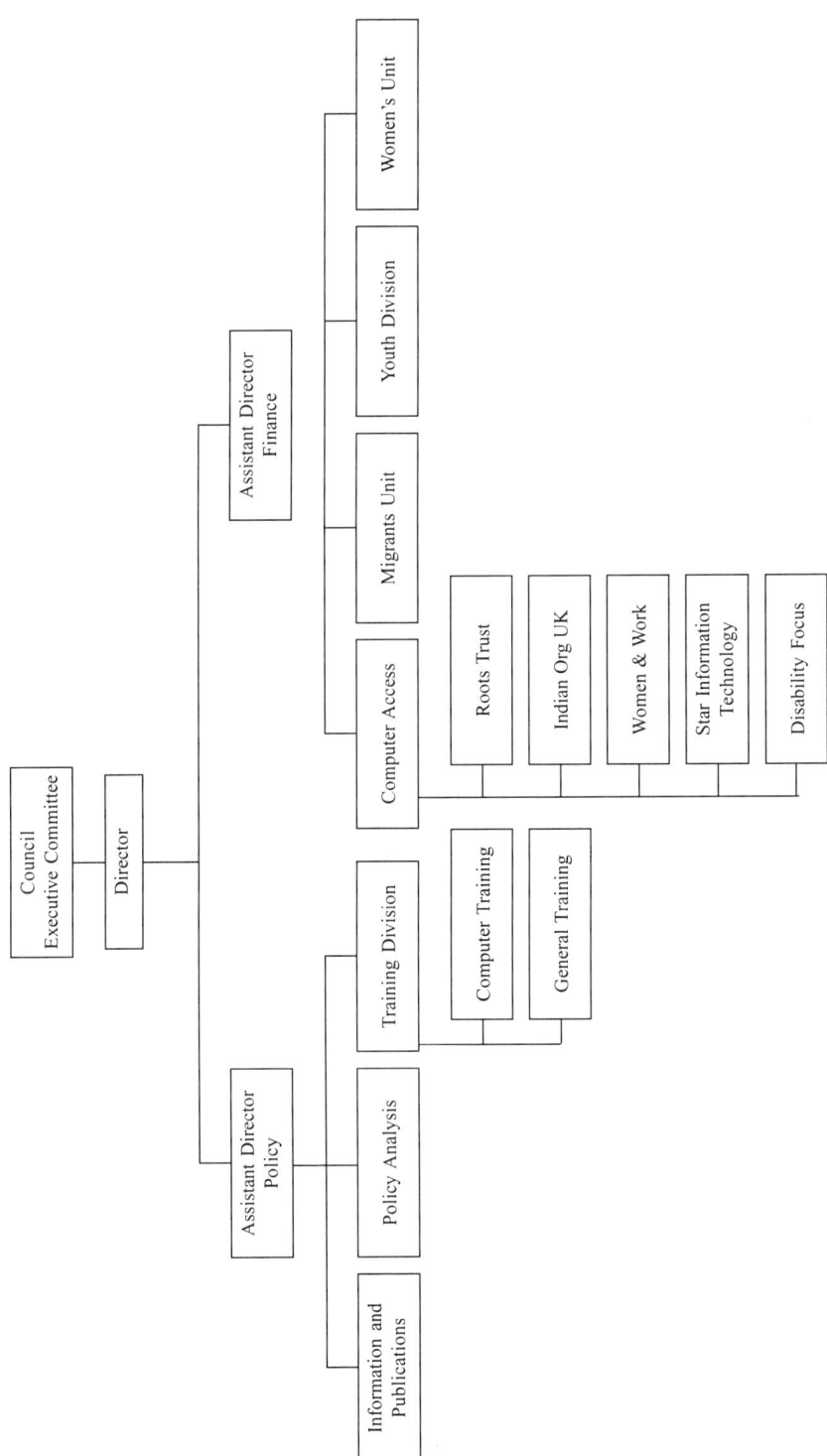

Figure 10.2a Voluntary Services Council: Organizational Structure

— 209 —

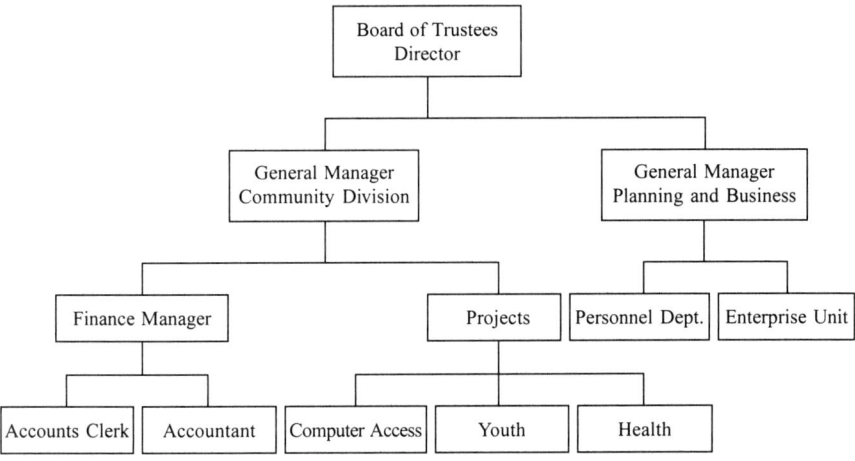

Figure 10.2b Roots Trust

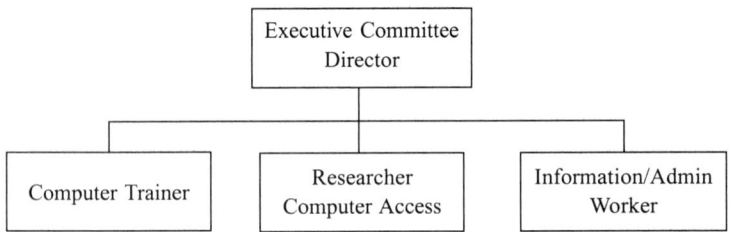

Figure 10.2c Indian Organization UK

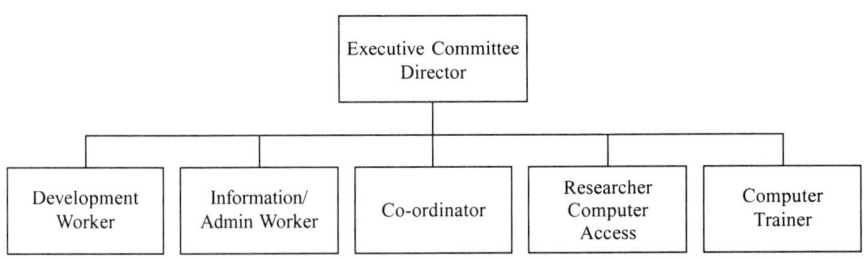

Figure 10.2d Women and Work

Thus, my unit within VSC was one of several constituent units each with a separate focus (see Figure 10.2a). As a member of VSC, I was expected to attend staff meetings and contribute to various organizational activities. At these meetings, I would give reports on my project and receive feedback from colleagues, many of whom did not have a research background. My line manager was not a social scientist nor had he undertaken research of any kind. He was the Assistant Director of VSC, responsible for finance. Out of the three members of the Directorate he was, at the time, the only one who had some knowledge of new computer technology and was assigned as my manager. He was motivated by economic rationality and therefore concerned with efficiency and effectiveness. Within a few weeks of my taking up the post, both the senior officer in the funding body responsible for the project and my own line manager at VSC asked for detailed bar charts with clearly identifiable performance indicators, such as number of interviews and training sessions which would be undertaken by specified dates. Regular research reports were required showing that there was progress in the project, and including recommendations for action even if these were based on circumstantial evidence rather than what I considered to be a solid body of systematically collected data. My manager tended to eschew social factors and issues of rigour and relevance of social research. His background was a direct contrast to that of the line manager I would have had as a researcher in an academic institution.

As the co-ordinator of the Computer Access project, my focus was almost exclusively on my project, whereas VSC and the local NGOs located the project within the context of the portfolio of projects and other activities for which each was responsible. For VSC, the Computer Access project was distinctive in three respects. First, it was the only research-based project amidst all the practice-based projects and activities handled by VSC. Second, it provided the first experience that VSC had of working simultaneously over a sustained period of time with multiple voluntary organizations. Third, the project had a very high status in VSC's portfolio of activities because its high level of funding had considerably exceeded the funding other projects had attracted, and it was hoped that it would be a precursor to further funding in the future. The combined result of the three factors was that the Computer Access project was perceived as VSC's 'flagship' – which placed considerable pressure on me and my team to deliver specific outcomes.

Within each of the local NGOs, the Computer Access project was differently located and its significance for the organization also varied. This meant that the interest in the project and its outcomes varied. Indeed, one NGO gave the impression that it was primarily interested in acquiring computer equipment to meet the other needs of the organization and only went along with the research and development objective because it was a vehicle for obtaining equipment.

Development and Politics

Management Structure: How are Organizations Managed?

Various management styles were evident in the Computer Access project. Thus, RT had an autocratic management structure with individuals at each level of the hierarchy having specific decision-making powers; SIT had a participatory management structure requiring consultation with various people prior to decision-making; WAW was a collective, working on a consensus model. The implications of these diverse structures was evident in the research process, particularly when a questionnaire was being drafted. I sent out a draft to all the five organizations. RT and IOUK returned theirs with comments within a couple of weeks as their researchers had the authority to make decisions on content and format. SIT returned the questionnaire within a month, as its management style required the project researcher to consult not only the other team members in the Computer Access project but various colleagues and committees in the organization. When the comments were all received, the SIT researcher made the final decision. A similar approach was adopted by DF.

However, WAW consulted everyone in their organization. Their ideological approach did not allow for distinctions to be drawn between professional and white-collar workers. This was reflected in the fact that all staff, irrespective of qualifications, type of job, and level of responsibility, earned the same salary. Furthermore, they were not ideologically comfortable with the distinction between paid and unpaid staff and, therefore, sought to involve unpaid workers in decision-making processes as much as possible. Consequently, as many people as possible were asked to comment on the questionnaire and several meetings were held to reach a consensus. Not surprisingly, the time required was over two months. As my research model was that all projects would work with the same basic questionnaire, none of the other four projects could commence work until there was agreement within and between the five projects.

Funding and Accounting Systems: How are Financial Matters dealt with in an Organization?

An organization's annual accounts will indicate the size of its budget and the allocation of funds for different activities. It may also indicate the number of people involved in various financial tasks. The five NGOs involved in the Computer Access project all had different accounting systems and the significance of this was brought out in the purchase of equipment for computer training. Thus, RT had a separate finance section who were able to process the accounts for the purchase of computers in a short space of time. IOUK took considerably longer because financial matters were the responsibility of one staff member who was also in charge of a number of other tasks. Furthermore, he had to obtain authorization from the executive

– 212 –

committee who worked in a voluntary capacity and were not always immediately available to deal with financial matters (see Figure 10.2c). Consequently, all the organizations did not have the computer equipment at the same time, and therefore could not simultaneously begin the computer-training activities which were to be subject to monitoring, review, and evaluation in accordance with the agreed research protocol.

Human Resources: How Many People are Involved in the Organization?

The number of people working for the organization, in either a paid or an unpaid capacity, gives an indication of its size. Furthermore, job titles give a clue to how human resources are deployed in the organization. However, common titles, such as 'manager' are not necessarily comparable between and within organizations.

The autonomy and authority of individuals in an organization also varies. Thus, in WAW, where there was no concept of a 'line manager' or of staff with certain levels of authority, decisions were made by consensus. In DF and SIT, role boundaries were blurred under an ideology of equality, and authority was invoked only when disputes arose. At RT, where there was a hierarchical management structure, line managers had to be kept informed of decisions taken by staff.

The staff working in the Computer Access project were managed jointly by the local NGOs and the central unit at VSC. This combined management of human resources was put to the test when a dispute arose between the RT researcher and his line manager, and the aggrieved worker was suspended from work. He rallied the support of colleagues at RT as well as the support of all the Computer Access staff who were located in the different NGOs on the basis that they were employees in a common project. The senior management of VSC and RT also became involved as they were jointly responsible for payment of salaries. As the Computer Access project was concerned with equal opportunities, the RT researcher, who it later emerged belonged to a left-wing political activist group, used the rhetoric of equal opportunities to frame his grievances. This strategy helped to mobilize a large number of workers as he was seen to stand for 'higher ideals' and, therefore, was a worthy cause to support. During the dispute very little research was done by any of the project staff as they engaged in 'strike action' against the alleged hypocrisy of senior management supposedly committed to a project whose principles were being violated in practice.

Communication Systems: How do People Communicate within and between Organizations?

Hardcopy, oral, and electronic communications play various and different roles in organizations. In some organizations, there is an expectation that everything will be in writing. In others, personal contact and oral communication – at both individual and group level – are more common. I began to realize that it is important to be aware of the way in which cross-cultural communication works: for instance, how people expect to be addressed; their preference for oral/written and electronic communication; norms about who should be kept informed, and whose views solicited; expectations about enquiries about their family, and other personal matters. It is a mistake to assume, as I found out, that if a report is sent to one person in an organization, it will be circulated to other relevant people who may have views or think they should be consulted. Often papers are not circulated and if a response is expected from a number of people in an organization, then copies should be sent to all. Failure to do so resulted in delays in the Computer Access project. In one case, a particular research approach had to be completely re-examined because one important individual on a committee claimed he had not been sent papers nor had his views been canvassed.

Expectations relating to the private and public domain are also significant. For instance, with IOUK, I always began telephone conversations with Indian staff with enquiries about their health, family, etc., as this provided a personal touch and demonstrated that I was thinking about an individual as a person rather than merely as a worker. On the other hand, the white British staff at SIT expected telephone calls to be restricted to business matters. While I do not wish to perpetuate stereotypes, it is important for researchers to be aware of varying cultural and sub-cultural norms regarding interpersonal communication.

Key Individuals: Who are the Key Actors in the Organization?

Key individuals may be the same as the names cited in the organization's literature. Alternatively, some people may be mere figureheads, and the power brokers not formally identified. It is important also to remember the gatekeepers, such as secretaries, who play an important role in facilitating or inhibiting access to those in positions of power. Key individuals may be identified by observing committee meetings and public events, and by listening to whose names are cited with greater frequency in informal conversations. It is important to cultivate key individuals because they may be important conduits to a network of contacts which will facilitate the research process and also play a role in the take-up of recommendations arising from research.

Power and Influence: What is the Basis for Power and Influence in the Organization?

At the risk of stating the obvious and for heuristic purposes, one may say that power is distributed in organizations in various ways and may emanate from:

- position: people in senior posts usually have more power;
- resources: the magnitude of resources under a person's control contributes to power;
- gender: women often have less power;
- race/ethnicity: non-white ethnic/racial minorities generally have less power. Expatriate white researchers/consultants, for example, often have, or behave as if they have, or are perceived to have, more power;
- personality: people with charisma often have more power.

It is important to pay attention to the 'official' or designated loci of power as well as to the capillaries of the organization through which power may be 'unofficially' dispersed. In the Computer Access project it was the honorary chair of the Trustees of RT, not the full-time paid Director, who had a great deal of power because he was a charismatic personality and because, by virtue of his position in the wider society, he had a network of influential contacts through which he was able to acquire public and private funds for community projects.

Intra-organizational Dynamics: How does an Organization Work in Practice?

The preceding points in the checklist will give some idea of the formal structure. However, organizational structure is the outcome of compromises and balances between conflicting but perhaps equally valid considerations. It is important to try to understand the balances and to work within them. It is worthwhile doing a rapid stakeholder analysis (see Mascarenhas-Keyes 1997: 173–83) in which primary and secondary stakeholders are identified, their interests, power, and influence ascertained, and their motives for participation in project activities explored. This should ideally be done at the beginning of the project and at regular intervals, as the dynamics of the situation rarely remain static.

Circumstances change fast and on-going awareness is needed of the internal and external political and economic climate in which research is being undertaken. It is important to understand and analyse the interests, the perspectives, and the constraints under which staff and other people connected with the organization work. Problems may be masked by individual personalities and styles of management. No organization is a monolith, however much it may be portrayed as such in its literature. Different and conflicting values may co-exist and the balance between these is probably constantly shifting. Power struggles, evident in confrontations and conflict, are inevitable in organizations. Goffman (1967) distinguishes between 'frontstage' and 'backstage' behaviour, and it is useful, to observe closely but unobtrusively, the backstage behaviour of individuals during informal gatherings over lunch, in the pub, or at office parties. These often reveal the power struggles which may not be mentioned in open conversations but which can be discerned from subtle verbal and non-verbal inter-personal communication.

Awareness of power plays and ideological dispositions, and of the knock-on effect outside the organization, for example, is useful when judgements have to be made for selecting recommendations for action. For instance, I suggested that students from the anthropology department of a local university could be involved in conducting interviews and undertaking other aspects of data collection and analysis. I saw this strategy as being of mutual benefit to the project and the students. While some of the staff at VSC agreed with this, others saw it as a way of depriving unemployed people from paid work, and as the exploitation of student labour. The students and supervisors saw the strategy as a useful opportunity to gain practical research experience. However, because of various ideological resistances, the idea had to be discarded.

Inter-organizational Politics: How do Various Organizations Relate to Each Other?

There are many different kinds of organization. It is therefore important to consider inter-organizational politics and to seek a variety of perspectives on this. This may help to determine which organizations are likely to favour or resist recommendations. In the Computer Access project, VSC and all five voluntary organizations had a stake in the project but the stake kept changing over the duration of the project. Short-term cliques emerged when there was a common interest, and there were continuous alignments and realignments throughout the project.

This organizational complexity was further complicated by two factors. First, about a year into the project, the borough's funds and the projects it was responsible for were taken over by a residuary body (RB) which had a different political agenda and a different way of managing projects. RB tried, eventually unsuccessfully, to terminate the project on the grounds that VSC's contract with its predecessor was *ultra vires*. VSC took legal advice and I was involved in briefing solicitors and lobbying through speaking on local radio programmes. Second, in addition to the fierce competition among voluntary groups to be chosen to participate in the Computer Access project, there was a great deal of competition among a variety of commercial organizations to obtain contracts to supply the computer hardware. Two main contenders were Mahab Computer Company and City Computers Ltd. They were owned respectively by Asian and African businessmen who argued they should be chosen because the Computer Access project focused on 'disadvantaged' people.

Organizational Time Frame: What Concept of 'Time' does each Organization Work to?

Organizations concerned with policy and practice want research findings to be translated into practical outcomes. Furthermore, these outcomes, such as new training courses, development activities, policy guidelines, articles, and research reports are expected at regular intervals. This approach to research was at complete variance to the one I had been trained for: the research exercise is undertaken over a long period of time, is completed first and subsequently written up. If I had adopted this approach, nothing substantial would have been produced in the Computer Access project until some time in the second year. The concerns at VSC regarding outcomes were replicated at the local level. The project had a different strategic location in each local NGO whose time-frames also varied. This meant that my model of synchronous research activities between the projects was very difficult to implement and was naive in its conception. My academic training had taught me not to be premature with publications but to wait until the findings had been analysed and digested, but this time-frame means that tangible evidence of research activity is not visible on an on-going basis to the diverse consumers of the research. This led to the erroneous view among some potential consumers of the research that the project funds were contributing to the 'fat cats' lifestyle of a chosen few staff, while the 'real' beneficiaries – that is, 'disadvantaged' people – were not reaping the rewards of the research. In hindsight, a better strategy would have been to organize the research into a number of discrete, clearly focused but interrelated components, each to be undertaken in a short time-frame of two to three months with specific policy and practice outcomes to be disseminated in a series of reports and workshops accessible to diverse consumers.

Research Outcomes: How can I ensure that Recommendations for Action are taken up?

Any report based on research work submitted to the organization should be in a format that is easy to read and which contains the summary and recommendations at the beginning of the document (Mascarenhas-Keyes 1997: 236–9). Busy executives do not have the time or the interest to read through detailed academic arguments eventually leading to a conclusion at the end of a lengthy document. The first research report I wrote at VSC was in the format of an academic essay of 4,000 words. It was 'torn to shreds' by the management committee who had a number of agenda items to get through at the meeting and had no time for a 'long' academic paper. Therefore brevity, limited use of academic jargon, an easy-to-read style and well-focused recommendations for action are the hallmarks of a research report for non-academics.

It is important to find out which officer in an organization is accountable to senior management for one's project, and build up a shared understanding with that person. The location of that person in the organization also needs to be determined: for instance, which section is he or she in? What are the strengths and weaknesses of that section? Is it under threat? Where does one's project fit into the officer's personal vested interests and intra-organizational politics? To whom does the officer report? How are actual decisions made, and by whom?

It is useful to identify the key players and keep in touch with them to discuss their ideas, as a project will have a history of accumulated agendas, only some of which will appear on the project description and terms of reference. It is worthwhile to have regular meetings with key individuals to share the progress of the research so that there are no surprises at the end. In the meantime, the officers with know-ledge of one's project will be able to lay the paths for the reception of the research when it is completed.

If at all possible, it is advantageous to talk through the research results with the people whose support is needed to get the recommendations accepted and acted upon. It is better to do this orally and informally before officials see anything of the final report on paper. This means that when the hard-copy version is submitted it confirms their expectations and they are ready to act on it. It is advisable never to give officials or politicians a shock by submitting the written report without a prior oral briefing session. They need to be familiar with the ideas before they see them written down. Furthermore, prior oral sessions enable one to test out orally which wordings are acceptable in order to communicate in a language that will not set up resistances.

Conclusion

It is useful to bear in mind three main points: first, the autonomy of the researcher; second, the purpose of the research; and third, the audience it addresses. These can best be illustrated by drawing on a contrast between my doctoral research and the work done at VSC. First, autonomy of the researcher: while researching and writing up the doctorate on a studentship, I was virtually my 'own boss' and free to pursue my own research interests. On the other hand, while working at VSC, my interests had to be balanced with those of my employers. Thus, there was a constant tension between reconciling my interests and views on how a research project should be run with that of the organization and the various constituencies that it served.

Second, the purpose of the research: my doctorate fitted in with the concept of 'pure' research in that it was a work of scholarship to extend the frontiers of knowledge for its own sake, and I could dictate the pace, theoretical and methodo-logical approach, analysis and interpretation of data. In the Computer Access project, on the other hand, the research fitted into the concept of 'applied research' in that the knowledge generated was to be used for policy and practice purposes. This had implications for the pace and scheduling of research activities. It required developing an awareness of the optimum moments within and outside the organization to channel the findings in order to promote changes in policy and practice.

Third, the audience for the research: with my doctorate, verbal remarks and written texts produced in a university setting were subject to comment from academics with a scholarly interest in the work. On the other hand, in the Computer Access project, the audience was very heterogeneous. It became necessary for me to cultivate an acute sensitivity to multiple interests and the often nuanced and subtle ways in which they were expressed. As I came to realize, my oral and written texts would be used by different sectors of the audience to drive their own agenda. If the texts did not meet individual requirements, then the strategy usually adopted was 'shoot the messenger'. The most common form this took was for criticisms to be voiced about the quality of the work. 'Quality' is a contestable concept. Whereas in a university environment there tends to be a fair amount of agreement about 'quality' and 'standards', outside the academy 'quality' is defined in multiple ways. Criticisms can be levied on a number of grounds, for instance personal vested interests; bias towards particular sections of the audience; questionable research methodology, usually related to whether informants constitute a representative sample; doubts about whether the data is genuine and reliable; and recommendations for action not being properly supported by 'real' evidence. In such situations, it is easy to be either completely dismissive of negative feedback or to become demoralized by such comments. While one develops resilience with experience, a strategy that I have found very useful, both when doing doctoral research as a native anthropologist, and when working in the Computer Access project and subsequently, is to adopt a reflexive stance. This means regarding Self as Informant (Mascarenhas-Keyes 1987), a method which involves constituting the Self as Other, and systematically and critically analysing feedback from other people and one's own responses to such comments. This approach has parallels with the psycho-analytical concepts of transference and counter-transference which Krause (1999) recommends that anthropologists may usefully adopt.

The strategy may reveal interesting information about the micro-politics operating within and between organizations, and may prompt one to exercise extra vigilance before engaging in oral and written communications. Furthermore, by subjecting one's own reactions to analysis, one is able to gain a deeper insight into how one's values and beliefs relating, for instance, to political ideologies, gender, sexuality, ethnicity, and the substantive content of one's research, all affect the way in which engagement in different aspects of the research process occurs. Thus the strategy both dispels anxiety and at the same time generates information which can be used for beneficial purposes in the research. Undertaking research and research-related activities within and for different organizations during one's career is extremely challenging, both personally and professionally, but the reward is that one may contribute to improving the quality of life of some people.

Acknowledgements

This chapter is based on an actual project, but all the names have been changed to preserve confidentiality. Certain sections have appeared in Mascarenhas-Keyes (1997). I am grateful for contributions from Sue Wright and Teresa Creswell.

References

Goffman, E. (1967), 'Where The Action Is', in E. Goffman, *Interaction Rituals: Essays on Face-to-Face Behavior,* Chicago: Aldine Publishing Co.

Krause, I.-B. (1999), 'Learning How to Ask in Psychotherapy and Ethnography', in D.N. Gellner and E. Hirsch (eds), *The Ethnography of Organizations: A Reader*, London: Department of Human Sciences, Brunel University.

Loder, C. (1992), *Support for Social Science Research: Setting the Scene*, Institute of Education, London University: Centre for Higher Education Studies.

Mascarenhas-Keyes, S. (1987), 'The Native Anthropologist: Constraints and Strategies in Research', in A. Jackson (ed.), *Anthropology at Home*, London: Tavistock.

—— (1997), *Professional Practice in Anthropology: A Curriculum Resource Manual for University Teachers*, Birmingham: National Network for Teaching and Learning Anthropology.

Part V
An Ethical Case Study

–11–

Participation or Observation? Some Practical and Ethical Dilemmas

Martin O'Neill

It is my intention in this chapter to outline some of the practical and ethical considerations that I have encountered while carrying out ethnographic fieldwork with a Welsh ambulance service. In doing so I hope that it will give rise to some wider considerations of the ethical position of the individual while conducting ethnographic enquiry. The purpose of this account of my experiences is that I believe, as Beales (1978) has argued, that although a formal code of ethics is of use to researchers, what is often more useful is the recounting of cases and their outcomes. Such accounts may be used as the basis of discussion, instruction, and assistance in the practical resolution of the ethnographer's dilemmas.

The fieldwork I describe here was the basis of my PhD (O'Neill 2000). When I first commenced my studies I was fresh from completing my first degree in anthropology and sociology and, as a diligent student, I had paid attention in my research-methods class during the lectures on participant observation. I had heard about Malinowski, Roy, Humphreys, and Bourdieu and felt that I had some understanding of the method. Later experience, however, was to teach me that although I may have had some grasp of the theoretical aspects of fieldwork, the practical implications of one's actions in the field were something that had to be learned on the hoof, as it were.

In order to understand the ethical dimensions of what I am to recount, a little personal history is necessary. Prior to going to university to study for my first degree I had worked in the ambulance service for some seven years. Therefore, within the environment in which I was conducting my research, I was known. Many of those who were to be the subjects of my research I had worked with 'on the road'. When I started out it was my aim to employ what one could call a classic qualitative approach, that is, unstructured and semi-structured interviews and observation of staff as they went about their daily routines. These were to be my main tools of enquiry. I approached the ambulance service with my research outline, detailing my approach and methodology, and they very kindly gave me free access to the organization.

As other studies of ambulance workers have identified (Hutchinson 1983), and as I knew from my own previous experience, ambulance work is characterized by high degrees of uncertainty and visibility. When an ambulance crew are dispatched to a call they have little idea of what they will actually encounter on arrival. Also, unlike the doctors or nurses at the hospital, they are unable to pull a screen around the patient as they administer treatment, often having to do so in the full public gaze. For crews to perform their duties and avoid negative consequences they are aware that they need, at the very least, to appear competent. Therefore, the Goffmanian (1967) concepts of 'front stage' and 'back stage' are particularly pertinent to the way that the crews cope with the uncertainty and visibility inherent in their duties. 'Back stage' behaviour is for the station or when they are alone on the ambulance; 'front stage' is when they are in the gaze of their audiences, be they the public or other healthcare or emergency workers. To do this successfully they have to project an identity as competent, which needs to be accepted by the audience. Aspects of this identity, particularly for the lay public, derive from the portrayal of the ambulance service and the 'paramedic' in popular media forms such as the television programmes *Casualty* and *999*.

In studies carried out in the USA, Mannon (1992), Metz (1981), Hutchinson (1983), and Douglas (1969) all found that management of the front stage was a central feature of ambulance work. My own research also supports this observation. From the individual members of staff who crew the ambulances on a day-to-day basis to the organizational displays of public scrutiny, such as Trust Board meetings, the ambulance service needs to appear competent at all times. They are aware that the consequences can be serious if they fail. For example, there was national public outcry after the failure of the London Ambulance Service control system on 26 October 1992, which resulted in questions being raised in the House of Commons and an NHS inquiry.

This culture of front management generates a procedure which Hutchinson (1983) has categorized as 'covering'. By this she is labelling that self-protective process which anticipates consequences, which staff themselves refer to as 'watching your back'. To avoid the possibility of personal and organizational negative consequences staff are socialized into this notion from their earliest induction training course. This, in turn, presents particular problems for a researcher in this type of setting. Douglas (1972) believes that parallels can be drawn between the study of ambulance workers and the study of deviant groups, as they construct such elaborate fronts to exclude the outsider. Indeed Metz believes that Douglas failed to get behind these fronts due to her ascribed categories of female and nurse. Hutchinson, another female nurse, also suffered problems in her research, in that the crews engaged in activities to intimidate and hinder her.

I was in a different position from that of any of the researchers so far mentioned. I had been, up to a few years previously, an insider. I still lived in the same town where I had worked in the ambulance service and had remained in contact with many of my former colleagues as friends and neighbours. However, this relationship that I had with my 'subjects' led to different dilemmas. In relation to the construction of fronts, one of my informants said to me early on in the research process: 'Well, it's pointless trying to hide anything from you as you've seen it all in the past.' I also knew the strategies that crews employed to obfuscate the appearance of any feelings of uncertainty or fear on their part, as I had done it myself in the past. But, there were now subtle nuances at play concerning my own self-identity, both internal and external. Although I had returned to an organization within which I used to be a true insider, I now had a new modified identity. It had aspects of being an insider but it also had aspects of being an outsider. This was to lead to multi-faceted dynamics within the research process for which no amount of classroom education could fully prepare me. What I want to consider in the next part of this chapter is how my state of mind and understanding, of myself as participant and observer, evolved at the very beginning of the fieldwork.

In the first few weeks of entering the field I carried a very naive conceptual model in my head: that I was now no longer an ambulance man; that I was now in the role of the 'researcher'; and that my subject was the ambulance service. The subtleties of the fieldwork situation were to teach me that the position could never be that simple. Early on in the fieldwork it became obvious that I could not just observe: I had to participate. What was I to do if the ambulance that I was on arrived at the scene of an incident with casualties and people in a state of distress? Surely, according to the classic theoretical model I should remain a detached observer, but as a human being I could not just stand by and watch: I had to become involved.

There were a number of dimensions to this. From the staff's point of view they knew me and knew I could 'do the job'. If I did not get involved they would resent me, not only because I hadn't helped them out, but what would they have thought of me as a person if I had stood by when someone was suffering and taken notes or spoken into my tape machine? What would the public have thought of me in the same situation and also, what would I have thought of myself? Several incidents in my first few weeks of fieldwork made me consider my ethical and legal position as both a citizen and as a researcher. One incident in particular compounded these concerns and caused me to retreat from the field for a while to rethink my strategy.

The incident happened during one day shift when I was with an emergency medical service (EMS) paramedic crew. We had arrived at the hospital and the crew were waiting for a piece of equipment to transfer the patient onto a trolley for transfer to a clinic. As we waited in the corridor an ambulance liaison assistant came running after us and said that a five-hour-old baby had stopped breathing some two miles down the road. The paramedic ran to take the details of the call from ambulance control, while the emergency medical technician (EMT) and I transferred the patient on to the trolley by hand and grabbed the stretcher.

Mannon (1992), in his study of emergency medical service ambulance crews in the United States, although acknowledging that it could be problematic, advocates that the participant observer in this situation should never let participation become so engrossing as to forget his or her analytic stance. On this occasion, in the heat of the moment, I completely forgot my 'analytic stance' and suspended my role as observer. It may be relevant here that Mannon had no background as a health-service worker.

The EMT and I ran through the corridors of the hospital toward the ambulance. I was in front, in civilian clothes, shouting at members of the public to get out of the way. When we got to the ambulance we threw the stretcher in the back. As various other studies of emergency medical workers have identified, incidents involving children elicit greater urgency, and on this call, all the stops were out. The journey to the incident was a very silent affair with none of the jokes or banter that often characterizes the journey to emergency calls. I felt sick; my heart was pumping and my mouth dry. The EMT and I prepared the equipment that we thought might be needed at scene. He, I, and the paramedic worked as a team of three; I was no longer 'the professional stranger' but was acting as a member of the ambulance crew. This may have been some sort of coping mechanism on my part to deal with the situation that I now found myself in.

On arrival at the scene of the incident, the EMT and I jumped from the vehicle and ran into the house, while the paramedic turned the ambulance around in case there was a need to depart quickly. Inside the house the EMT ran into the kitchen where the baby was, while I stayed near the door of the house, ready to run to the ambulance to get any equipment that he might need. As I stood there the grand-parents of the baby came out of the kitchen, obviously very distressed, and I tried to calm them down. At this time the midwife also arrived and went into the kitchen. It was very tense for everyone concerned. The paramedic stayed near the vehicle with the doors open. All three of us knew from past experience that if it were not possible to get the baby breathing again quickly at scene, the other option was to run with the baby as fast as possible to the hospital, which was why we had adopted the positions we had. I stayed with the grandparents trying to reassure them. We all looked to the door of the kitchen expectantly. When the EMT did emerge he told us that the baby was breathing again. This was a source of great relief to us all. The paramedic and the EMT then went into the kitchen to attend to the baby with the midwife. I stayed outside comforting the grandparents. Obviously they were now a lot more relaxed and they asked me who I was and what was I doing there. We had just been through a very stressful time together, probably for them one of the most stressful events of their lives. When I explained that I was a researcher from Swansea University they seemed confused at first, perhaps because

I was one of the first people that they had seen arrive at the house. I then said that I had in the past worked in the ambulance service and this seemed to explain matters. Although the baby was now breathing, it was not breathing normally so it was conveyed to the hospital for a check-up. The journey back, although a lot less fraught, was still full of tension. The EMT and I sat in the back. The baby was continually monitored in case there was a need to start resuscitation.

When we arrived at the hospital the baby and mother were taken into Casualty. I sat in the back of the ambulance with the EMT and talked about the incident. By this time I had my researcher's hat back on and my head was full of ethical and legal concerns. What if I had dropped the patient when transferring from the stretcher to the trolley? In gaining access I had told nobody that I would be touching patients, as at that time it had not been my intention to do so. What if I had prepared a piece of equipment incorrectly en route to the call? When I worked in the ambulance service that had always been a concern, but now I didn't work for the ambulance service and felt that I should not have been doing such things. What right did I have to be in these people's homes observing them at times of intense emotion and grief? As far as the ambulance staff were concerned I had their informed consent but the patients had not invited me into their houses. What if the baby had stopped breathing in the back of the ambulance? I knew I would have got involved in the resuscitation, if I felt I could have helped. I knew the ambulance crew would have expected me to, and that if I had not, they would have been disgusted with me. But I was now supposed to be the researcher; I felt that I had no right to be attempting to resuscitate people's babies, probably the most precious thing in their life. As I sat there in the back of the ambulance sharing these rantings with the EMT he said something that made me put my concerns about research ethics back into perspective. He said, 'We worked as a team and who gives a fuck as long as the baby is all right?' I realized then that that said it all. Whatever my role or responsibility as a researcher these were secondary to my roles and responsibilities as a human being. If I could help, I had a duty to help, regardless of any arguments concerning research ethics; the ethical issues in this situation were a lot deeper.

This realization, however, had various implications for my research strategy. I had been given permission to observe ambulance crews, not to lay my hands on and treat patients. This raised new ethical problems regarding the informed consent of patients to be treated by a researcher. Until I resolved these issues I decided to retire from the field. I felt it was time to consider my ethical position reflexively and then to approach the medical research ethics committee of the health authority. Although the focus of my research was not the patients, events had shown that I couldn't help interacting with them on many levels. I consulted the literature of others who had been involved in this type of research to see if they had had to resolve such dilemmas. Although there were no similar studies from the UK, there were three studies that I could draw upon of emergency medical services in the

USA. As stated earlier, however, I felt that Mannon was in a different position, as he had no medical background. Metz (1981) also was in a different position, as he was employed as an EMT when he conducted his study, and therefore was in the position where it was his main role to provide medical care with the research role being secondary. The only researcher in a similar position to my own was Hutchinson (1983), as she had trained as a psychiatric nurse prior to conducting her research. However, her main concern in this area was how she should deal with what she believed to be bad practice in the treatment of psychiatric patients by ambulance crews.

In the end it turned out to be Metz who gave me the most guidance. He found that there were many times when being a participant on an ambulance got in the way of observing. The demands of the moment can prevent the researcher from casually surveying the surroundings, or reflecting on the behaviour seen. One's actions are being judged by others who are involved in the situation and the researcher's emotions come into play and influence judgement. What is central to any incident is that the patient's well-being is at stake; the focus necessarily is on that goal, because one is human (Metz 1981: 225). This I took in conjunction with the observation made by Reinharz (1984: 183) that if the researcher does not accept the members' perspective then he or she will appear indifferent, hostile, or ignorant and will be tolerated only briefly. These observations and my own previous experience helped me to consolidate in my own mind what role I had as a participant and what role I had as an observer.

Due to the area my research covered I had to attend two research ethics committees and both posed the same hypothetical question. What would I do if I arrived at the scene of an accident and there were three casualties? What extent of care would I give? What equipment from the ambulance would I use? My answer to such questions was that I would provide first aid as any citizen who had a knowledge of first aid would. I would not use any equipment from the ambulance unless directed to by a member of the ambulance crew. That is how I resolved the situation both for myself and to the ethics committee. I felt that I was no longer qualified to offer anything more, but due to the fact that I knew some first aid I was under an obligation to use those skills. Relating it to the position I recounted earlier, as a parent myself I felt if there was anyone who could help in keeping my child breathing, be they researcher or anything else, I would want them to do so.

Normally in the presentation of aspects about my research I do try to resist the gory or dramatic story, as I feel that these often contribute to the misrepresentation of what the ambulance service is about. However, on this occasion the purpose of using a dramatic story is that in this incident, what was of concern was very precious, a child's life. As mentioned already, however, I had begun to have these concerns for some time in my fieldwork, often while involved in more routine ambulance duties. I found I was in the position, as every ethnographer is, of being involved in social relations with others who occupied the field, not only ambulance staff but patients, hospital workers, and members of the public.

This incident compounds a concern that I had during the whole research process and one that I feel that other researchers should consider. We, as researchers, are parasites on our subjects. As this incident illustrates, I was using a period of intense emotional trauma as data for my PhD thesis. This, in turn, poses both practical and ethical concerns that should be addressed. The question that researchers need to ask themselves, reflexively, is: What's in it for them? If we just stand back and observe for our own purposes then we are failing to address these concerns. Lofland (1971: 98) talks of the need for 'immediate reciprocities': the need for the researcher to make a contribution to the informal social network in order to be accepted and to be able to observe and record what people are doing. In other words, reciprocity is necessary in order to achieve one's practical ends. However, I would suggest that ethnographers, in considering such reciprocities with their 'subjects', should address the question of ethical reciprocity as well.

Over the years there has been much debate as to how much the anthropologist should get involved with his or her subjects; this is not, however, the main focus of this chapter. What I have recounted here is an ethical dilemma as to how much to get involved, which in turn is similar to the arguments that surround the question of anthropological advocacy. Ethical decisions made during ethnography are often problematic, as they are in everyday life. Akeroyd (1984: 154) has stated that in an 'increasingly pluralist discipline, consensus about ethical behaviour and research practice is unattainable and compromise seems inevitable. The social researcher must make compromises . . . between roles as scientist and citizen, commitment and impartiality . . . The onus for making such decisions rests on the individual researcher.' I do believe that my experiences in the field have shown this dichotomy between the role of the individual as a researcher and as a citizen. The experience has made me believe that it is essential that researchers consider the humanitarian implications of their actions in the fieldwork situation, although addressing this problem is rarely straightforward. All I feel that we as researchers can do is to try to resolve these ethical dilemmas as best we can. To do this we need to consider these decisions reflexively and discuss them openly, not only with our colleagues, but also in a wider arena. What I hope to illustrate by using this concrete example from my own research is that there are times, as Hammersley and Atkinson (1993: 286) have identified, where the researcher should stop being a researcher and engage in action that is not directed towards the goal of producing knowledge. By its very nature ethnography forces us into relationships with people: this in turn has an impact on how we behave; or, more germane to this case, actions arise through obligations in another role, in my case not only as a former ambulance worker, but I think more basically as a citizen and as a human being.

References

Akeroyd, A.V. (1984), 'Ethics in Relation to Informants, The Profession and Governments', in R.F. Ellen (ed.), *Ethnographic Research: A Guide to General Conduct*, London: Academic Press.

Beales, A. (1978), 'Ethical Dilemmas in Anthropological Fieldwork', in G.N. Appel (ed.), *Ethical Dilemmas in Anthropological Enquiry: A Case Book*, Waltham, Mass.: Crossroads Press.

Douglas, D.J. (1969), 'Occupational and Therapeutic Contingencies of Ambulance Services in Metropolitan Areas', unpublished PhD thesis, University of California Davis.

—— (1972), 'Managing Fronts in Observing Deviance', in J.D. Douglas (ed.), *Research on Deviance*, New York: Random House.

Goffman, E. (1967), 'Where The Action Is', in E. Goffman *Interaction Rituals: Essays on Face to Face Behavior*, Chicago: Aldine Publishing Co.

Hammersley, M., and Atkinson, P. (1993), *Ethnography: Principles in Practice*, London: Routledge.

Humphreys, L. (1975), *Tearoom Trade: Impersonal Sex in Public Places*, New York: Aldine de Gruyter.

Hutchinson, S.A. (1983), *Survival Practices of Rescue Workers: Hidden Dimensions of Watchful Readiness*, Washington: University Press of America.

Lofland, J. (1971), *Analyzing Social Settings: A Guide to Qualitative Data and Analysis*, Belmont, California: Wadsworth.

Mannon, J.M. (1992), *Emergency Encounters: EMTs and Their Work*, Boston, Mass.: Jones and Bartlett.

Metz, D.L. (1981), *Running Hot: Structure and Stress in Ambulance Work*, Cambridge, Mass.: A.B.T. Books.

O'Neill, M. (2000), 'Carriage with Compassion: An Ethnographic Study of a Welsh Ambulance Service', unpublished PhD, University of Wales, Swansea.

Reinharz, S. (1984), *On Becoming A Social Scientist: From Survey Research and Participant Observation to Experimental Analysis*, New Brunswick: Transaction.

Roy, D. (1973), 'Banana Time', in G. Salaman and K. Thompson (eds), *People and Organisations*, London: Longman.

Afterword

Afterword:
Natives 'R' Us: Some Notes on the
Ethnography of Organizations

John Van Maanen

This chapter is designed to wrap up this collection of readings by suggesting in broad terms what readers might take away from the preceding writings and what might be made of them all in terms of the promise and prospect of organizational ethnography. This is a field growing fairly rapidly in both North America and Europe and the work presented here provides a reasonable sample as to what anthropologists are up to in the area and thus tells us something about the current state of the art (and science) of organizational ethnography.[1] The chapters mix story and explanation with theory, critique, and advice but most tell, in some detail and with bite, about what it is like to be someone else. The natives of these tales are not, however, the alien and exotic others of faraway lands put forth in the classic monographs of cultural or social anthropology but, rather, oddly familiar domestic others who might be our cohorts at work, our next door neighbors or even, gasp, ourselves.

This shift in locale is at least partly a consequence of the relatively recent spread of the specialized and formerly insular disciplinary aims of anthropology (and, to a lesser degree, of sociology). Growing interest in the distinctly modern idea of culture – as something constructed both thick and thin by all self-identifying human groups – has put ethnography in play across the intellectual map. No longer is ethnography ordered by familiar categories that cut across times, places, and peoples; nor is it confined to single-site studies of supposedly isolated or at least

---

1. The Atlantic, it seems, separates rather than connects the organizational research worlds of Europe and English-speaking North America. Unlike organization studies in Europe, organization studies in the United States stands on its own as a rather autonomous field, complete with internal rifts and divisions between and among those who are called macro- and micro- organization theorists. It is a field that represents a growing assembly of rather diverse scholars frequently working in business schools and held together by convenience, will, and a few summer meetings. For better or worse, organizational research in Europe, notably in Britain and France, is tied more closely to reference disciplines, especially sociology and psychology. Useful recent discussions of these matters are found in Koza and Thoenig (1995), Child (1995), Chanlet (1994), and Hinnings (1988).

conveniently restricted ways of life. With market globalization, enhanced communications, the rise and spread of vast human migrations, the increased ease of transport, and so forth, comes an inevitable and yet largely unprecedented – but closely observed and theorized – shuffling and interpenetrating of modes of thought and action as people, ideas, and goods move back and forth across the world.[2] Ethnographic studies reflect such breaching and blending processes, mixing parasitic and novel elements with traditional interests such that the trade is shaped as much by timely, topical, and pragmatic concerns as by disciplinary goals or theoretical worries.

This eclecticism is neither a scandal nor (necessarily) a strength. But, for better or worse, ethnography is now being carried on in a seemingly limitless number of organizational settings. In this volume alone, we have learned something about corporate worlds, lab science, museum work, medical practice, rural development projects, community planning and more. For most organizational researchers – few of whom claim anthropology as their reference discipline – ethnographic work of this type represents travel over a field of study. Travel is of course not enough (even for an anthropologist or, for that matter, a geographer).[3] But, students of

---

2. Although I will not touch much on these matters, globalization refers to the apparent intensification of worldwide social relations which link distant localities in such a way that local happenings are shaped by events many miles away (and vice versa). In both anthropology and sociology, the idea of the whole, integrated, self-contained social group and way of life gives way to a flexible, open view of culture that operates in a continually changing environment. Clifford (1997), among others, argues that the world has changed and changed dramatically as a result of globalization. Culture (and therefore identity) is not longer stable but is now fluid and more or less consciously constructed. Ethnography must then offer a variety of discordant voices, never come to rest, and never 'essentialize' (a favorite term of abuse) a people or a culture. Just how globalization is playing out in different parts of the world is of increasing interest to anthropologists generally and to organizational ethnographers specifically. Examples of how various aspects of globalization might be treated ethnographically include Appadurai (1997), Passaro (1997), J. Watson (1997), Hannerz (1992), Kahn (1995), Zabusky (1995), Lamphere (1992), Fox (1991), and Featherstone (1990).

3. I do recognize that a prestige of place has long been associated with anthropological work. What Gupta and Ferguson (1997) refer to as a 'hierarchy of purity' still obtains within the trade such that some field sites are taken as more anthropological than others. The question 'Where are you going to do your research?' remains an important one in anthropology and the reply 'across the street' is not likely on its own to generate an enthusiastic response from colleagues. Fieldwork at home is sometimes seen as an avocation – akin to tending one's garden – rather than a vocation and some notable figures in anthropology have gone out of their way in the past to stigmatize the practice. Geertz (1995: 102) for example remarks that ethnography in one's own society was once known derisively as 'gas station anthropology'. This has of course created a good deal of opportunity for the ethnographically inclined without proper anthropological credentials – myself among them – to contribute to various interdisciplinary fields such as organizational studies. Anthropologists have never been totally absent from the field, of course, but their numbers have been few and the status of their at-home work within the discipline rather suspect. This is changing as the ethnographic literature associated with organizational life grows.

organization at home or away who have never – even vicariously through reading – been exposed to everyday work in a clinic, a business firm, a research lab, a divorce court, or a civil service agency have probably missed something. Their generalizations about organizations are quite apt to be based on far too narrow a selection of the field. Taking readers to places where they presumably have never been is then very much a part of organizational ethnography as currently practised and understood.

Yet, as anthropologists know only too well, the burden of ethnography – to represent culture, fragmented or whole, at home or away – has over the past several decades become heavier, messier, and less easily tied to a specific set of analytic categories and narrative conventions. To suggest in writing what it is like to be someone else has of course never been a simple matter, but the task appears almost Herculean these days given the problematic of personal and social identity associated with the conditions we so nervously call postmodern. Moreover, the theories, practices, and rhetorics associated with ethnography continue to evolve (or, at least, shift) in recognizable and presumably irreversible ways. Although I have no cranky epistemological fits to throw on these pages, I suspect that most of us would now agree, for example, that all ethnographies owe whatever persuasive power they can muster to contingent social, historical, and institutional forms and no meta-argument can question this contingency.

But, as the dust settles on this ethnography-as-text argument, most of us are also coming to realize that if we are to continue to do our work, this sublime contingency – and other similar ones put forth by the annoying but necessary epistemological hypochondriacs among us – matters very little since any particular ethnography must still make its points by roughly the same means that were available before the contingency was recognized. These means include the hard work of securing access to study sites (by whatever sneak means possible), becoming saturated with first-hand knowledge of the research setting, gathering and putting forth evidence, providing fresh interpretations, inventing and elaborating analogies (crisp or otherwise), invoking authorities, working through examples, calling out theories, and, in general, marshaling the tropes such that attractive work is produced. This is simply to say that while the nature of ethnographic work, evidence, explanation, metaphor, authority, example, and rhetoric may shift over time, the appeal of any single work remains tied to the specific arguments made within a particular text and referenced to a specific, not general, substantive domain, analytic approach, and narrative style.

The work of ethnography, then, goes on in much the same way as it did before textuality came into fashion. To some, perhaps, the discourse surrounding the textuality of ethnographic facts and the factuality of ethnographic texts is paradoxical (discomfortingly so). But I think the paradox vanishes with the realization that ethnography – like any other form of social research – does not soldier on because its facts, methods, genres, theories, and so forth all survive the passage of time (and, most assuredly, they do not) but because in the midst of change an audience still looks to it for the performance of a given task. In the case of ethnography, what we continue to look for is the close study of culture as continuously worked out and lived by particular people, in particular places, doing particular things at particular times.

This mandate has, if anything, grown in recent years. Cultural self-consciousness is on the rise and everyone, it seems, now has a culture well worth presenting if not defending (or challenging) – including, for instance, nation-building groups of Hawai'ians or Québecois, dedicated corporate tribes of Motorolans or Decies, and spreedsheet warriors of Anderson Consulting or the London Business School.[4] Such worlds of meaning and apparent solidarity are not only felt but increasingly inscribed in both popular and scholarly forms. Cultural insiders create engaging lay ethnographies such as Lewis's (1990) treatment of Wall Street traders in *Liar's Poker* while cultural outsiders write scholarly ethnographies such as Albolafia's (1998) examination of these same creatures from Planet Finance in *Making Markets*. The ethnographic mandate has spread well beyond any neatly ordered disciplinary borders and now accommodates a rather astonishing amount of topical, theoretical, and stylistic diversity thus serving to question if not subvert what Malcolm Chapman, in Chapter One, rightly calls the 'vain hope' associated with intendedly authoritative definitions and portraits of culture. While the anthropological market share in the cultural portrait business may be down, the market itself is booming.

For ethnographers trained in either (or both) anthropology or sociology, the rise of interest in culture ever so broadly defined means that more subject matter is opened up, more attention is paid to neglected or marginalized areas of social life at home and away, more opportunities are created to cross traditional disciplinary and topical boundaries, more play with forms of reporting is possible, and more ways to frame research questions are available today than has been the case since Ur-anthropologists like Bronislaw Malinowski took up residence in the Trobriands or W. Lloyd Warner landed a job on the Hawthorne Studies research team at the Western Electric plant in Cicero, Illinois. Moreover, the audience for ethnographic narrative and the pleasure, puzzlement, and provocation such writings provide continues to grow in various applied and multidisciplinary fields such as

---

4. This spread of culture shows up occasionally in the most unlikely places. For example, Milton Friedman, the patron saint of free-marketeers and hard-line economic rationalists, when asked by a reporter why he thought the University of Chicago economics department had been so productive and prominent over the years, responded without a trace of irony that it was not the hardy individualists who were attracted to the department nor the rewards put in place to motivate them but rather, in his words, 'the culture of the place' that was responsible for the group's success (*The Economist*, 1996: 72).

education, law, communications, management, social work, criminal justice, and public policy. I think it fairly safe to say that there are now fewer rules for ethnographers to follow but more work to do. This seems to me a far better world for practising or wannabe ethnographers than one with less work and more rules.

There are of course problems. Not the least of which surrounds what kind of studies we are comfortable calling ethnographic and just how we are to assess their quality. Such matters appear to be very much on the minds of the contributors to this volume. All recognize the distance they have traveled from the so-called cultural island perspective and the one-site, one-tribe, one-scribe conceits associated with such work. All recognize that they have cut back on the rather timeless culture concept to fit a restless, shifting, multicultural world populated by natives not so very different from themselves. All recognize the tensions that arise as research sponsors unfamiliar (or perhaps too familiar) with ethnographic research clamor for timely and useful results. And all recognize that the unblinking ethnographic eye celebrated in Latour's (1993) much-mentioned call for 'symmetric anthropology' is not so easy to bring off in those highly segmented worlds of self-interested organizational actors who not only can read the reports of research conducted on their turf but may actually wish to do so (with the exception perhaps of some of the randy managers studied by Alex Ouroussoff in Chapter Two).[5]

Yet grumbling about the difficulty of doing ethnography while doing it is a rather well-established narrative ploy (Van Maanen 1995). We should not make too much of it for it signals a rather high and I think welcome degree of self-awareness on the part of ethnographers who realize at the outset of their work that they have already acquired at least some, if not a good deal, of the culture they are going to the field to study. It also reflects the troubles that come with working in league with sometimes remarkably patient but understandably chary and occasionally resistant informants who know quite well that ethnographers as pesky social researchers are out to interpret what they say and do in ways they might not find agreeable.

How ethnographic work is understood and (sometimes) read by various audiences is a matter on which all authors in this collection have something to say. In Chapter One, for example, Malcolm Chapman, wanting to overcome the 'lingering primitivism' his new colleagues in a management school ascribe to

5. A handy little book edited by Caroline Brettell called *When They Read What We Write* (1993) might well be placed in the ethnographer's backpack (or laptop bag). Ethnographic authority of the classical sort thrived in part under a cloak of distance and difference. The natives never knew what was written about them. Today they do, and we write more circumspectly as a result or risk being upbraided and run out of town. To wit, 'natives' have become 'members' or sometimes 'clients'. And 'primitives', 'savages', and 'subjects' are thankfully long gone, as well maybe as 'informants' (an increasingly ugly and troublesome label for those who knowingly aid us in our studies).

anthropology, goes well out of his way to tutor – with apparent success – a skeptical colleague trained in the dismal art of economics. David Mosse in Chapter Eight bluntly suggests that the more independent, critical, and unrestricted the work of the ethnographer in the field, the less legitimacy and practicality the work is likely to have for those who make the study possible.

More generally, it seems that readers outside anthropology, sociology, and the relatively small ethnographic circles that form on the periphery of other social science disciplines and professional pursuits are rather accepting of the so-called ethnographic facts. These same readers are, however, sometimes suspicious of ethnographic interpretations which they read as intentionally subversive, confused by empyrean clouds of theoretical vapor, or, most crushing of all, too obvious for words. For a good number of readers outside the field a trustworthy ethnography is a straightforward realist tale focusing largely on what people say and do as witnessed by the author who displays the expected courtesy of staying out of the way when the ethnographic facts are neatly bundled up in writing. No more, no less. No spin. Thank you very much.

Such response is tied partly to the sacralization of culture that I think goes with the concept's popularization at large as well as what we might call the cult of authenticity associated with heightened cultural sensitivity and awareness. A broad misunderstanding of ethnography results and anything other than the native's point of view as put forward by the native – in Geertz's (1983: 17) memorable phrase, 'an ethnography of witchcraft by a witch' – is read as less than the real thing. To wit, the enormous popular appeal of Studs Terkel's tape-recorded (albeit extensively edited) interviews such as *Working* (1974) and *The Good War* (1984) or Tracy Kidder's hanging-out form of literary journalism in *The Soul of the New Machine* (1981) and *Among Schoolchildren* (1990). Many if not most readers take writings of this sort as indisputably authentic cultural accounts devoid of insidious interpretation. While there are certainly many good reasons to call into question various ethnographic narratives, authenticity is rarely one of them.

Whatever else it may be, ethnography is an interpretation. It is something added to all the wondrous facts that are collected or stumbled on during a period of fieldwork. The purposes of ethnography do not normally spring from the settings in which fieldwork is conducted but come (and leave) with the ethnographer. In Chapter Six, for instance, Simon Pulman-Jones tells us that while he is not the only social theorist in the children's behavioral clinic he studied, he is the only one for whom the theories of others serve as data rather than competition for his own. His work entails the interpretation of interpretation and his aims in the setting sharply differ from those of his temporary colleagues however convenient it may be for all to forget such matters for a time.

It helps to keep in mind that we never observe or study a culture directly since the term 'culture' does not denote any concrete reality. It is an abstraction and, as commonly used, a vague – but still useful – abstraction.[6] Culture is to ethnographers as life is to biologists, force is to physicists, or God is to theologians. We learn of the customary talk and behavior that goes on among those we study and then artfully categorize what we've heard, seen, and felt according to our own interests, training, skills, and insights. To be sure, we rely heavily on others (both in and out of the studied settings) but, in the end, it is the ethnographer and not the native who develops and takes responsibility for whatever cultural accounts and representations mark the study. To position one's self at an angle, to provide a 'cross-eyed' vision and independent voice, is of course what we count on and expect ethnographers to provide as an intrinsic component of their work. It is also what makes ethnography a good deal more complicated than simply a method of collecting data.

Let me now turn to classification and briefly delineate some – although surely not all – of the substantive interests followed by those intrepid ethnographers of organizations including most of those represented in this book. What do they study? What problems seem to focus their research? Where does their work fit into what is known (or thought to be known) about organizational life? These are of course big questions I am not about to fully answer. But some inkling where this once and future field has been and is going comes from examining topical domains.

Four areas of inquiry are I think sufficiently well established – indeed prominent – so that a crude picture of field can be drawn despite considerable theoretical and stylistic variation that exists within each domain. I must, however, add a proviso that no one study fits a single category perfectly. Ethnographers are an integrative and ambitious lot and ethnographic holism has not retreated entirely or lost all of its appeal. Nonetheless I do claim that most ethnographic studies of organizations

---

6. I realize that some influential modern work on culture suggests that we might be best off avoiding the hyper-referential word altogether and write more specifically about knowledge, practice, tradition, technology, discourse, ideology, or habitus. There is much to be said for such a tactic. It may dispel the totalitarian overtones and perverse idealism that sometimes surround the use of the term 'culture'. But substituting alternative concepts merely defers, and does not solve, the analytic difficulties. Kuper (1999) suggests that such difficulties become most acute when 'culture' or any other stand-in term shifts from something to be represented, interpreted, or even explained to a source of stand-alone explanation – beyond established social institutions and political or economic conditions – for why people think and act as they do. As suggested by some of the contributors to this volume (e.g. Bob Simpson in Chapter Five and Simone Abram in Chapter Nine), ethnography sometimes suffers from a myopia that sharply delineates behavior at close range while obscuring the proximate and less visible structures and processes that engender and sustain behavior. A fetish with fieldwork may deny the legitimacy of social observation beyond the tête-à-tête of interpersonal interaction. Other sources of information exist and the best – and most responsible – ethnographies are perhaps always interdisciplinary. This ethnographic broadening is effectively preached and demonstrated by Nash (1993), di Leonardo (1998), and, most recently, Burawoy and Verdery (1999).

are sufficiently focused individually but varied enough collectively that the following taxonomy is neither pointless nor pat.[7]

Studies of Organizational Processes and Informal Relations

Fieldwork of the ethnographic sort is intended to be largely unobtrusive and, at least at the time it is carried out, non-reactive. Ethnographers listen, observe, participate, converse, lurk, collaborate, count, classify, learn, help, read, reflect, and – with luck – appreciate and understand what goes on (and maybe why) in the social worlds they have penetrated. It is an unspoken methodological paradigm that is generally effective in not scaring away the phenomenon of interest and is more or less at odds with the no-nonsense discovery of truth by experimentation, survey, or highly-formatted call and respond interviews, techniques which most fieldworkers believe ignore context and create reactions. Preserving the apparent naturalness and everyday character of what is being studied is the stock and trade of ethnographic work on the ground (and in writing).

Nothing puts these precepts and trade skills to test more than the study of organizational processes and informal relations. Such processes and relations concern the way members of organizations individually and collectively come to terms and cope with, but seldom solve, the recurrent problems and contradictions they face when going about their daily tasks. Research interest might center on how work is patterned, decisions made, control exercised (or thwarted), or autonomy carved out. Organizational processes come in a variety of cultural forms including routines, rituals, dramas, and games.

---

7. There are of course many other useful ways to categorize organization studies including classification by type of organization (business, science, public service, and development) as put forth in this book. I am drawn to the topical order because I have used it once before to classify a somewhat broader sampling of research in the field (Van Maanen 1999). It also allows me to shake and bake the previous chapters in a different way than editorially arranged. I realize of course that some quite interesting ethnographic work is going on at the edges and between my categories. Worth mentioning in this regard are ethnographic studies examining narrative in organizations (e.g. Czarniawska 1997; Ewick and Silbey 1995), the impact of gendered expectations in the workplace (Garson 1975), the role of emotion work in organizations (e.g. Leidner 1993; Hochschild 1983), and the time and place norms associated with work (and non-work) activity (e.g. Nippert-Eng 1995; Perlow 1997). It is also worth noting that what might be called the ethnography of amusement or pleasure (and of the entertainment, leisure, and tourist organizations that make up this enormous industry) is a growing area of study (e.g. Fjellman 1992; Davis 1997) as is the cultural response to cultural products and the organizations that produce them (Radway 1997; Lutz and Collier 1992). While this is no place for a literature review, my point is simply that ethnography of the worthy sort David Gellner and Eric Hirsch outline in their introductory remarks to this book has become of central feature in organizational studies (a cross-disciplinary area that is itself expanding).

Informal relations refer to the so-called 'underside' of organizational life – those adaptive but sometimes hidden and unofficial arrangements by which things get accomplished (or ignored). Some are tightly scripted, rather predictable, and governed by well-established social rules and cognitive schemes. Some are not. Most probably fall somewhere in the middle, identifiable as human ways of fleshing out the skeletal, formal chains of command and task structures of an organization by distributing various levels of responsibility, trust, fealty, and interpersonal control among members – workers, supervisors, customers, clients, managers, and so forth. Both organizational processes and informal relations are tractable by a logic embedded in what people are trying to do but they are also forever and always subject to considerable situationally specific variation.

Perhaps the most well-regarded and well-known study of such matters – in the United States at least – is Melville Dalton's (1959) classic *Men Who Manage.* Seeking 'to get as close as possible to the world of managers and to interpret this world and its problems from the inside' (p. 1), Dalton noted that the gaps between prescribed and observed behavior and the competitive relations among individuals and groups aspiring to power in the organization were not simply fleeting departures from standard operating procedures but patterned, predictable, and potent ways of doing things together which sometimes supported official organizational goals and sometimes did not. His findings, however, could only have derived from a method able to track the subtleties in both meaning and action as they emerged on the ground.

The processes that caught Dalton's attention – decision-making, communication, cooperation (or lack thereof) – and the informal relations that characterized the performance of various managerial tasks are of course quite general. Indeed, his findings and approach have since vividly informed a number of other organizational ethnographies such as Kanter's (1977) study of gender relations in the workplace and Jackall's (1988) justly acclaimed portrait of the relativist bureaucratic ethic that governs managerial choice in large business firms. While studies in this domain are typically focused on contextualized, specific, and most often unarticulated local practices and rationalities as displayed by members of relatively small and de-marked organizational units or groups – of clerks, machine operators, police officers, doctors, and so on (and on) – the results are cast in highly general terms subject only to the potential ethnographic veto arising from a parallel future study.

The field guide for studies of this sort – providing a set of analytic categories and a theoretical rationale – is Erving Goffman's *The Presentation of Self in Everyday Life* (first published in 1956). The empirical center of the book is a partial community ethnography derived from Goffman's dissertation research, supervised by W. Lloyd Warner, in the Shetland Islands. But it is well worth keeping in mind that Goffman also thought of the work as something of a handbook for examining organizational behavior – '(for studying) behavior that goes on within the confines of a building or plant' (p. xi). The sensitizing notions conveyed in the work – such as front- and back-stage regions, impression management, and teamwork – have led to a lasting image of an organization as built up and sustained by the ritualized performances of organizational members. Goffman went on to do fieldwork in mental hospitals and publish *Asylums* (1961), a monograph that evokes the everyday grit and grind of organization (under)life like no other.

In this volume, the work of Sharon Macdonald (Chapter Four) and Simon Pulman-Jones (Chapter Six) neatly fit my organizational processes and informal relations category. Both studies focus on work groups in a single organization. Both closely examine the on-going negotiation and facework that routinely occur in these settings as tasks are situationally defined and carried out. Macdonald looks to the way new exhibits are developed in a science museum and finds not only a good deal of indeterminacy built into the process – thus effectively blunting some of the critical if not paranoid intellectual discourse that surrounds cultural production and museum work – but also suggests that the hedge on change and creativity in the museum stems from members who understandably fall back on certain long-standing institutional routines and recipes when in a pinch. A kind of organizational regression takes place as staff members charged with coming up with an innovative and client-friendly exhibit lose their enthusiasm for certain ideas and approaches as resource constraints, management oversight, and rather traditional assumptions surrounding the 'accessibility and clarity' of museum displays come into play.

Pulman-Jones also concentrates on routine interaction and teamwork. The interest here is on the labeling, evaluating, explaining, and, when possible, helping of children with chronic behavioral problems. As the sadly inconclusive story of Gemma makes clear, the clinic is a not-so-total institution whose staff struggles to meet a mixed, sometimes contradictory, set of organizational goals. Staff members are segmented however, assigned membership to either the core team or the psychiatric team, and the differences between the two animate the clinic. While Pulman-Jones notes that the two groups are in theory complementary, each doing what the other cannot, in practice the two are regularly at odds and, in the end, the work of the clinic suffers and its place if not survival in the larger social-service world is left in doubt.

Both studies examine first-hand the political and social worlds of quasi-professional work and focus on the gaps between official and unofficial practice as well as on the relations between groups vying for influence within the organization. The activity supported by informal relations does not necessarily resist or oppose what is organizationally prescribed – at times it may even buttress official procedures – but it flows from a local logic of institutionally segmented and stratified groups trying to accomplish what they regard as their real work. Laying out such logic and the constraints that seem to keep it in place is what studies of organizational processes and informal relations do best. Studies of this sort can easily make a quota of formal generalizing remarks sufficient to satisfy all but the most obsessed of theory fans. But what is perhaps most memorable and valuable is not the analytic work or the bold generalizing but the particularizing as authors report on specific episodes that serve as small epiphanies to readers. The human logic attached to organizational processes is thus made apparent, rather vivid and concrete, allowing a degree of ethnographic charity to be granted to those whose behavior might otherwise appear as odd, alien, lazy, malicious, conformist, mendacious, uninformed, or simply inexplicable.

Studies of Organizational Identity and Change

The roaring success of the American comic strip Dilbert reminds us of the mocking contempt many employees have for their bosses and the popular management theories they import willy-nilly into the workplace. Such theories often come christened with silly acronyms, tarted-up in fancy scientific language, and, so fast do they rise and fall, written in disappearing ink. Much high-flying and mass-marketed management theory is thin gruel indeed. Full of vapid rationalization and superficial fad, more than a few best-selling management books offer little more than an intellectual, if not ideological, justification for the foolhardy, flavor-of-the-month notions top executives rain down on lower- and mid-level employees. Airport bookstores are today stuffed with organizational salvation texts preaching the latest gospel of business process re-engineering, downsizing (or, as some say, rightsizing), knowledge-based organizational design, economic value-added analysis (EVA), and (fading fast) total quality management.

Nowhere is the penchant for fad and folderol more prominent than in the discourse surrounding organizational identity and change. The popularity of advice tracts and change manifestos seems to reflect an acute, widespread, and apparently pressing need among managers for guidance as venerable cultural patterns associated with organizational life unravel with innovations in technology, alterations in governance structures, the decline of bureaucracy as a model of organizational form, and the internationalization of markets and communications (e.g. Friedman 1999; Handy 1996). Stability, it seems, has given way to variability, and it should be no surprise that top executives trapped in unsettled times are on the lookout for ways to swiftly redirect and alter the character of organizations over which they assume responsibility and for which they are increasingly held accountable. Yet where heads of state agencies or chief executive officers (and their consultants) get their Masters-of-the-Universe ideas probably matters less than the consequences of putting such ideas into play. On this matter, a good deal of scholarly ink has been spilled.

Studies of organizational identity and change are often – perhaps most often – ethnographic in character. Because symbolic meaning and unfolding history are critical to any account of collective identity, there is perhaps no other substantive area for which ethnography is more suitable as a method of study. While there are a variety of theories floating about to explain identity and change, few can claim much predictive success and most are largely descriptive, basing their claims on the interpretation of a carefully laid-out case or set of cases. Narrative is the name of the game and students working this domain increasingly draw on methods and styles originating in the humanities and arts as well as anthropology and the social sciences. Over the years, the writing about organizational identity and change seems to have avoided much (but not all) of the mischief engendered by the sort of runaway positivism of variable analysis and hypothesis testing that afflicted organizational studies more broadly. At any rate, when well done, studies of organizational identity and change provide an elegant mix of representation and interpretation as authors balance the interaction of events, groups, ideas, institutions with the intentions and feelings of human actors and do so in a historically sensitive fashion.

Such studies inevitably involve the notion of organization culture(s) and this creates something of a problem for ethnographers. Culture is now, as noted earlier, a rather well-worn accounting device, available as an explanatory mechanism not only to ethnographers but to organizational members (and their many professionally interested observers such as consultants, reporters, stock analysts, social critics, politicians, competitors, prospective employees, and so on). It can be and is used to explain if not justify such matters as sterling or poor organizational performance, the success or failure of mergers and acquisitions, or the presence or absence of harmony among members. In some organizations, upper-level managers studiously work up explicit cultural values that are trickled down to the ordinary folks in the operational trenches who are presumed to then take their social and behavioral cues from their betters.

This consciousness of culture may even be promoted by an officially sanctioned (and budgeted) cultural engineering department charged with making sure the organization is a happy and productive one. Culture can thus be codified, posted to a wall, and cheerfully presented to an ethnographer as a way to ease the burden of organizational study. Home-grown culture claims are usually far more inchoate, contested, and ambiguous than these terse examples suggest, but cultural descriptions – whether appearing on the back of business cards or emanating from boozy lunchtime encounters – are quite common these days. Such raw material serves of course as an ingredient for a cooked ethnography (of the sort represented in this book) and thus represents yet another symbolic domain to be contextualized and interpreted by the ethnographer.

It is worth noting, however, that organizational members who give such an honored place to culture are themselves helping to displace the loony but surprisingly successful modern idea that organizational life is dominated solely by a secular, rational, matter-of-fact, means-ends logic and is therefore beyond or above culture – an economic notion that if true would allow us to dismiss matters such as custom, myth, ceremony, and ritual as unimportant and insult our boss's most recent convention speech with impunity. While we cannot afford to take member depictions of culture at face value or assume, for instance, that what some organizational members call traditions are in fact traditional, we can certainly count on the presence of organizational participants who are altogether prepared to take culture seriously, having dabbled a bit in some cultural analysis themselves.

All this is to say that there is widespread interest in culture as expressed in organizational settings. Ethnographers have been at the game of cultural representation for a long time and are altogether aware that the conventional talk and behavior from which their own portraits of organizational identity and change are derived serve also as interpretative resources to organizational members.

One of the best works to walk the fine line between ethnographic and member accounts is Gideon Kunda's (1992) study of 'culture control' in a high-tech firm. Examining the daily corridor and office talk, formal meetings and assemblies, offsite gatherings and written ideological materials on view in the firm (e.g. e-mails, posters, employee handbooks, etc.), Kunda argues that Techies (his term for organizational members) are active rather than passive recipients of the organizational culture. Paradoxically, however, the longer Techies remain with the firm and the higher they rise in the hierarchy, the less likely they are to experience and appreciate the culture as their own (although they may still post it on to others). The end result is widespread cynicism such that the very processes put to work creating a strong and desirable work culture undermine its existence.

Several chapters in this volume examine organizational identity and change. Most explicitly, Alex Ouroussoff in Chapter Two sketches out the corporate culture of Bion International (a pseudonym like almost all of the organization names used in this collection) where ideas associated with the capacity to manage and being a man are tightly interwoven and the successful high-flying managers in the firm must display toughness, potency, and an almost insatiable appetite for decisive action. This is compared to the culture of a non-profit firm called C&R where the identity between the capacity to manage and being a man is lacking and the successful manager need not demonstrate toughness, potency, or bold action. The contrasts could not be any more striking and Ouroussoff concludes that the profound differences between the two studied organizations give readers a good indication of the cultural diversity that exists among organizations in Britain. More provocatively, the chapter suggests just how difficult it is to imagine changing and perhaps improving the work situation for both women and men in an organization like Bion where 'libidinal desire and economic performance are unconsciously experienced (by male managers) as integral to one another'. At Bion, gender is social structure.

Christine Hine also looks at organizational identity in Chapter Three. In the confessional mode of an ethnographer who had to work long and hard to normalize her outsider presence in the lab, she takes up the work and careers of research scientists with a studied appreciation for how wider narratives – of competition for funds, findings, degrees – were drawn on by organizational members to make sense of the mundane events occurring in the organization. She notes just how the culture of the lab and the scientific results that are produced there are shaped by the notion of being in a race against competing labs. Hines enters the lab knowing something about the computer systems designed to aid the work of lab scientists and uses such knowledge to good effect as she looks closely at how such systems are put into practice in the lab. This dual-sited ethnography allows her to 'follow a thing' (information technology) across design and implementation settings discovering in the process just how its meaning shifts.

Another study of organizational identity and change is provided in Chapter Seven by Melissa Parker who takes us into the sexually charged world of a clap clinic in London. Here we learn the status order of diseases and patients as established by an unruly mix of organizational members segmented by rank, training, sexual orientation, and current organizational assignment. Like the two studies above, there is a good deal of culturally shaped work going on in the clinic. AIDs patients, for example, are actively sought out since they bring added resources to the clinic in both money and prestige. Common clap patients do not and are hence treated with dispatch and (relatively) poorly. The organizational culture itself is an unstable one as funding falls in some areas and jobs are lost, as the emotional detachment associated with the work occasionally gives way or as new members come into the organization more or less equipped with new ways of doing old things. Still, sexuality remains an attraction for most employees and serve as an important integrating bond across hierarchies in the clinic.

The three studies summarized here cover a good deal of ground. All are interested in how members of an organization produce, reproduce, and, to a degree, alter the symbolic meanings associated with what they do. Organizational identity is in the foreground of each chapter with change in the background but the two are inherently linked. Moreover, each study suggests that incremental shifts and repositionings of the organizational order are the rule and not the exception. Individuals and groups constantly adapt in response to new problems and this in turn pushes adaptations elsewhere in the organization.

Not represented in this collection are studies of organization change that go beyond modest shifts in the work order and reach deep into organizational structures and cultures. Some fine work in this regard exists. Consider, for example, Barley's (1986) ethnographic portrait of organizational change in two quite similar radiology laboratories where the same new technology was adopted (computerized scanners) but quite different and largely unintended organizational structures emerged as a result. Consider too Julian Orr's (1996) superb look at Xerox repairmen and how the workplace culture shapes their response to both organizational and technological change. Ethnographic work on organizational identity and change cannot but grow in the coming years.

Studies of Organizational Environments

Interest in how the world outside influences the world inside organizations (and vice versa) has occupied organizational theorists for a good deal of time. Much of this work is devoted to defining, characterizing, and categorizing certain alleged features of the social and institutional domains within which organizations, as human creations, operate. This taxonomic focus is hardly surprising. Organizational environments are conceptual fictions that cannot be put under bell jars to have their physical features observed, probed, tested, and measured. Their being is not obvious, their features not given but assigned. Still, there is no shortage of students willing and eager to take up the naming and framing tasks necessary to illustrate, conceptualize, and textualize this domain.

Ethnographic studies of organizational environments are plentiful. Some focus on how ritual practices spread from organization to organization, how broad cultural understandings of proper form and action influence the structural arrangements and socio-economic fortunes in and among organizations, and how new technologies are understood, utilized and in various organizations (often reshaping both the technology and so-called adopting organizations). All suggest that open borders are now far more salient than closed communities.[8] In addition to fieldwork, studies of this sort rely on a variety of credible secondary data sources including economic indictors, government reports, official statistics, and organizational records. Quasi-historical narratives – in pinched or expansive form – are written to provide meaning and texture to broadly descriptive but not so easily defined environmental constructs such as an institution, regulatory sphere, network, societal norm, industry, field,

---

8. Broad ethnographic treatments of the environment(s) in which organizations operate are often pitched as occupational, sometimes institutional, studies. See, for example, Rubinstein (1973), Latour and Woolgar (1986 [1979]), Gamst (1980), Applebaum (1981), Estroff (1981), Becker (1982), Kolb (1983), Dubinskas (ed.) (1988), Biggart (1989), Smith (1990), and T. Watson (1994). Some of the most interesting recent studies focus on upheavals in the international order and the resulting impact on organizations and their members. A wonderful display of such work is Glaeser's (1999) multi-sited ethnography on the merging of the east and west Berlin police forces that took place on the fall of the wall. See, too, Gusterson's (1996) splendid work on weapon designers in the post-cold war era at the Lawrence Livermore National Laboratory in California, and Milkman's (1997) careful study of workplace shrinkage in the American auto industry.

governing order and so on. These are all, like organization and culture, conceptual entities but, as well done studies demonstrate, they are as real in their consequence as air quality on health. How such entities form and assert force in the world is the kind of study in which determinative objectivity is a chimera and absolute relativity is self-defeating. Good ethnographic studies do not choose between these poles but walk the tightrope between them.

An example in this regard is Gary Alan Fine's (1996) work in the restaurant industry showing how life in restaurant kitchens emerges from choices made outside those settings. Working in three quite different organizations, Fine demonstrates that what is served (and how it is served) is shaped by the customer niche of the restaurant and the labor and food costs as filtered through the decisions of managers responding to what they regard as market pressures. Another quite different example is Malcolm Young's (1991) close look at police practices as they occur on the ground in urban areas. A career officer who read anthropology rather than law while seconded at mid-career to the university, Young provides a stunning portrait of British policing that cuts across organizations and organizational segments and leaves the reader with a sharp if disturbing symbolic analysis of a most insulated and conservative institution.

Walter Powell's (1985) comparative ethnography of publishing organizations provides a final illustration of work focused on organizations and their environments. Powell places publishing houses in the center of a network of ties that link authors, libraries, booksellers, editors, readers, scholars, and members of parent corporations together. Social ties shape publishing decisions as editors use their network positions to advance their careers, meet organizational goals, and achieve aesthetic aims of publishing high-quality yet marketable books.

In this volume, several chapters provide studies of organizational environments. Most apparent perhaps is Chapter Five where Bob Simpson discusses his multi-sited ethnographic work on divorce and separation in Britain. His study takes place in what he calls a 'kaleidoscope of organizational cultures' involving judges, social workers, barristers, welfare and benefit officers, mediators, doctors, counselors, and many more, including, most critically, members of the families that are splitting up. Sponsored in the research by those wanting to take into account the ever-so-difficult-to-locate 'client's point of view', Simpson notes – with some longing for a fixed research site wherein he could be anthropologically at home – that there is no community of the divorced. His work turns on the metaphors of conflict and separation used by various interested parties in divorce proceedings as a way of ordering and analysing the disorder in a fluid and continually changing organizational field.

In like fashion, David Mosse in Chapter Eight finds himself swimming in multi-organizational waters as he considers the role ethnography plays and might play in rural development projects. The problem for the would-be ethnographer of development institutions lies in balancing the demands for engagement in an agency with the critical analysis of the purposes and practices of such an agency. To take part in a development project is to put forward an agenda that presumably one believes in. Simultaneously to analyse that agenda as, say, an instance of how thought and practice are structured by development work is, then, a bit like attempting to push (or stop) the bus that one is currently riding on. Mosse takes us through a bewildering array of participative approaches that have currency in the field and concludes that none of them effectively solves the ethnographic dilemma of how to reflect critically on a project while trying to achieve its goals. In the end, the ethnographer as a member of a development team is probably best served by thinking of social research as a means of testing, refining, and building consensus across groups and organizations party to a development project rather than as a way of analysing and explaining institutional performances and relationships.

Such a position is shared by Simone Abram who, in Chapter Nine, tells a terrific tale of planning and its discontents in a southeast English village. Acting as an ethnographer of policy and policy implementation, Abram works with planners, politicians, local residents, landowners, and developers, all of whom have a stake in the outcome of a housing estate planning process. Like Mosse, Abram is quite aware of the trade-offs involved in practising advocacy ethnography but, in this case, opts not to work with any one group or organization and thus to suspend loyalty while trying to achieve something of a neutral position among those she studies. And, as we might expect, some are accepting of her inquiries (planners) and some are not (politicians). The ethnography that results is not apolitical, of course, but Abram notes it is intendedly disinterested and designed (as the work is being done) to follow through the process by which one view becomes dominant over others.

These three studies of quite complex organizational environments are all rather loose methodologically. This is probably to be expected in multi-sited work for which no apparent format yet exists. The authors tells us about their sources but little about how they sorted out and drew on these sources. As with all ethnographic writings, a good deal of silent selectivity stands behind a writer's decision about what plot to follow, what details to include in a story, what organizing concepts to use, what events to highlight, and so forth. And, as we all know only too well, the facts, even ethnographic ones, do not speak for themselves but must be given significance and weight by interpretive nerve and sharp argument. The craft of organizational ethnography, no less than ethnography in any other domain, is a writer's craft which is learned but not taught. While there may be rules for writing evocative, powerful, persuasive ethnography, rest assured: no one knows what they are.

Studies of Organizational Morality and Conflict[9]

What people (in groups) consider right and worth fighting over cannot be separated from the organizational (or societal) contexts in which conflict appears. In some situations, individuals may act as self-interested, more or less atomized rational actors who seek to maximize their gains or cut their losses. In other situations, people may fight over communal values and beliefs or seek social justice with enormous determination. Those who differ may prefer to negotiate or bargain, turn to a mediator, attack one another, or simply lump their differences and carry on. Ethnographic studies of organizational morality and conflict examine real and imagined breaches in the normative order associated with organizational life. The focus is on disputes – of a mundane or spectacular sort – and the playing out of ruling relations in organizational life.

These can be cut into two types of study. The first focuses on the grievances, conflicts, disputes, and illicit practices that arise in 'legitimate' organizations such as business firms, government agencies, charitable societies, and service groups. The second type examines organizations considered illegal, countercultural, or otherwise beyond the pale given conventional societal standards, such as urban gangs, drug-dealing cabals, groups of flying saucer fanatics, family crime organizations, and religious cults. The line between the two is, however, anything but hard and fast, for ethnographers (and others) continually discover that the boundaries between the legitimate and illegitimate, appropriate and inappropriate, the harmonious and conflictual, the good and bad are everywhere habitually blurred, thus undermining any absolutist or rationalist understanding of normative behavior.

A good deal of work of the first type tracks back and through the anthropology of law. The 'trouble case' method is a familiar strategy for examining conflicts of all sorts and there exists a rich ethnographic literature concerned with how members

9. This category is lifted from a useful literature review of ethnographic contributions to organizational sociology by Morrill and Fine (1997). An enthusiastic and historically informed push for the ethnographic study of conflict in organizations is provided by Barley (1991). A wonderful example of work in this category is Morrill (1995). Disputes and conflicts in organizations are not of course ignored in other research domains but what sets studies of this category apart from others is the ethnographer's focused and intense interest in the moral order of the setting or settings under examination. Conflict, as treated in, for example, ethnographies of informal relations in organizations is interesting insofar as it animates group dynamics or marks and solidifies social boundaries in the organization but it is not the centerpiece of the work. In organizational identity studies, conflict among self-interested groups is interesting insofar as what is at stake is the character of the overall organization, but how conflicts routinely arise and how they are settled among organizational members are of secondary interest. Conflict is considered common, but the moral basis on which it turns is not of central concern.

of various societies and cultural groups handle their disputes (e.g. Nader and Todd 1978). A recent organizational ethnography making good use of such an approach is James Tucker's *The Therapeutic Organization* (1999). The setting for this study is a self-labeled 'post-bureaucratic' business firm that has tried with some success to decentralize and flatten hierarchical lines of authority, reduce specialization, and promote strong personal relationships and goodwill among employees (who are a relatively homogeneous lot in terms of class and race). Tucker's interests lie in how employees of a firm emphasizing teamwork and cooperation in a work world marked by considerable (and intentional) ambiguity define and respond to deviance in their midst. He finds they do so rather sympathetically, turning interpersonal and intergroup troubles into intrapersonal afflictions of the sort that self-help, counseling, and friendly third-party coaching can typically resolve. Conflict does not of course vanish but is shaped, managed, and constrained by subtle, informal means initiated by fellow employees diagnosing and treating one another (and themselves) for personal lapses and inadequacies. Tucker concludes with the entirely plausible thesis that therapeutic means of dispute resolution – and a morality system based on self-help, personal character, and individual responsibility – thrive under conditions of equality and intimacy.

Of particular interest to ethnographers in this subdomain is the social organization of what might be thought of as systemic deviance. A number of striking ethnographic studies explore persistent negligence, incompetence, mismanagement, rule-bending, and rule-breaking in organizations as diverse as ministries, hospitals, sports teams, universities, and business enterprises. Sometimes it is a single case that organizes a work as in Diane Vaughan's (1996) ethnographic look at the working norms and practices of various operational and engineering groups in NASA leading to the Challenger disaster. Other times, corporate misconduct (or dirty business) is simply business as usual and ethnographically portrayed in precisely such a way (Punch 1996; Mars 1982). Perhaps nowhere is the friction between the espoused aims of a collectivity and the evasive social reality of daily interactional life revealed as more problematic than in ethnographic studies of organizations created to uphold moral systems such as the police and the courts (e.g. Manning 1981; Conley and O'Barr 1990).

Just as ethnographers of supposedly legitimate organizations illustrate their unseemly or deviant sides, ethnographers of deviant organizations illustrate their seemly or normal sides. This anthropologizing of unconventional and alien occurs in organizational as well as societal contexts. One such study is Jankowski's (1992) ethnographic treatment of urban gangs as quasi-rational business organizations in which Weber's venerated entrepreneurial spirit, not risk, turf, or violence, is the driving force in the organization. Another example of the contextualization of the seemingly exotic is Anne Allison's (1994) linking of male dominance and organizational culture to playing out (and with) gender identities in the hostess clubs associated with corporate nightlife in Japan. Hostess clubs of both the respectable and not-so-respectable sort are in Allison's view not peripheral play palaces for upper-level Japanese *sarariimen* out for a good time but rather central establishments for the creation of bonds among white-collar men which help to forge a masculine identity that suits the needs of the prestigious organizations that foot the bill.

In this volume, commentary on organizational morality and conflict is part of the background of most chapters (most apparent perhaps in those by Ouroussoff, Pulman-Jones, and Parker) but comes to the fore only in two. And, in both, the deviance and conflict (largely submerged) to be accounted for is our own. In Chapter Ten, Stella Mascarenhas-Keyes looks at some of the difficulties ethnographers run into when working with and for non-academic institutions. The call for short-cut or time-efficient research methods is familiar to ethnographers who have written needs assessments, market appraisals, or set forth intervention strategies and prescriptions for change at the bequest of others. But is speedy ethnography – what Rist (1980) calls 'Blitzkreig ethnography' – possible? Can it answer the kinds of questions the movers and shakers of policy worlds have in mind? Mascarenhas-Keyes is not altogether certain but documents a fair number of mistakes she made in the field as a way to gently remind readers that research purpose(s) and quality are quite flexible, contestable matters, irrevocably linked to political and moral concerns.

Martin O'Neill, in Chapter Eleven, worries about the proper role of an ethnographer when studying one's own kind and having therefore the skills and interests that may help others in times of need. In theory, O'Neill notes, the ethnographer is the 'detached observer' attending first and foremost to research. In reality, as O'Neill discovered, such a stance is not only impractical and likely to cause resentment, but immoral if suffering results. The brief case study O'Neill puts forward recounts an episode in which he more or less forgot his research role and joined with those he was studying in the handling of a professional (and urgent) task. It is a case that reminds us that the role of an ethnographer always competes with other roles we play – as citizens, as friends, as parents, or, in O'Neill's case, as a former ambulance worker quite able to offer aid and assistance if needed on the scene of an emergency. And, as O'Neill comes to realize, to embrace fully a research role would be to reduce ethnography to a soulless, empty, technocratic pursuit, devoid of recognizably human obligations and attachments.[10]

---

10. It seems the moral dilemmas of fieldwork become increasingly of interest to ethnographers as they move closer to home. With such a move has come the somewhat belated recognition that participant-observation is yet another brilliant addition to our repertoire of ways to make ourselves (and others) uncomfortable when in close contact. That there are no special moral codes available to fieldworkers (or special dispensation from them) is a point well and movingly made by Behar (1996), Wolfe (1992), and Rosaldo (1989).

Both O'Neill and Mascarenhas-Keyes remind us of a few of the ethical and moral dilemmas that seem to be particularly linked with organizational ethnography. Along with other contributors to this volume, they also remind us that there may be some larger-scale changes at work that bode ill for ethnographic scholarship. As we try, for example, to find ways to speed up our performance, accept the dictates of research review boards without principled resistance, reduce our aims to the representation of mentalities or points of view not contextualized by class, race, gender, politics, or economics, or adopt without question the aims of research sponsors as a kind of tax burden necessary to carry on our work, ethnography become less distinct, adventurous, and valuable as a research endeavor. Ethnographic work will certainly continue in the foreseeable future, but of what kind?

Some Final Words . . .

The four areas of organizational study highlighted above serve mainly as templates to organize research materials. But they can also be thought of as thematic tensions (or temptations) built into organizational ethnography. Each offers a seductive way to frame ethnographic materials. Lengthy periods of fieldwork allow for considerable topical selectivity and range. As a relatively artistic, improvised, and situated model of social research, a good number of authorial choices are required when writing up (or down) the results of a study. A single-sited study could result in a research report focused on any one or several of the following: organization culture and sub-culture, power and authority, managerial decision-making, feuding occupational enclaves, environmental pressures and influence, change (and resistance to change), and so on. Thematic choices among many possibilities are required and any given study could go in a number of substantive directions. Moreover, since ethnographies are typically designed while they are being accomplished, what begins as, say, a focused probe of informal relations on the shopfloor might well end up as a study of new recruits to the organization or the response of the workforce to a new production technology or form of management.

There is, in sum, a rather intractable unpredictability associated with ethnographic studies. Templates can be bent, stretched, and combined in a variety of ways. Where the research will lead is often up in the air throughout a fieldwork stay and beyond. Sponsors of ethnographic research may regard this as perverse but few ethnographers will argue that it could or should be otherwise. Trying to chart a direction in a scholarly field that emphasizes particularism over universalism and regards the playing out of chance and indeterminacy more highly than causality and correlation is therefore a risky business. But, like the economist who predicted nine of the last two recessions, I will bring this meandering to a close by considering (quickly) a few areas where I think ethnographic work might in the near future concentrate and prove particularly helpful and timely to both organizational researchers and practitioners alike. These are limited to broad alterations now taking place in the workplace (and in the nature of work itself) and address the rather general 'flies in amber' critique leveled occasionally at ethnography for too often presenting a rather static view of social life and soft-pedaling flux, change, and historical agency (e.g. Marcus 1998; Clifford 1988)

Most pertinent perhaps is the blurring of practical and conceptual boundaries surrounding the workplace as work careers, jobs, firms, hierarchy, and the division of labor change in character and meaning.[11] Sharpness and clarity give way to fog and uncertainty. Where exactly is the workplace? What is a firm? Who is a manager? Societal-level changes are afoot here as well. Take for example the many public agencies that are now expected to operate according to market principles. How are they doing? Or, what is happening to those public services once thought to be the sacred preserve of the state but which have been turned over to profit-making firms? What is a public good? How is it dispensed? Who wins and who loses?

A good deal of conceptual mischief is also occurring on both sides of the conventional boundary separating home and work. Policies, practices, and opportunities continually arise to integrate or collapse these worlds. Increasing amounts of paid labor are now forms of 'remote work', performed at home, in the car, at a client's office, in hotel suites, in conference centers, or, more generally, out of the traditional plant or office. And home moves toward work as well with fashionable 'quality-of-life programs' of on-site day care, elder care, satellite schools, and flex-time programs appearing in the workplace. A result is that some of our most tenaciously held assumptions about the proper organization of work and the proper work of organizations are being questioned.

Organizational ethnographers are well equipped to examine local and broad shifts taking place in what it means to be a 'good' organizational citizen, to put forth a 'fair' day's work, or observe the 'right' of privacy (e.g. 'Have you had your urine test today?'). What does a supervisor do in a 'post-bureaucratic' world? What of those protean yet ever-more-elusive middle managers in organizations? How are managers and non-managers distinguished when 'self-directed' work arrangements push supervisory responsibility to front-line employees? Is the difference merely a parking space, a style of dress, the size of a pay check, access to certain

11. It is here perhaps where postmodernism plays an obvious and useful analytic role. As Marcus (1998) suggests, postmodernism finds its subject matter and audience where meanings are fluid, where stable identities are difficult to find, where the boundaries that structure identity such as work, family, home, and state are apparently collapsing, and where the experience of liminality is seemingly widespread. Such conditions give postmodernism its exaggerated, hyperreal character as well as its apocalyptic flair. With a few exceptions, ethnographers have been wary of postmodernism, approaching it not so much as a poisonous or dastardly narcotic but as a temptation still somewhat out of reach. This cautious stance of ethnographers toward postmodern social theory is taken up by Graham Watson (1987) in his wonderfully titled article, 'Make me reflexive – but not yet'. See, also, the essays collected in Brown (1995).

scarce resources or, as Nippert-Eng (1995) argues, the right to blur boundaries that others cannot? Does it mean that the manager becomes simply a financial overseer (untrained in the specifics of the work or organization)?

Systems of meaning are the bread and butter of ethnographic research and they are anything but stable. With structural and technological change, work arrangements and the interaction patterns that support them shift as individuals and groups face new problems that both reflect and promote broader cultural changes that in turn influence organizations in new ways. Telecommunication technologies for example alter interaction patterns in and between organizations but we know little of such matters. Ten years ago few of us had even heard of, much less used, the internet, voice mail, cell phones, e-mail, video conferencing, and the like. Changes are no doubt both subtle and dramatic but they are seemingly taking place on a grand scale. What might an ethnography of an organization look like if the work studied involved computer technicians writing programs in the morning in Beijing and sending their work at the end of the day to a similarly trained group in Seattle who pass it on at the end of their day to another group in Bangalore who, after putting in their efforts, then send it back to Beijing? Messy ethnography indeed.

Consider, too, the use of teams in organizations. Teamwork is something of a current buzzword in a number of organizations large and small. Work teams typically cut across occupational divisions of labor, operational units, and, sometimes, hierarchical ranks. Occasionally government regulators, consultants, suppliers, and customers or clients to the organization are added to the mix, vastly complicating the work lives of employees. A person's job becomes embedded within a greater variety of others' work such that just who is responsible for what becomes difficult to determine. Moreover, the same individual may serve on several teams simultaneously. Teamwork of this sort may demand new skills and create new group alignments and loyalties that slide and collide with one another at various times in various places both inside and outside the organization. What this might mean in terms of one's identity (or lack thereof) as an organizational member, a worker, a manager is clearly an open question.

Relatedly, shrinkage of the workforce in organization is also of much current interest. What are we to make of across-the-board reductions in force? With fewer resources to support their work, the presumed lucky ones left seated after a sharp cut may well be asked to stand and do a good deal more than they have previously been accustomed to do – to fix computers, move furniture, monitor the phones, polish the floors, run copy machines, host visitors, create their own desk-top-publishable reports, and turn off the lights on the way home. Fewer permanent employees may well do the same amount of work required in the organization but the way they think about, interact, and carry on with their duties will surely change. And what of the downsized? Where do they go? What do they do? How does a laid-off working mother of three feed her family?

Figuring out where the organization begins and ends and just who belongs to it is yet another area that is likely to be increasingly problematic in the future. The growing use of part-time workers and consultants, the 'out-sourcing' of services, the tightening of connections between clients and providers or vendors and buyers all lead to ever more slippery and amorphous organizational borders. If workers are 'leased' between NatWest in the UK and Bank One in the US for months, even years, at a time, for whom do they work? Does it matter? What are we to make of occupational gypsies or transients – whether machinists, fishermen, software engineers, or university professors? Are organizational structures and cultures becoming increasingly homogenized or isomorphic as permeability advances or are they increasingly diverse? How are power centers shifting?

By raising these questions, my purpose is simply to underline the point that the study of contemporary organizations is and will remain a vibrant area. It is a (somewhat) delimited domain of social life richly and, I think, especially fit for ethnographic representation. The work presented in this volume is testimony to the ethnographer's pledge to take us elsewhere and thus helps us learn what certain groups of people who are more or less stuck in organizational conditions they did not entirely choose are doing and why. This is 'getting out the news' – telling what lab scientists do, how some managers get ahead, what development planners are up to, how certain clinics are organized, and so on. It is storytelling to be sure, but remains firmly in a scholarly, non-fiction division and when done well carries a good deal of persuasive clout and may well expand our sense of human possibilities through the study of how people do things together.

While there are pressures on ethnographers to produce detachable conclusions and weave ever more intricate analytic webs, these are stymied by the storytelling or narrative basis of the trade and resisted with style. Narrative is not an ornamental or decorative feature designed to make ethnography more palatable or audience-friendly, but a cognitive instrument in its own right. Realism, as a representational, tale-telling practice, plus a belief system grounded on a witnessing ideal and tied to a methodology that remains improvisational and loose, still marks the trade. This is not to be dismissed. It may well be what ethnographers do best. There is much to be done.

References

Albolafia, M. (1998), *Making Markets*, Cambridge, MA: Harvard University Press.
Allison, A. (1994), *Nightwork: Sexuality, Pleasure, and Corporate Maasculinity in a Tokyo Hostess Club*, Chicago: University of Chicago Press.
Appadurai, A. (1997), 'Fieldwork in the Era of Globalization', *Anthropology and Humanism*, **22**: 115–18.

Applebaum, H. (1981), *Royal Blue: The Culture of Construction Workers*, New York: Holt, Rinehart, and Winston.

Barley, S.R. (1986), 'Technology as an Occasion for Structuring: Evidence of CT Scanners and the Social Order of Radiology Departments', *Administrative Science Quarterly*, **31**: 78–108.

—— (1991), 'Contextualizing Conflict: Notes on the Anthropology of Disputes and Negotiations', in M.H. Bzerman, R.J. Lewicki, and B.H. Sheppard (eds), *Research on Negotiation in Organizations*, **3**: 165–203.

Becker, H.S. (1982), *Art Worlds*, Berkeley: University of California Press.

Behar, R. (1996), *The Vulnerable Observer: Anthropology that Breaks Your Heart*, Boston: Beacon Press.

Biggart, N.W. (1989), *Charismatic Capitalism: Direct Selling Organizations in America*, Chicago: University of Chicago Press.

Brettell, C.B. (ed.) (1993), *When They Read What We Write*, Westport, CT: Bergin and Garvey.

Brown, R.H. (ed.) (1995), *Postmodern Representations*, Urbana: University of Illinois Press.

Burawoy, M. and Verdery, N. (1999), *Uncertain Transition: Ethnography of Change in the Postsocialist World*, NY: Rowman and Littlefield.

Chanlet, J.-F. (1994), 'Francophone Organizational Analysis (1950–1990)', *Organization Studies*, **15**: 47–79.

Child, J. (1995), 'Guest Editorial' (Special Issue: The European Perspective on Organization Theory), *Organization Science*, **6**: 117–18.

Clifford, J. (1988), *The Predicament of Culture: Twentieth-Century Ethnography, Literature, and Art*, Cambridge, Mass.: Harvard University Press.

—— (1997), *Routes: Travel and Translation in the Late Twentieth Century*, Cambridge, Mass.: Harvard University Press.

Conley, J.M. and O'Barr, W.M. (1990), *Rules versus Relationships: The Ethnography of Legal Discourse*, Chicago: University of Chicago Press.

Czarniawska, B. (1997), *Narrating the Organization: Drama of Institutional Identity*, Chicago: University of Chicago Press.

Dalton, M. (1959), *Men Who Manage: Fusions of Feeling and Theory in Administration*, New York: Wiley.

Davis, S.G. (1997), *Spectacular Nature: Corporate Culture and the Sea World Experience.* Berkeley: University of California Press.

di Leonardo, M. (1998), *Exotics at Home: Anthropologies, Others and American Modernity*, Chicago: University of Chicago Press.

Dubinskas, F. (ed.) (1988), *Making Time: Ethnographies of High Technology Organizations*, Philadelphia: Temple University Press.

Economist (1996), 'Nobel Savages', 30 March, 72.

Estroff, S.E. (1981), *Making It Crazy: An Ethnography of Psychiatric Clients in an American Community*, Berkeley: University of California Press.

Ewick, P. and Silbey, S. (1995), 'Subversive Stories and Hegemonic Tales: Toward a Sociology of Narrative', *Law and Society Review*, **29**: 197–226.

Featherstone, M. (ed.) (1990), *Global Culture*, London: Sage.

Fine, G.A. (1996), *Kitchens: The Culture of Restaurant Work*, Chicago: University of Chicago Press.

Fjellman, S.M. (1992), *Vinyl Leaves: Walt Disney World and America*, Boulder, CO: Westview.

Fox, R.G. (ed.) (1991), *Recapturing America: Working in the Present*, Santa Fe, NM: School of American Research Press.

Friedman, T.L. (1999), *The Lexus and the Olive Tree: Understanding Globalization*, New York: Farrar, Strauss, and Giroux.

Gamst, F.C. (1980), *The Hogshead: An Industrial Ethnology of the Locomotive Engineer*, New York: Holt, Rinehart, and Winston.

Garson, B. (1975), *All the Livelong Day: The Meaning and Demeaning of Routine Work*, Garden City, NJ: Doubleday.

Geertz, C. (1983), *Local Knowledge: Further Essays in Interpretive Anthrpology*, New York: Basic.

—— (1988), *Works and Lives: The Anthropologist as Author*, Stanford, CA: Stanford University Press.

—— (1995), *After the Fact: Two Countries, Four Decades, One Anthropologist*, Cambridge, Mass.: Harvard University Press.

Glaeser, A. (1999), *Divided in Unity: Identity, Germany and the Berlin Police*, Chicago: University of Chicago Press.

Goffman, E. (1959 [1956]), *The Presentation of Self in Everyday Life*, New York: Anchor.

—— (1961), *Asylums: Essays on the Social Situation of Mental Patients and Other Inmates*, New York: Anchor.

Gupta, A. and Ferguson, J. (eds) (1997), *Anthropological Locations: Boundaries and Grounds of a Field Science*, Berkeley: University of California Press.

Gusterson, H. (1996), *Nuclear Rites: A Weapons Laboratory at the End of the Cold War*, Berkeley: University of California Press.

Handy, C. (1996), *Beyond Certainty*, Boston: Harvard Business School Press.

Hannerz, U. (1992), *Cultural Complexity: Studies in the Social Organization of Meaning*. New York: Columbia University Press.

Hinnings, B. (1988), 'Defending Organization Theory: A British View from North America', *Organization Studies*, **9**: 2–7.

Hochschild, A.R. (1983), *The Managed Heart: Commercialization of Human Feeling*, Berkeley: University of California Press.

Jackall, R. (1988), *Moral Mazes: The World of Corporate Managers*, New York: Oxford University Press.

Jankowski, M.S. (1992), *Islands in the Street: Gangs and American Urban Society*, Berkeley: University of California Press.

Kahn, J. (1995), *Culture, Multiculture, Postculture*, London. Sage.

Kanter, R.M. (1977), *Men and Women of the Corporation*, New York: Basic.

Kidder, T. (1981), *The Soul of the New Machine*, Boston: Little, Brown.

—— (1990), *Among Schoolchildren*, New York: Avon.

Kolb, D.M. (1983), *The Mediators*, Cambridge, Mass.: MIT Press.

Koza, M.P. and Thoenig, J.-C. (1995), 'Organization Theory at the Crossroads: Some Reflections on European and United States Approaches to Organizational Research', *Organization Science*, **6**: 1–8.

Kunda, G. (1992), *Engineering Culture: Control and Commitment in a High-Tech Corporation*, Philadelphia: Temple University Press.

Kuper, A. (1999), *Culture: The Anthropologists' Account*, Cambridge, Mass.: Harvard University Press.

Lamphere, L. (ed.) (1992), *Structuring Diversity: Ethnographic Perspectives on the New Immigration*, Chicago: University of Chicago Press.

Latour, B. (1993), *We Have Never Been Modern*, tr. C. Porter, Cambridge, Mass.: Harvard University Press.

—— and Woolgar, S. (1986 [1979]), *Laboratory Life: The Construction of Scientific Facts*, Princeton: Princeton University Press.

Leidner, R. (1993), *Fast Food, Fast Talk: Service Work and the Routinization of Everyday Life*, Berkeley: University of California Press.

Lewis, M. (1990), *Liar's Poker: Rising through the Wreakage on Wall Street*, New York: Penguin.

Lutz, C. and Collier, J. (1992), *Reading National Geographic*, Chicago: University of Chicago Press.

Manning, P. (1981), *The Narc's Game*, Cambridge: MIT Press.

Marcus, G.E. (1998), *Ethnography through Thick and Thin*, Princeton: Princeton University Press.

Mars, G. (1982), *Cheats at Work: An Anthropology of the Workplace*, London: Unwin.

Milkman, R. (1997), *Farewell to the Factory: Auto Workers in the Late Twentieth Century*, Berkeley: University of California Press.

Morrill, C. (1995), *The Executive Way: Conflict Management in Corporations*, Chicago: University of Chicago Press.

—— and Fine, G.A. (1997), 'Ethnographic Contributions to Organizational Sociology', *Sociological Methods and Research*, **25**: 424–51.

Nader, L. and Todd, H.F. (eds) (1978), *The Disputing Process: Law in Ten Societies*, New York: Columbia University Press.

Nash, J. (1993), *Crafts in the World Market*, Albany: State University of New York Press.

Nippert-Eng, C.E. (1995), *Home and Work: Negotiating Boundaries through Everyday Life*, Chicago: University of Chicago Press.

Orr, J.E. (1996), *Talking about Machines: An Ethnography of a Modern Job*, Ithaca: Cornell University Press.

Passaro, J. (1997), 'You can't take the Subway to the Field', in A. Gupta and J. Ferguson (eds), *Anthropological Locations*, Berkeley: University of California Press.

Perlow, L.A. (1997), *Finding Time: How Corporations, Individuals and Families Can Benefit from New Work Practices*, Ithaca: Cornell University Press.

Powell, W.W. (1985), *Getting into Print: The Decision-making Process in Scholarly Publishing*, Chicago: University of Chicago Press.

Punch, M. (1996), *Dirty Business: Exploring Corporate Misconduct*, London: Sage.

Radway, J.A. (1997), *A Feeling for Books: The Book-of-the-Month Club, Literary Taste, and Middle-Class Leisure*, Chapel Hill, NC: University of North Carolina Press.

Rist, R.C. (1982), 'Blitzkrieg Ethnography: On the Transformation of a Method into a Method', *Educational Researcher*, **9**: 8–10.

Rosaldo, R. (1989), *Culture and Truth: The Remaking of Social Analysis*, Boston: Beacon Press.

Rubinstein, J. (1973), *City Police*, New York: Farrar, Strauss, Giroux.

Smith, V. (1990), *Managing in the Corporate Interest: Control and Resistance in An American Bank*, Berkeley: University of California Press.

Terkel, S. (1974), *Working: People Talk About What They Do All Day and How They Feel About What They Do*, New York: Random House.

—— (1984), *The Good War: An Oral History of World War II*, New York: Random House.

Tucker, J.C. (1999), *The Therapeutic Organization*, New York: Oxford University Press.

Van Maanen, J. (1995), 'An End to Innocence: The Ethnography of Ethnography', in J. Van Maanen (ed.), *Representation in Ethnography*, London: Sage.

—— (ed.) (1999), *Qualitative Studies of Organizations*, London: Sage.

Vaughan, D. (1996), *The Challenger Launch Decision: Risky Technology, Culture, and Deviance at NASA*, Chicago: University of Chicago Press.

Watson, G. (1987), 'Make Me Reflexive – But not Yet: Strategies for Managing Essential Reflexivity in Ethnographic Discourse', *Journal of Anthropological Research*, **43**: 29–41.

Watson, J. (ed.) (1997), *Golden Arches East: McDonald's in East Asia*, Stanford, CA: Stanford University Press.

Watson, T.J. (1994), *In Search of Management: Culture, Chaos and Control in Managerial Work*, London: Routledge.

Wolfe, M. (1992), *A Thrice Told Tale: Feminism, Postmodernism and Ethnographic Responsibility*, Stanford, CA: Stanford University Press.

Young, M. (1991), *An Inside Job: Policing and Police Culture in Britain*, Oxford: Clarendon.

Zabusky, S.E. (1995), *Launching Europe: An Ethnography of European Cooperation in Space Science*, Princeton, NJ: Princeton University Press.

Name Index

Abram, S. 4, 5, 9, 239, 249
Akeroyd, A.V. 229, 230
Albolafia, M. 236, 256
Allen, I. 151–2, 155
Allen, J. 187, 202
Allison, A. 251–2, 256
Alvesson, M. 87, 95, 179
Appadurai, A. 172, 179, 234, 256
Applebaum, H. 247, 257
Ardener, E. 20, 32
Asad, T. 13
Atkinson, P. 89, 95, 229, 230

Bagadion, B.U. 173, 179
Baland, J.M. 177, 179
Barley, S.R. 246, 250, 257
Bate, S.P. 1–2, 6, 9, 13
Baumann, P. 177, 179
Beales, A. 223, 230
Beck, U. 103, 104, 114
Becker, H.S. 247, 257
Beck-Gernsheim, E. 103, 114
Behar, R. 252, 257
Berreman, G. 89, 92, 95
Bicker, A. 183, 203
Biggart, N.W. 247, 257
Boddy, D. 64, 74
Bourdieu, P. 223
Boyacigiller, N. 21, 33
Brettell, C. 237, 257
Brown, R.H. 254, 257
Buchanan, D. 5, 13, 64, 74
Buckley, P. 20, 22–3, 25, 27, 32–3
Buerk, M. 2
Burawoy, M. 239. 257
Burke, K. 56, 57
Burton, L.B. 103, 116

Cahoon, L. 177, 179
Casson, M. 22, 32

Chambers, R. 2, 13, 165–7, 179
Chanlet, J.-F. 233, 257
Chapman, M. 4, 6, 7, 10, 13, 37, 92, 94, 236, 237
Charlesworth, M. 72, 74
Child, J. 233, 257
Clifford, J. 4, 7, 13, 93, 95, 234, 254, 257
Coase, R. 22, 32
Cochrane, A. 187, 202
Cohen, A.P. 90, 95
Collier, J. 240, 259
Collins, H.M. 72, 74
Collins, J. 107, 114
Conley, J.M. 251, 257
Corlyon, J. 101, 114, 115
Cullen, S. 199, 202
Cunnison, S. 35, 57
Czarniawksa, B. 240, 257

Dalton, M. 241, 257
Davidson, A.I. 200, 202
Davis, G. 109, 114
Davis, S.G. 240, 257
de Beauvoir, S. 42, 57
Denning, P.J. 62, 74
Descola, P. 37, 58
di Leonardo, M. 239, 257
Dicken, P. 19, 32
Donegan, E. van 137, 155
Donnan, H. 113, 114
Douglas, D.J. 224, 230
Douglas, M. 134, 135
Dubinskas, F. 247, 257
Du Gay, P. 82, 95
Dunning, J. 19
Durkheim, E. 4

Edwards, J. 4, 14, 199, 202
Edwards, M. 177, 179
Errington, F. 82, 95

Name Index

Schneider, D.M. 105, 115
Schön, D. 107, 115
Sekaran, U. 21, 33
Serres, M. 200
Silbey, S. 240, 258
Sillitoe, P. 183, 203
Silverstone, R. 79
Simpson, B. 4, 8, 9, 239, 248
Sinclair, S. 1, 14, 137, 156
Smith, V. 247, 260
Stack, C. 103, 116
Stocking, G. 1, 2, 14
Strathern, M. 6, 7, 11, 12, 14, 47, 58, 94, 96, 103, 105, 116

Terkel, S. 238, 260
Thoenig, J.-C. 233, 259
Thornton, R. 7, 15
Timms, N. 2, 14
Todd, H.F. 251, 259
Tonkin, E. 27, 33
Traweek, S. 72, 76
Tucker, J.C. 251, 260
Turnbull, C. 10, 15

Uphoff, N. 164, 181

van Gennep, A. 134, 135
Van Maanen, J. 4, 10, 15, 260

van Velsen, J. 171, 181
Vaughan, D. 251. 260
Veneración, C. 173, 181
Verdery, N. 239, 257
Vike, H. 185, 199, 03
Volken, H. 164, 181

Walker, J. 101, 109, 114, 115, 116
Watson, G. 254, 260
Watson, J. 234, 260
Watson, T.J. 247, 261
Weber, M. 2–3, 251
Weiss, C. 102, 116
Werbner, P. 82, 96
Williamson, O. 22, 33
Wilmott, H. 37, 58
Wolfe, M. 252, 260
Woolgar, S. 11, 37, 58, 64, 70, 72, 76, 247
Wright, S. 3–4, 15, 175, 181, 183, 186, 203, 220
Wylie, L. 30–1, 33

Yim, D. 37, 58
Yiftachel, O. 185, 203
Young, M. 1, 15, 248, 260

Zabusky, S.E. 234, 261
Zonabend, F. 180, 203

Subject Index